# Eric Gill: Autobiography

*Also published by Lund Humphries*

Eric Gill
AN ESSAY ON TYPOGRAPHY

Judy Collins
ERIC GILL: SCULPTURE

Jan Tschichold
THE FORM OF THE BOOK

Jan Tschichold
TREASURY OF ALPHABETS AND LETTERING

Ruari McLean
JAN TSCHICHOLD: TYPOGRAPHER

Edward Johnston
FORMAL PENMANSHIP

Herbert Spencer
THE LIBERATED PAGE

# Eric Gill: Autobiography

With a New Introduction by Fiona MacCarthy

Lund Humphries
London

This edition of Eric Gill's *Autobiography* published 1992
by Lund Humphries Publishers
Park House, 1 Russell Gardens, London NW11 9NN

*British Library Cataloguing-in-Publication Data*
A catalogue record for this book
is available from the British Library

ISBN 0 85331 613 9

*Publishing History*
Eric Gill's *Autobiography* was first published in 1940
by Jonathan Cape Ltd, London. For this edition a new Introduction
by Fiona MacCarthy has been added.

Printed in Great Britain by
Biddles Ltd, Guildford, Surrey

*To*
*M. E. G.*
*and*
*E. P. J. and G.*

# CONTENTS

|  | INTRODUCTION by Fiona MacCarthy | 5 |
|---|---|---|
|  | PREFACE | 11 |
| I | HOLES IN OBLIVION | 15 |
| II | THE SCHOOLBOY AT SCHOOL | 23 |
| III | THE SCHOOLBOY AT HOME | 35 |
| IV | CHICHESTER | 73 |
| V | IN AN ARCHITECT'S OFFICE | 94 |
| VI | THE MONUMENTAL MASON AND LETTERCUTTER | 131 |
| VII | POSTSCRIPT — (1) THE BUSINESS WORLD AND THE ARMY | 193 |
|  | (2) T.O.S.D. | 205 |
|  | (3) CAPEL-Y-FFIN AND SALIES-DE-BÉARN | 215 |
|  | (4) JERUSALEM | 248 |
|  | (5) ESCAPADES | 260 |
| VIII | CONCLUSION | 278 |

# INTRODUCTION

ERIC GILL began writing his *Autobiography* in the afternoon of 28 February 1940. At the time he was staying in Wales, in the Black Mountains, in the Gothic monastery formerly occupied by Father Ignatius of Llanthony, where he himself had lived with his family and entourage in the 1920s. His daughter Betty now ran it as a Guest House. For Gill it was a place full of history and memory. Gill wrote fast and fluently and by the end of that evening, as he noted in his diary, he had completed Chapter One, an achievement celebrated with an interlude of lovemaking, the way Gill liked to celebrate all noteworthy events. The next day he continued what he called his 'Auto' book, although by this time he was ill in bed with flu.

Gill's memoirs have a special place in any history of twentieth-century biography. They were not conceived as autobiography in the conventional sense of a day-to-day record of events. Gill had set out to write a history of mental adventures rather than physical ones: 'in as much as certain *influences* made themselves felt at that place and time they must be written about'. He had read G. K. Chesterton's autobiography soon after it was published in 1936 and had much admired it. Whether consciously or not his book resembles Chesterton's. It is Gill's personal story of his intellectual journey from Brighton to Jerusalem. It is a book about the gestation of ideas.

When Jonathan Cape, the publishers, first approached him in the early 1930s, Gill had been flattered but unenthusiastic. Their exchange of letters is a classic correspondence between importunate publisher and reluctant author. Gill pleaded lack of time: he could not take a six-month holiday. He claimed to disapprove in principle of autobiography published in a subject's lifetime. By 1936 Cape had got no further than extracting a promise from Gill to jot down some notes in between his work on carving the great League of Nations sculpture in Geneva. Needless to say this promise was not kept. But by 1940 Gill's whole attitude had altered. It was wartime, a lean period for sculptural commissions. He was ageing, almost sixty. His health was now precarious. He returned to the idea with sudden energy and urgency. One feels there was a sense in which he wanted to get the whole thing down before his death.

Gill had a wonderful talent for throwing himself into the job in hand, whether letter-cutting, wood engraving, chopping wood or having sex. He had superhuman powers of concentration and could cut himself off from his surroundings when working, almost in a trance. Once he started the *Autobiography* he wrote it obsessively, anywhere and everywhere. 'Wrote a bit sitting in field on mountain side in afternoon', a Capel-y-ffin diary entry runs. His other work continued. He was at that time carving the reredos for Westminster Cathedral; he was producing his preliminary sketches for the Guildford Cathedral crucifix; his Peace Pledge Union pamphlets were almost a production line; he was writing a new book of anti-capitalist essays, *Christianity in a Machine Age*. But his diaries suggest the 'Auto' book took precedence. By 3 March he was reporting back to Cape: 'by the way, I'm well started with it – rum stuff'.

In the context of the rest of Gill's literary output the *Autobiography* is indeed an oddity. He abandons the thumping style of his polemic writings for something much more personal and lyrical and charming. 'It is clear, lucid, shining', as Richard Church described it at the time in his *New Statesman* review. Nowhere else in Gill's work does one find anything comparable to those short, impressionistic scenes of South Coast childhood in his opening chapter, with their clear-cut infant's vision of the sweet and the bizarre. There are signs that Gill himself was taken by surprise at the mood of wistful memory. A third of the way through he wrote to Cape a little anxiously: 'I cannot imagine whether it is the kind of thing you are either expecting or wanting. It seems to me to be a very innocent affair.'

Through the spring and early summer of 1940 Gill was back at Pigotts, his own home near High Wycombe. He had never managed

6

to shake off the string of illnesses of earlier that year. German measles had been followed by bronchitis and lumbago. Then the doctor had discovered slight congestion in the lung, a recurrence of Gill's lung problems of 1936. (He never seems to have attempted to cut his smoking down.) He told his brother Cecil he was glad to have some writing work to get on with at a time when he was unable to do anything more physically strenuous. He still complained of feeling '*rotten* weak', and he wrote much of the *Autobiography* in bed or on a kind of daybed rigged up in the garden. Considering Gill's physical condition, the ebullience of his writing as the book progresses and the zest with which he glorifies man's sexual appetites are remarkable indeed.

On 1 June he finished the manuscript: 100,000 words in total. It was handed over to Dr Patrick Flood, the resident Chaplain, for typing and for a general lookover, to keep Gill, as he put it, 'on the theological rails'. How much Dr Flood may have influenced the general tenor of the book is a fascinating question, for there are signs that Gill originally intended a more revealing book than the one finally delivered. 'I very much doubt whether you would dare to publish what I should dare to write for I do not see how my kind of life, which is not that of a big game hunter, could be written without intimate details.' This was what Gill wrote to Cape in 1933.

One longs to know exactly what Gill had on his mind, sifting through old memories in that first spring and summer of the war he so detested. How did he come to write about that innocence of childhood in Brighton and in Chichester without being painfully aware of his incestuous relations with his sisters? (With Gladys they continued on into the 1930s.) How did he describe Ditchling's idyllic domesticity without recalling incidents of incest with his daughters, his growing alienation from his adopted son Gordian and the final bitter quarrels that split the religious craft community he founded? How could he embark on those rapturous descriptions of a life at Capel that came very close to paradise, without being inhibited by a whole domestic history of adulteries and sexual complexities? These are questions one can now ask with the benefit of hindsight. Gill vociferously supported sexual candour; yet he was not able to address it in his book.

Gill failed to persuade Cape to call his book *Autopsychography*. They feared that such a title would 'puzzle and deter' the unsophisticated reader. They turned down his subsequent suggestion of *Autopsy*. In the circumstances this too was just as well. Gill in the end settled fairly happily for *Autobiography*, which after all bore out his plain man's slogan, frequently repeated, that 'an A is an A'. Gill's words on the title page are *Quod ore sumpsimus*: what we have taken with our mouth. This is the beginning of a prayer in the Mass referring to the body and the blood of Christ. Gill uses it, of course, in a wider sense referring to all bodily and sensual experience. His wood engraving shows two lovers' fingers touching. In a way the frontispiece is more explicit than the text.

By the end of October Gill's illness was much worse. An X-ray had shown up a fibrous growth in his right lung. It was obviously cancer. Before he was taken into hospital for an operation he wrote to Cape to say 'As I hate wasting time I am wondering whether it would be possible for you to hurry up the printers, so that I can do some correcting while I am in bed'. Cape agreed and he sat up in bed in Harefield House Hospital in Middlesex reading Wilenski's *Ruskin* (as a result of which he added a last-minute footnote) and finishing the proofs. Professional to the end, he sent Cape his apologies for holding up the schedule: 'I don't think I'll be able to get on with the Index until the end of the week – it depends how I react to the knife!'

Gill's last words on his *Autobiography* were 'It's not going to be such a bad book as I imagined'. This on 10 November 1940, a week before he died. Over the years his optimism has been justified and we would be foolish to discount the breadth and richness of a classic of its period by concentrating on the things that Gill left out. His book is a pungent statement of his views on art and politics, morality and workmanship, and it was to have enormous influence on successive generations of artists and craftsmen. Like Ruskin and like Morris, Eric Gill must be regarded as a practical prophet who actually showed people the direction they should go. With so much revived interest in hand-making, in ecology, and in the viability of small communities, Gill's views begin to seem more relevant than ever. Few people this century have delved quite so intrepidly into the troubled waters of religion, art and sex.

Gill wrote the way he spoke. Someone who knew him very well said he was astonished by the way the book recaptured Eric Gill's authentic manner. The jokes, the provocations, the pistol-shot delivery. He could hear Gill talking. We still can.

Fiona MacCarthy
1992

# PREFACE

I HAVE given way to the reiterated request of my publisher that I should write an autobiography. But I cannot write a record of doings and happenings; for nothing particular has happened to me — except inside my head. I have done nothing in the way of remarkable deeds. The only kind of autobiography I can possibly write must be an autopsychography, a record of mental experience. Such reference as I shall make to physical doings and events will be but incidental, the accidents and not the substance of my tale.

It is exceedingly difficult to know what you really think and what you really feel, and especially what you really thought and felt in the past, and it is even more difficult to put it down in words. How many people have really tried to do so? Jean-Jacques Rousseau tried to, and his book is a most valuable document. But he was a very peevish and disgruntled person, he spent too much space writing his complaints of other people. The same may be said of Monsieur Nicholas Restif; and he was such a liar and braggart. And, to leap from the low to the high, there is St. Augustine. Yes, the *Confessions* is the master-work in this line of business, but St. Augustine had a better and surer basis on which to write. He was not an upstart philosopher like Rousseau. He could know himself better, know better than Rousseau or Restif what kind of creature it was who confessed. For the question is not only: who am I? but what am I?

Therefore I preface this book with the statement that man is matter and spirit, really both, conjoined and inseparable. The record will be concerned with the spiritual as informing the material and with the material as manifesting the spiritual. What sort of a person was this son of a parson? What adventures of the spirit did he suffer? What to the best of my remembrance has gone on in my mind during these fifty-eight years of life?

11

But alas! it is a hasty record and lacking in calm. Of necessity I have had to wedge the writing of it in between other things. I have had to write it almost exactly as it came, neither going forward nor going back. And not only is it lacking in calm; it is lacking in humility. I am sorry. By all that I have written I belie my firm conviction that I am in the wrong. Please believe me – I believe that. It is the key to human life. If only we could admit that we are in the wrong!

Man is matter and spirit. But I don't want to give the impression that I think I know what those words mean. I do not. They are as unknowable to our finite minds and as inexplicable as time and space. We say that so and so is so many years old and that such and such is so many miles long! And we think we know what we mean. Our whole notion of things is vitiated by this delusion. I only know that there seems to be a being I know as myself and that there seem to be beings that I know as not myself. I know that in final analysis the only thing we can say is that matter is in some sense measurable, whereas the spiritual is not. Measurement implies a standard and one that is changeless, otherwise the word has no meaning. But nothing known to us is changeless except that which is not measurable. So what? The philosophers can probe this matter. My only point here is to disarm the suspicion that I think I know the secrets of the universe.

But if I am to write this book at all, it must be on the level of ordinary human speech and thought. We can say nothing true about God but he is not this; he is not that. Shall we therefore keep silent? God forbid; for he has bidden us to praise him. And I am quite perfectly certain that the ultimate truth of the created universe is that which is implied in the saying of Julian of Norwich: 'It lasteth and forever shall, for God loveth it', and that as the actuality of everything is dependent upon God's will, so everything is sustained in being by his love.

Nevertheless, these seemingly independent loves, this body, these bones, this earth, these beasts, these storms of snow and rain, these pleasures — God! what pleasures, these pains — O God! what pains, these things encompass us and are the condition of our spiritual being. Let us grant that in any ultimate sense they have no independent existence; but here and now, in this book, I accept them as they seem and write accordingly. Do not even the hermits eat their daily bread and do their daily doings? *Vanum est vobis ante lucem surgere.* It is useless to pretend that you have got further than you have.

# CHAPTER I

## HOLES IN OBLIVION

THOSE little isolated visions which alone remain from early child-hood – unconnected with anything, surrounded by darkness! Some people have many such memories. Some people can remember much earlier happenings than others can. These things, it seems to me, must have some importance in such a record as this. They are very odd little things. You can't tell why they should have remained, and remained alone, while much more important things, as one would suppose, must have been happening. Such things must indicate something. If I remember such and such rather than something else, it must be because I'm a different sort of person from what I would have been if I had remembered other things. I sometimes ask other people; we all sometimes ask other people what is their very first memory. It is curiously revealing.

I

The very first thing I can remember happened in a house in a street in Brighton called Prestonville Road[1] – I don't know if it is still so called – the railway went under it in a tunnel just before entering Brighton Station – the church of St. Luke with blue bricks in patterns set in red brick walls was nearby. At the back of our house there was a wooden staircase leading down from the back sitting-room into the garden. The other houses in the same row also had such stairways. All the gardens ran down to the ends of the gardens belonging to the houses of the Dyke Road, which was parallel with Prestonville Road. It must

[1] This was the second house we lived in in Brighton. The first, which we left soon after I was born, was No. 3 Hamilton Road, with a back garden overlooking the sidings outside Brighton Railway Station.

have been early summertime because everything was bright green and there was a misty shimmer of warmth in the air — not the shimmer of great heat but that of warm sunshine after rain, with a sense of everything growing and blooming. My father was standing by me at the top of the stairs. I think he had probably brought me there. He had a great eye for the loveliness of the earth and of trees and flowers and sky. Wooden staircases, red brick walls enclosing little flourishing suburban gardens in the Brighton of 1883, or thereabouts. A shimmering summer afternoon. A little boy and his father. Big trees somewhere in the background. Low bushes and small trees here and there, and we stand looking at it all and my father has brought me to see it. We stand facing rather north-westwards. My father points to a friend of his — a neighbour working in his garden, just like Mr. McGregor in the distance. I think it is all very beautiful. I have thought so ever since. I can see it now and think so still.

II

One afternoon, in the same house and I suppose about the same year (for we moved to another house in 1884), we are having tea in the front room in the basement. The street level is about six feet above the basement floor. It must be about that because sitting at the tea table and looking out across the narrow 'area' I can see the sky. But the pavement railings are well above my head and there is an iron gate and a flight of about ten steps leading down to our lower front door. I think it is a nice afternoon and we are having a nice tea — my mother and my elder sister and me and my baby sister, Cicely, if she was big enough to sit up to table — I don't remember, but I know it is a family tea. My father wasn't there at the time, though I know he was somewhere about the house because in the middle of the meal my mother called out to him saying: 'They've sent the bath back' and I see, coming down the brick steps into the area, a man, or a boy, with a hip-bath, and he is carrying it over his head like a vast bonnet. I don't remember his delivering the bath. As far as I am aware he is still just half-way down the steps, one hand steadying the bath, the other holding the iron railing, though at the time he wasn't a man at all, he was a hip-bath walking. What a nice tea-time it was when such marvels occurred!

### III

It was about this time that I had another vision. But this time it was purely imaginary. I don't know what occasion he had to tell me, perhaps there had been a child drowned at Brighton about that time, or perhaps it was only 'in the paper', but I remember my father saying that he had dreamed he saw a group of men coming along Prestonville Road carrying a shutter (one of those long panels which at that date were used to cover shop windows at night and on Sundays — you had a dozen or more and they stood on end, fastened top and bottom. It was good to watch the shop keeper putting up the shutters in those days) and on the shutter was a body, covered with a sheet. And they came nearer and then, in the dream, he saw the sheet taken off, and the body was me, drowned. It was only my father's dream; but I find it difficult to believe I didn't see that procession with my own eyes. I can see the red brick pavement, wet with rain. I might have remembered brick pavements and shutters for all sorts of other reasons; but no, I must needs remember them only because they figured in someone else's dream.

### IV

We moved to Cliftonville Road about 1884. By that time there were father and mother and one boy and two girls. As at the house in Prestonville Road there was a basement floor which was a little below the street level. We played in the sitting-room on this floor, at the back. You could just see the garden if you stood on a chair. And I can remember a small boy, and I can remember

17

what he felt about it, standing, by order, close up to and facing the easternmost wall, with the garden window on the right, and on the wall, hung on a nail, is a pair of his small knickerbockers — very wet and smelly. This was to teach him not to.

## V

And in that same room, this time there is a sewing-machine in the middle, I remember dancing up and down, howling with agony because I had put my finger into the place where the bobbin went to and fro while my mother was working and I very nearly got the tip of my finger wrenched off. The effects are still visible and horrid, and the small boy is still dancing and howling. But I don't remember in the least what the pain was like.

## VI

In the same street, a few houses further east, towards what is now called Brompton Avenue, the minister lived.[1] My father was his 'curate' and one Sunday afternoon my elder sister went to tea with the old gentleman. This must have been a memorable occasion; for the minister, who said 'methinks' at intervals in his sermons, was a great and mysterious figure of an upper world. When the time came he brought my sister home and I and my mother happen to be looking out of the front sitting-room window, the drawing-room window, the one above the basement. To my wonderment they pass by our house, the minister holding my sister's hand. The houses were all alike and the old boy didn't know which was ours — forgotten the number. But you can imagine the awful situation. The ship approaching harbour and being swept past the friendly and inviting and imploring entrance — swept into who knows what unpredictable disaster. So it seems to me — not in those words but with that emotion. Presently back they come again and this time they turn into our

[1] The minister of the Countess of Huntingdon's chapel, in North Street.

front gate. I suppose no one but I felt the magnitude of the escape. The grown-ups just thought it was funny – funny to hold a child by the hand and lead her past her own home.


### VII

And upstairs in that same house, in one of the back bedrooms, the westernmost of the two bedrooms on the first floor, I was in bed one morning. It is quite light. I don't know why I am not up and about. I think things must have been a bit abnormal; for as I sit there someone comes in and says: 'You've got a new baby brother' or words to that effect. I just remember the curious light in the room – as though it were lit by a yellowish skylight, but it can't have been, and me in bed and the person bringing the news. (That was Max, that was. So it must have been October 6th, 1884.)


### VIII

Some time after that we moved to Preston View, Dyke Road Drive. We lived there until 1897 when we moved to Chichester. From 1888 onwards my memory becomes more or less coherent but before 1888 there are just holes in the oblivion. I don't know the order but as two of them are visions of events occurring at the time of Queen Victoria's Jubilee they must have been in 1887. One was on the occasion of the visit of the Shah of Persia to Brighton. We had been told about this world-shaking event for weeks or perhaps months beforehand. I was taken when the day came to a house on the Marine Parade – whose house? who knows? – and we all looked out of a window on the first or second floor. The street is filled with people. There are red plush and gilding on the furniture in the room. Presently a carriage drives by and everyone cheers. That was the Shah of Persia!

## IX

And on the night of the Jubilee, as a most special treat, I was taken to see the fireworks which they let off from the West Pier. The night was black, but fine. There were lots of fireworks, even a curious and, to me, extremely boring thing called a 'set piece'. I remember the shapeless, stupid glare of it. But near the end of the show they sent up a thing which went soaring in a stupendous curve into the sky and, bursting, sent a golden shower over the whole black world. First there is the rushing hiss and then the grand, great curve mounting higher and higher and then that marvellous slowing down as the thing reaches its apogee and then a myriad new curves of light rushing towards you in all directions of perspective with new-born speed. 'That's golden rain' they said and seemed content. But I went home miserable because there was no more of it. And it's the kind of fireworks I really love best now — that and Catherine Wheels.

## X

And somewhere about that time I had the only ride on a horse I've ever had. I was the hindermost of about seven children who were given a ride on the horse which pulled the mower in the tennis ground at the bottom of the Nunnery Drive. I sit on his tail supported by some other children's nurse. I have never so much as sat on a horse's back since then. But I went to Marsaba on a donkey, and nearly died of the heat. . . .

## XI

And about that time I was taken to stay with an old friend of my father's near Blackheath. She was known to us as Aunt Sophie. I screamed and refused all comfort when my father left me there. I remember screaming and at the same time rolling a little wooden locomotive up and down the wall in their sitting-room while my father said good-bye. But I got used to it and I remember sitting up in Aunt Sophie's bed one morning while she had a bath in a hip-bath in the middle of the room. I can see everything except what she looked like. Later on, as a growing boy, I often thought it almost culpable that I did not take more notice! She was very kind, she had big front teeth and we picked flowers somewhere near her home – near a railway bridge.

### XII

I can give a definite date to what I regard as the last of these 'holes'. It was about 11 o'clock in the morning of February 22nd, 1888. It was my sixth birthday. I had been sent out to amuse myself before being taken down to the town to buy a promised present. Our house was immediately over the entrance to the tunnel which the railway line went through on the loop line between Preston and Hove and the loop line joined the main line about three hundred yards from the entrance thus forming a big triangle of which the base was our road.[1] This land was empty and sloped up steeply from the railway. It was fenced off from our road by a wooden paling, through which you could see the trains, for the palings were a few inches apart (nice to run along them with a stick). It was naturally very exciting to see a train coming out from the tunnel and they came very slowly because it was quite noticeably uphill. On one side of the line just outside the tunnel there was a steep chalk embankment (trees on the top at that time, but since built on with the usual cheap suburban houses) and the chalk slipped down from time to time and gangs of navvies came and shovelled it on to low trucks labelled mysteriously BALLAST. Well, then, while I watch the trains, a train comes snorting and puffing up out of the tunnel and stops. And it isn't an ordinary train of ballast trucks but a train of trucks and passenger carriages mixed. And the doors open and a regiment of soldiers in red coats gets out and they all start

[1] See diagram opposite p. 81.

shovelling the loose chalk . . . Now there was a mysterious happening for a sixth birthday morning. It would have been exciting enough to see ordinary passengers daring to get out of a train where there was no station — but a lot of soldiers . . . This is not perhaps a mere hole in oblivion automatically appearing — it is a memory consciously preserved and treasured. The train is still snorting from the tunnel, the red-coats are still climbing out, still shovelling.

## XIII

But there is yet one more. It is at a kindergarten somewhere near Montpelier Road. As far as I can remember I only went there for one day. But this can't have been so. Why only one day? I am in an upstairs room. There is no sun, the sky is grey and gloomy. We have been making little mats by interweaving strips of shiny blue and white paper — not exciting but at least intelligible. Then the teacher starts us on clay modelling. She gives me a lump of greyish clay, about as big as a plover's egg, and suggests that I shall make something by squeezing it about. She shows me how to do it but doesn't tell me what or why. I am miserable and bored. I remember clearly the grey light and my impotence. If only I could have told her that it wasn't in my line!

# CHAPTER II

## THE SCHOOLBOY AT SCHOOL

CONSECUTIVE and coherent life began for me when, having finished with nursery and kindergarten lessons and having very nearly learned to read, I was sent to a real school. I remember my first day very vividly because in the playground one of the bigger boys almost, as it felt, twisted my arm off. But I remember very little about the first years. Spelling lessons were the first and chief business and 'little Arthur's History of England' – 'Now you know, my dear little children, that the country you live in is called England' – that's how it goes. But the first important educational experience I remember was the result of overhearing the mistress who taught the very small boys saying to one of the masters (it was on the landing outside one of the upstairs class-rooms), referring to *me*: 'It's a pity he's so easily led'. Of course I didn't worry much at the time, but it stuck in my memory like a fishbone in the throat. And of course I took it, as I'm sure it was meant, as a statement of moral inferiority. It stuck in my mind all through my schooldays – it echoed like a knell: he's so easily led, he's so easily led. And of course it meant led astray, led by evil companions, led into sin. And I knew it was more or less true. Well, there it was, and if I didn't get into any real trouble during all the years I was at school, and if, all my life, I have been a timidly law-abiding person, it is probably the consequence of that salutary memory. But, as the years passed, the words gradually came to have a quite different significance. Gradually I rose superior to the suggestion of moral inferiority. Gradually I came to see that, in colloquial terms, it was 'a jolly good thing' to be easily led and not a pity at all. I think I had long left my schooldays behind me before I properly realized it. I think it was not until I became a pupil to an architect in London.

But I came to see that to be 'easily led' might be a blessing in disguise, and a very thin disguise too. For what did they want? Did they want me to be an obstinate bounder of a boy who listened to no one? I came to see that there was virtue in being easily led – provided you had good leaders. That was the point and the discovery was an immense illumination and a sun-shining release. Moreover it turned the tables on them. Their rebuke became matter for praise or, at any rate, thanksgiving. If they said 'He's easily led', I could retort, 'Yes, but see how good are my leaders'. For choosing your leaders is a comparatively easy matter – you can almost do it by reason; but being a leader is a much more doubtful matter and I was quite happy to acknowledge that I had no talents for it; moreover I came more and more clearly to realize that to be a leader was the last thing anyone should wish, and that, for example, to go into Parliament ought rather to be forced on people than sought by them.

So I look back on my schooldays without any ill feeling. I was taught nothing in such a way as to make it difficult to discard. I learnt elementary arithmetic, algebra and Euclid. In the course of my seven years I got as far as the Tudors in the history book – beginning at Julius Caesar's invasion. There was no history before that and no foreign history at all. I didn't get further than the Tudors, and perhaps James I, because as we were moved up from class to class we were always beginning again. The whole idea of history was dates, when things happened – nothing else seemed to matter. Geography was much the same in style and was taught out of a book in the same series – 'Gill's History of England', 'Gill's Geography' – 'where and what noted for?', lists of rivers and their tributaries, mountain ranges and drawing-maps. I don't see much harm in the idea though, if I were to teach History and Geography I should want to go a lot further. I should, to start with, want my pupils to have a good comprehensive view of the world in general. I should want them to understand the nature of man, his spiritual nature, his reason of being and his eternal destiny, and to view all the growth and decay of nations and races in the light of that understanding. I don't think I should care whether they ever learnt the dates of the battles of the 'Wars of the Roses' (incidentally, I should take pains to ensure that they never heard such a phrase) but I should see to it that they could 'place' an event, put a more or less accurate date to it, simply by judging the kind of event it was – just as you can 'date' a building by a look at its general structure. And as to Geography, physical geography would be the chief thing and only as springing out of that, the names of towns and countries and seas and rivers. And then mathematics – when you consider the enthralling and exciting nature of arithmetic, algebra, Euclid . . . (it was only Euclid in our school) it is astonishing that schoolmasters are content to teach them as though they were nothing but another kind of physical drill. But I suppose few teachers in boys' preparatory schools in those days really wanted to teach. I suppose the great majority of them hated the job and were only doing it for lack of any other means of livelihood. It may be entirely different to-day. I rather guess it must be so. But in the little preparatory schools of the 1890's in Brighton, and there were many, that was the style – cheap text-books which you went through, page by page and chapter by chapter, and weary young masters who cared little or nothing about education. Perhaps my memory is unjust to them. Perhaps they were keen, intelligent young fellows, filled with zeal to impart knowledge and under-standing. Perhaps I was stupid and lazy. It may well have been so.

Then there were the classics! And here I know it was very much my stupidity. I had no gift whatever for foreign languages. I was completely fogged. It seems to me now that Caesar's wars in Gaul must have been very interesting matters and the poets of Greece and Rome . . . But it was no good. My brain is active enough in some directions, but when it is confronted by foreign languages it retires from the fray like a snail into its shell – it goes all blank – a film like that on a pigeon's eye comes over it. And it's the same to this day; for though I'm familiar with the Mass and a lot of the Psalms in Latin, and know many of them by heart, it's only noises to me which have to be translated before they mean anything. *Te Deum, Laudamus* . . . a grand and sonorous noise (if pronounced properly, of course) but almost meaningless, except that, almost instantaneously, it becomes 'You, God, we praise' and that means a heaven of a lot. And *divites dimisit inanes!* I cannot understand how, to any English ear, those words can herald such a stupendously revolutionary threat as that which they do in fact convey. So the Latin prayers and psalms are good, not because they mean anything much to me in Latin, but because each word is a kind of box containing precious jewels. And of course that is why, anticipating what I discovered later, the Latin Liturgy is good – it is a treasurechest out of which an infinite number of different things can be got, 'new things and old', and you are not more or less compelled to confine yourself to one necklace.

And English and French (no German at our school) and English Grammar – we learnt languages as we learnt our multiplication tables! There was nothing else in it – something to be learnt so that you could give the correct answers to questions, in class or in 'examinations'. We learnt bits of Shakespeare and 'The Lay of the Last Minstrel' in exactly the same way. The whole of my education was simply that – learning things out of little books and being able to remember enough to answer questions.

And, finally, there was Religion! There was very little of this in our school. It was, I think, assumed that if religion had any important meaning at all, that meaning was imparted from the pulpit or at home. Religion in school was only another form of 'tables'. Wars of the Israelites instead of Wars of the Roses, or: Who was Joshua and what was he noted for? But, as I say, at our school there was very little of this and, if faith was taken for granted, morals were simply a matter of learning the ten commandments off by heart – and no explanation.

But games were the real business of school life and here there was understanding and enthusiasm on all sides. I wish I could write about this with the fullness the matter is patient of. In the matter of football and cricket (there were no other games at our school except a bit of hockey and rounders at odd times) and, through them, the whole world of games generally, we were really and truly and admirably educated at our school. Of course I can only write about this as it seems to me. I have very little idea at all what the other boys, or even the masters, thought. We talked about football and cricket a vast amount and studied the games technically and theoretically with real understanding and enthusiasm; but we didn't talk about them philosophically and aesthetically. In such ways we were entirely inarticulate, and so were our masters. Games were a real job of work, like farming or engine-driving. And they were founded upon living traditions, traditions accepted by all and revered. It was not a matter of book-learning, but of practice, and the practice was unquestioned. We were in the tradition and shaping it. It was truly our affair and we were responsible for our part in it. The locomotives of 1892 were unquestionably better than those of 1882. They were newer and therefore *must* be better; because they embodied the latest improvements. You wouldn't think of going back to an earlier style even if you could. That would be a kind of blasphemy, a disloyalty to the spirit. And so it was in football. We played better football in 1892 than they had in 1890. We knew the latest things about it. We were responsible for carrying on the good work. It was not merely a case of letting down the school, but of letting down the game! I say we didn't talk about it like this. Of course we didn't. We weren't grown up enough. But I know that that is what we really thought about it and the masters too; for we were all in it together. And it was not only a job of work in which we took a responsible part – winning a game against another school, scoring goals or runs – there was also the actual, the intrinsic quality of the physical thing itself. There are ways of doing things with a ball and your foot which have in them a physical perfection, intensely lovely, intensely illuminating – whether you do them yourself or see them done. It is the same in all the trades and crafts, but, in the nature of things, it is more poignantly seen in games. For in games we are more free to consider action in itself and are less concerned with its effect – the particular quality of a 'stroke' at cricket, the intricate perfection of the combination of the exactly right power with the exactly right angle and curve and deflection . . . It becomes absurd when such things are reduced to words; they do not exist except in actuality. The point here is that games at school when properly taught have the highest educational value. And it is not that we go to school to learn such things because they are useful. It is not like that at all. We do not go to school to *learn* football but to *play* football. We are educated by the doing not by the learning. And that is, in my mind, the whole secret of education, whether in schools or in workshops or in life. The actual business of learning (by which I mean the acquiring the use of tools without using them – as one might learn multiplication tables without ever doing 'sums', or the ten commandments without ever leaving the nursery) is the very smallest part of a proper system of education. A certain small amount of mere learning is probably necessary, but it should be reduced as much as possible. And as this is obviously true in the avocations of grown-up life, so it is true in childhood and at school, in the nursery and in the home.

I shall have more to say about grown-up avocations when I come to deal with my mental adventures in such matters as art and industry and commercialism and industrialism. At this place I am only concerned to note the remarkable contrast, at our school, between the playground and the class-room. In the former the education was almost entirely by doing; in the latter there was properly speaking no education at all but only the acquiring of the use of tools – tools which were never used. I think, looking back on it, that this was a bad business. It need not have been so. It should not have been so. But, on the other hand, I am very far from complaining. In the circumstances of the 1890's any other sort of 'education' would have been much worse. The information they supplied was often misleading and unintelligently imparted.

for MEG from EG Christmas 1927          EG 20.12.27

ERIC GILL, SELF PORTRAIT (1927)

MARY ETHEL GILL (1940)

INCISED ALPHABET (HOPTON-WOOD STONE) 1932

ELIZABETH, PETRA AND JOANNA GILL (1914)

GORDIAN GILL (1920)

THE ENGRAVER (1928)

J. O'C

ERI

FATHER O'CONNOR
(THE VERY REV. MGR. JOHN O'CONNOR)
1929

THE DEPOSITION
(BLACK HOPTON-WOOD STONE)
1925

BAS RELIEF FOR THE LEAGUE OF NATIONS PALACE AT GENEVA
(1938)

The picture of the world which they more or less sketchily put before us was a product of every sort of myopia and was in some respects grossly untrue to nature — inept misrepresentation and no mere caricature. What a blessing then that, in effect, they taught me nothing at school but a lot of more or less useful facts and a lot of more or less useful tricks. Reading, in the simple sense of knowing one word from another at sight, writing in the simple sense of acquiring the ability to mark paper neatly and legibly with letters, arithmetic in the simple sense of knowing the elementary rules of calculation. History, a mass of dates — but, after all, mere dates do give you a sort of time map, even if the particular points marked turn out to be less important than your teachers seemed to suppose — otherwise a view of England's development which I could hardly have acquired otherwise, a sort of fairy-tale which if I had not read it at school I should not have read at all.

So I do not complain. On the contrary I feel exceedingly thankful to my schoolmasters. I don't feel as though they did anything at all to coerce my mind or drive me up wrong roads. They were too mentally timid, too devoid of any enthusiasm — except in the playing field. But I did get a vision of the possibilities of tools — the things that help you to make. And somehow or other (but this must be due to my father and mother) I did get a liking for precision and order. Arithmetic and Euclid I found very satisfactory subjects. Right and wrong, true and false — these things are physically and visually manifest in mathematics. Grammar — the precise use of words — a very satisfactory acquisition. Perspective drawing. I do not say that I was conscious of these grounds of appreciation, but I certainly did appreciate them. I *liked* arithmetic and I remember very clearly the kind of liking it was. And I liked things to go together — the lay-out of the figures and the neatness of the writing all combining with the orderliness of the proceeding — statement of problem, working out, conclusion.

So, considering all things, I incline to think that our school was really a very good one. I can't imagine anything less 'high-brow' or less concerned to bring up the boys according to plan. There was no plan at all – no general view of the universe or of society – at least there was no plan or general view which they took any trouble to teach. Such things were taken for granted. The British Empire existed – the inevitable growth of centuries, the inevitable consequence of the inferiority of all other peoples . . . But as far as I can remember, such things were quite as much insisted upon by the boys as by the masters. And the boys got them at home as much as at school. And it was the same with religion. You didn't learn religion at school; you brought it with you. It was no part of the school's business to interfere. If you didn't get religion at home, you didn't get it at all – the most you got was a small amount of Bible history – very, very small – and the ten commandments without any explanation. The boarders went to church on Sundays, but I was only a day-boy so I saw nothing of that. My memory may be faulty – I can only say I don't remember anything about religion at school except the small amount I have described. Religion and politics, philosophy, any sort of general view of life or any explanation of the meaning of things – all this you got from your parents if you got it at all. It was no part of school teaching. And I say this seems to me, in the circumstances of the 1890's, a very good thing. They taught a lot of quite useful things, very unintelligently but almost completely without bias. I did learn to read, I did learn the elements of numerical calculation; I did learn the declension and conjugation of Latin nouns and verbs; and even the little I learnt about Latin was well worth learning and saved me the trouble of learning it since. I did learn ordinary 'copperplate' handwriting. And in the learning of these things I did get a sort of mental 'physical jerks'. That seems to me all to the good. And I was fairly happy at school – not uproariously so, but happy enough. I was able to keep up with other boys in class and even to pass them in some things, and though I had no special talent for games I enjoyed cricket quite a lot and football was an enthralling love.

And just because I was no particular good I was able to enjoy them in a disinterested manner. The headmaster, as I have said, was keener on games than on books. He sneered at books; but he never sneered at football. And he had special genius, it amounted to that, for training a team. Our school was one of the smallest in Brighton; I do not remember there being ever more than about thirty boys. But we beat every other school in the town and neighbourhood, including the Junior school of Brighton College. We didn't merely beat them; we just ran over them. We were the only schoolboy team in those parts which was really well trained and had any real discipline. But I admit that our success was partly due to the genius of two of the small boys. Some of the things they did at the age of thirteen or fourteen can, for perfection of skill, only be compared with the performances of the greatest music hall 'stars', and I'm not talking nonsense, for one of them afterwards played 'three-quarter' for England. These things live in my memory as things to praise God for. Even at the time, though I didn't talk about praising God, I quite certainly worshipped. I only wish I could write them down as clearly as I can see them happening even now. But though the team owed much, especially in spectacular appeal, to those two boys, we should never have been able to 'sweep the map' as we did without the genius of the headmaster as trainer.

And while I am thus writing about the beauty and impressiveness of technical prowess I cannot, for it made an immense difference to my mind, omit the famous name of Ranjitsinghi. Even now, when I want to have a little quiet wallow in the thought of something wholly delightful and perfect, I think of 'Ranji' on the County Ground at Hove. Our school was alongside the ground and the whole lot of us had 'passes' for all the matches. There were many minor stars, each with his special and beloved technique, but nothing on earth could approach the special quality of 'Ranji's' batting or fielding. There are whole books about this, so I need not describe it, even if I could. I only place it on record that such craftsmanship and such grace entered into my very soul.

Don't think I'm making too much fuss about this. This is an essential and very important part of my schooldays. My only trouble is to find how to convey the immensity of its importance. We won matches because we couldn't help winning them – but that is not the point. Who cares whether 'Arnold House' did or didn't beat Ovingdean School in the year 1896 by eleven goals to nought? For that matter, who cares whether the New Zealand rugby players beat every team brought against them a few years ago? It is not the result in scores that matters. We won matches because we had superior training and discipline. But, again, it's not the winning I want to insist upon. It's the discipline – that's the point – and it's not discipline as a morality but discipline as a technique that I want to write about. It was the technique of discipline that I found so admirable and so appealing. If you hold a broad pen in a certain way it will, if you've got some ink in it and if you pull it along the paper, make a certain kind of lines because it is its nature so to do. The more accurately you sharpen the pen's edge, the more accurately you obey the nature of the instrument, the more admirable will be the resulting writing. As far as possible the craftsman must suppress and efface himself – and not for reasons of morality, of humility, not because 'showing off' is morally bad, but for the sake of getting the best out of the pen – the best, that is to say, the thing which the pen, by reason of its own material nature, is most completely adapted to produce. That is the discipline of penmanship; you can call it the technique. And that is the thing I mean when I say that what so enthralled me as a schoolboy was seeing the results of discipline on the football field – not the scoring-board results; though, naturally, I wanted to win as much as anybody, but the technical results, the improvement in the game as a thing to be done, as a thing to be made and as a thing to be seen and known and enjoyed in the mind. I do not claim that I was unique or even very special in this respect. I dare say all schoolboys appreciate the thing I'm talking about. Certainly very large numbers do so. But I know I did. And I appreciated it so much that even as a small boy at an inferior preparatory school I deliberately sought the place in the team where there was least chance of success being due to personal prowess – where 'playing the game' was most called for. There was nothing virtuous or unselfish about this; for I hadn't got any personal prowess. But just for that reason it was more necessary to rely on something else. It was a sort of rationalism. Playing the game! This phrase has been horribly exploited and misused. But I don't think it is misused by schoolboys. I say nothing against its moral applications. They are right and proper. A selfish, vainglorious, showing-off sort of person is an abomination and schoolboys don't need much prompting to grasp that fact; but it is not his abominable moral nature that spoils a game of football but his fatuous lack of appreciation of what is required of him. He may be wicked – who knows? The point is that he is a nuisance and a defect. 'What I ask of a painting', says M. Maurice Denis, 'is that it shall look like paint.' The same principle runs through the whole of life and work. You may use a painting for good or bad purposes, but to be a good painting it must be done according to the nature of paint. A schoolmaster may use a football team simply as an advertisement of his school, but football is football and a good game must be played according to the nature of the game, whatever your ulterior motives may be.

Looking back then on my schooldays I see that I was extremely fortunate. I was not educated, except in games, but I was given the tools by which, if I wished to do so, I could educate myself, and in an elementary sort of way, I was shown how to use them.[1] And talking about tools, I must, before it is too late, record in gratitude the memory of the only boy at school who, as I imagine,

[1] My father wanted me to go on to a 'public school', and I was put up for a scholarship at Bradfield College. I sat for the examination, a bleak experience, but failed miserably in it. I did all the arithmetic and other mathematical papers pretty well, but the Latin floored me completely. So that was that.

had any influence on me – any influence that lasted beyond my schooldays.[1] He was a tall, lanky, clumsy, unpopular boy. He had the effrontery to have political views at variance with the blind jingoism of the rest of us.[2] We mostly hated and despised him. He was a day-boy like myself and against my inclination, and yet hating myself for hating it, I went sometimes to his house and he showed me his carpentering shop. I learnt about tools from him and I learnt about moral courage – he was of the stuff of which martyrs are made.

I guess most of the boys at our school went 'into business' when they left school. Some of them may have gone to bigger and better schools and even to the university. I never heard anything about it and from that day to this I have hardly ever met one of my old school fellows. The school itself disappeared; the headmaster, so I was told, became a cigar merchant. What a blessing – there was no 'old school tie'.

[1] Francis Wedd.

[2] My favourite author at that time was G. A. Henty, and the only prize I ever got at school was *Through the Sikh War*. I remember walking home in the moonlight with my father and mother after the prize-giving and school concert in a daze of exaltation and pride.

# CHAPTER III

# THE SCHOOLBOY AT HOME

MY first recollections of discipline are connected with a lady called Alice Blanche Carpenter — 'A.B.C.'. But the only recollection I have of her is being bathed by her and dissuaded from sucking the sponge. This seems like nursery days, but I know she taught us our letters and that we were very intractable. Then somewhere about 1888 my sisters were sent to a small kindergarten school 'kept' or 'run' by two or three sisters called Miss Browne, daughters of the illustrator of Charles Dickens, known as 'Phiz', and I was sent too, in an 'off and on' sort of way. I don't know why this was. Perhaps it was because I was very backward about learning anything. I couldn't read before I was eight and, even then, only words of three letters. I don't remember why I was so backward. So far as I can recollect anything at all about it, I have merely a vague memory of simple boredom in the presence of something devoid of rhyme or reason — English spelling. I hope I'm not praising myself unduly; but I can't think of any more likely reason. I wasn't specially lazy. The cleaning of the knives and boots was my special job and laying the table for meals (though these jobs may have been put on me at a later date) and I was always drawing 'engines' and signals and railway lines going into tunnels like the one under our house. But I do recollect the boredom of reading and it is of very much the same kind as that I experienced later when expected to construe Latin sentences. There didn't seem to be any certainty about it. It seemed too much like guess work. It seemed to be necessary to have a 'flair' for it and I don't and never did like 'flairs'. How can you like what other people score over you with, especially when it's a 'gift', something you can't get by trying? Well, be that as it may, I couldn't be bothered to learn to read and I don't see that it matters.

Everybody agrees that there's much too much printing done
and many too many books; then why not agree that there's
equally too much reading and that the longer children can be
kept off it the better. And our irrational spelling ought to be a
great help to this end. Irrational it is and irrational it will
remain. And all the games they get up to to rationalize it only
make it worse. I am pretty certain that that was what chiefly
annoyed me about the job of learning to read – that my teachers
clothed it in a false garb of reasoning. H A T spells the noise
which we use to signify the things we wear on our heads. Well
and good – Okay by me. And then they tell you that when you
add an E at the end, the A sound becomes longer and you get the
word signifying the opposite of love and that the E is not to be
sounded. Now that is *not* okay by me. It's obviously irrational
and absurd. I knew this before I was eight but I didn't know how
to say so. The A in HAT does not become longer when you add
the E. It's a different sound altogether. And however much it
may be the English custom to use a mute E to signify long vowels
it's absurd to talk about it in terms of cause and effect. I don't
want to write all I could write about the teaching of English
spelling. I only want to explain why, in my opinion, learning
to read English must be of its nature boring to rational creatures
and that it is only made more so by the irrational attempts of
teachers to make rules and regulations for teaching it. The only
way to learn to read English is by sight, and that's what we all do
in the end. Every word makes a different sort of pattern and we
have to learn these patterns by heart. I will only add this: that
I don't believe there can be such a thing as correct or incorrect
spelling, but only good spelling and bad, unless by 'correct' you
simply mean 'standard'.

So I didn't learn to read and I went very irregularly to the
school of the Misses Browne. They were dear kind people and
living with them were a nephew and niece (children of Gordon
Browne, illustrator of G. A. Henty, but it's only the nephew I
remember distinctly), through whom I first got the experience of

friendship. Children's friendships are commonly looked upon as
signifying very little. And it is certainly true that as their parents
move from one house to another and they go from one school to
another, children do seem to throw off such ties with a minimum
of heart-break and very little regret. Nevertheless, when I look
back on the friendships of childhood they do not seem to differ
in either quality or intensity from those of grownup years. We
can only have talked about childish things, we can have had little
experience of places or things, yet the relationship in itself was
precisely the same in kind as that between grownup people and
we delighted in one another's company and shared one another's
pains and pleasures with an even greater frankness and simplicity.
When I ask myself what friends have I known and who were my
very first? I answer: my sister Cicely and 'Bunny' Browne. And
then when I consider those friendships and ask myself how they
differed from friendships I have had with grownup people, I can
only say that I can discover no difference whatever, unless it be
that those friendships of childhood were even better than any
others, clearer, brighter, lovelier, more unselfish, more unalloyed. They were a union of minds, of souls. And they were
human too. There was nothing of the disembodied spirit about
them. In a real sense we enjoyed one another's bodies too. We
shared the same games and enjoyments. We did the same things,
went the same walks, enjoyed the same sights and sounds. We
were in complete accord. And our enjoyments, though more
limited in physical scope, were, within those limits, as intensely
felt and as consciously known as any that grownup people can
know – or, for I can only speak for myself, as intense and as
conscious as any that I have known since. We loved the flowers
and the hills. We loved the sunsets and the birds and beasts.
We loved one another. And will anyone tell me that we did not
love those things as much as we have learned to love them
since? And we loved one another. Will anyone tell me that
that love was in its quality any different and any lower than the
love of men and women or than the love of man for man and

woman for woman? I believe the difference is only quantitative. We can share more things when we are older, because we know more things. And we can talk about it more, because we know more words. But the friendship is the same in kind and the friendships of childhood are only different from those of grownup people as being finer in quality and simpler in their quantitative demands. What I should like would be to walk about in heaven with my sister Cicely as we walked about on the Downs above Brighton with the harebells blowing in the short turf, and the smell of it; with the other children dragging along behind and mother and tea waiting for us at home. And this is no low class enjoyment, such as you can buy for money in the town, but the absolute high level of human possibility. What more do the stars mean for me now than they meant for us then? Are flowers any more beautiful? Are hymns and songs any holier? What truth about the nature of things have I since learnt which was outside my comprehension then? 'God is love', 'little children, love one another' – I knew those things then. Our father and mother had taught us and we believed. If I have learned more since, it was implicit in what I learnt as a child. The flower of knowledge and understanding unfolds but it is the same flower. The child wills and knows and loves. It is a person. And we are the same persons, now as then.

It must have been about the year 1890 that a small incident occurred which, to the amateur of psycho-analysis, might seem to have a grim significance. Near where we lived was a bakery. It was, from a business man's point of view, a progressive affair and was organized on factory lines. I remember the tea-table excitement when about this time they put up on the roof a great big sign with letters against the sky proclaiming CLARK's MACHINE-MADE BREAD. I thought little about it. I had no opinions about such things at that time. Mother's cake was always held to be better than anything bought at the shop – nice and hot and crusty from the oven – Madeira cake was generally held to be only less of a bore than 'Seed' cake and as for 'Fairy' cakes, unless hot and crisp, they are nothing but a suburban nastiness. But the mere word 'machine-made' didn't signify quality, either good or bad. But one day Mrs. Hart came to call on my mother — you don't know her, never mind, she came to tea — afternoon-tea in the drawing-room, and I was brought in to say 'How d'you do?'. As I went in they were talking about Clark's Steam Bakery and I overheard Mrs. Hart saying in a horrified whisper, 'And do you know — *there was a black beetle in it* . . .' Nothing more was said, but I dimly gathered that Mrs. Hart was airing a generally acceptable notion that such a happening was a divine punishment upon those who thus profaned the domestic arts. Nothing more was said, but the atmosphere was one of horror. There was a clear implication of worse horrors to come if housewives persisted in patronizing such black arts as machine-bakery. It was all very mysterious. I have the impression that, with a child's delight in horrors, I must have asked questions about that beetle; for I have the impression that I was told to be quiet. I remember the air of mystery. Where did the beetle come from? How did it get there? Was it alive? Was it poisonous? Was Mr. Clark a very wicked man? Were all the people wicked who bought his bread? Would they all die? And none of these questions were answered. From that day to this I am still wondering. The atmosphere of dread has never been dispelled. What can the psychologist get out of that? I dread to think. Perhaps all my later attempts at a rational discussion of the question of machinery were nothing but an attempt to rationalize a childish fright. . . .

But years afterwards, when I was grown up, I revisited the scenes of my childhood and I happened to pass Clark's Bakery. There was the same factory building, grown a bit perhaps but not visibly much different. There was the tall chimney, its smoke advertising the still running steam engines, and there against the sky was the big advertisement. But how times had changed! Mrs. Hart had won. (Poor Mrs. Hart, poor nineteenth century, poor England, poor human race, how we are deceived!) For there against the sky, dark against the setting sun, in bigger letters than before was the monstrous proclamation: CLARK'S FARMHOUSE BREAD.

But in spite of this grim recollection, I hunt in my memory for anything that really sullies the picture of those years. It is quite certain that there must have been many dark moments. But it is hard to recall them. They do not stand out in my memory. By the time I was ten years old I had seven brothers and sisters and I was the eldest but one. I suppose we quarrelled among ourselves. I know we did and, particularly, we quarrelled with our eldest sister. This, now I come to consider it, really was a dark cloud in our sky. We never seemed to be able to do or say the right thing for her and we clubbed together against her. But my fear is that this made life worse for her than it did for us – the dark cloud however frequently appearing in our sky, must have been a much bigger and darker one for her . . . But sister Cicely generally managed to make peace. She was the good one in our family and she was strong and happy and intelligent – I think she was completely perfect. I do not remember the slightest thing wrong with her.

Apart from our childish selfishness, what else sullied the picture? Well, there was of course the dark cloud of poverty. But this was not so much a cloud in the sky as a constant subterranean rumble, a rumour of insecurity, eight children and five more to come and a regular salary or stipend of £150 a year was, even in those pre-war days, too great a disproportion. So there was the perpetual rumour of bills and summonses, and the perpetually hovering suspicion that the attitude of the baker or the butcher or the grocer was not as friendly as, to us children, ready to be friends with anyone, would have seemed natural. But somehow they 'managed', and it's impossible to be a poor relation without having rich relations. We had several of these and they were generous to the poor curate with his large family – they even sent congratulatory telegrams on the arrival of each new baby.

Those were the days before children were regarded as disasters. I suppose the people of to-day are quite unable to imagine that frame of mind. In those days boys and girls, young men and women regarded marriage and children as being inseparable things — the one an inevitable consequence of the other. We, of course, in the years I am writing about, had not the faintest idea how babies came, but we welcomed them without question and even with enthusiasm. Mother's got a new baby — of course, mothers always do have new babies. And as soon as they were old enough, we pushed them out in the pram, and took them out for walks. They were recruits for our little army, initiates in our masonry. We formed a little clan, we surveyed the world together and shared our discoveries, our raptures even — for it is not exaggerating to say that on the whole we were enraptured with life. The evil of life was only a rumour, an April cloud. We were sad if our parents were sad. It was gloomy and miserable when father was unjustly angry with mother, as, it seemed to us, he sometimes was. It was gloomy and miserable when mother was fretful and snappy with father — but these things though not infrequent, seemed natural enough even if unnecessary, and they were only passing troubles. I think we were wise enough, even as tiny children, to realize that our parents had plenty to worry them and that life was not easy for the poor. But they never complained about poverty as though it were an injustice. And they never put the pursuit of riches before us as an occupation worthy of good people. As I grew up I came to have many disagreements with my parents. There came a time, as I shall have to tell, when I seemed compelled to disagree with everything they said or thought, with their religion, with their politics, with their ideas of work and life, with their whole social scheme. But in these years of our childhood such a turmoil of the mind as overwhelmed me in my twenties was not even adumbrated. It cast no shadow before that I can recollect. Our parents, though fretful from time to time, were practically infallible and morally perfect. A rose seems no less a rose because it has a fly upon it, and the perfect goodness and wisdom of our father and mother seemed to us (for without talking about it, I know we children all agreed) to shine through any loss of temper or mistake in judgment.

However radically I disagreed with my parents when I grew up these things are perfectly clear. They have been perfectly clear to me always. There has never been a time when I have not known or even when I have forgotten that the main lines of their teaching and example were the main lines of the road to heaven. They taught us nothing of the theology of poverty, they never even praised it. They did not despise the rich or riches, on the contrary they revered the rich as persons whom God had blessed. They had no political bias in favour of the poor.[1] The thing that I am trying to say is this: that they made poverty holy — not in theory but in their daily lives.

I am trying to discover what I think and why I think it, what I love and why I love it. I must necessarily consider what our parents taught us and what example they gave. I am their child; what I know and love must be largely a consequence of what they were and what they taught. See my mother then: a beautiful black-haired young woman, such as a small boy would love to look at. She had a lovely big contralto voice and sang, as we thought, and I don't suppose we were wrong, divinely. She had been a singer in an Opera Company before she married and I think it was as an opera singer that my father first met her. She played the piano as well as we supposed it could be played. And she worked all day and all night. Sometimes we had a maid-servant or a 'mother's companion' (perhaps that is what 'A.B.C.' really was) but mostly we hadn't, because my mother wasn't good at keeping servants. She worked them too hard and didn't

[1] My father was, in those years, a liberal in politics and Mr. Gladstone was a hero to him, but that, I think, was mainly or entirely because my father was a non-Conformist in religion and, in a general way, all non-Conformists were liberals. But he never talked politics with us children or even in our hearing, as far as I can remember.

suffer fools gladly enough. She wasn't one of the mild and patient kind when it was a matter of work to be done. Cooking, sewing, darning, housework, and then she found time for reading her favourite George Meredith and George Eliot and to practise her singing. Her father, Gaspar King, was the manager of a timber-yard on the riverside at Brentford. And to that side of our family I owe the inestimable blessing of good 'working class' blood. I wish I knew more about him, but though we enjoyed going to the timber-yard, where he lived with a maiden daughter who taught the piano (I believe she was a good musician in a gentle way), our visits were very rare and they were very poor people indeed. Dear Grandpa King . . . he had a complete outfit of teeth which clacked as he spoke and a large library of more or less worthless second-hand books, all of which he had re-bound himself. But he was a proper respectable 'lower-middle' or 'upper-working-class' man and his house was entirely removed from the oppressive and fearsome masterfulness of the aristocracy of non-conformity on our father's side. Grandpa King and Aunt Lizzie were *good* people and we were not afraid of them.

And see my father: a rather good-looking, bald-headed clergy-man with a trim beard. A very kind man and a conscientious visitor of the poor. In those days I could never properly under-stand what good it did, but I accepted it without question that the sick expected the clergyman to visit them and that it was the right thing to do. My father often took me with him on these visits, and through them I became acquainted with disease and suffering. Poor old men in bed with sores that would not heal and that stank. Bedraggled women surrounded by children in rags—dirty rag-a-muffins, newspaper boys, pick-pockets just out of jail. And sometimes, to such a small boy as I was then, these walks seemed very long and weary. I don't remember a word of anything my father said to me, but I remember the gist of it very well indeed. He was, I thought even then and I can't help think-ing so still, very sentimental. As children, we were very con-siderably embarrassed by the things he said. But the substance of his teaching was doctrinally sound enough in an evangelical kind of way and I never doubted but that he had the word of God in him.

I shall have to say more about this later; what I am trying to do now is simply to describe him as a person so as to explain the sort of influence he had on me. In comparison with my mother, my father was a rather vain and lazy person. But she was so exceptionally the opposite that the comparison is unfair. By ordinary standards he was a very hardworking clergyman and it was not due to much fault in him if, by her standards, he seemed lacking in strength of character. Moreover, in his own line of business he had as much strength as she had. She was more intellectually combative and readier to fight verbally for her opinions and convictions; but the convictions and opinions were very much of his making or the result of his enthusiasm. He seldom or never argued with anyone and put on a more-in-sorrow-than-in-anger air when opposed; whereas we argued things with our mother constantly and she fought hard and loyally for the opinions she had to a large extent (as I can't help supposing) got from him. I say, it wasn't very much his fault if, compared with her, he seemed lazy and vain, for she consistently pampered and spoilt him. It was impossible to escape getting the impression that father's work was terribly important and terribly tiring. Father must not be disturbed; he's writing his sermon. Father must not be wakened; he's very tired after his Sunday work. Father's shoes or slippers must be warmed. In these and in countless hardly remembered but pervasive ways my mother built up in our minds the immense importance and dignity of the minister of religion and the father of the family. It was not at all his fault if he more or less basked in this sunshine, and so much so that even his admiring and loving children were, in an entirely unmalicious way, amused and sometimes faintly annoyed. I can well remember the slightly peevish feeling – the unexpressed 'I wish he wouldn't'. None the less we admired and loved him and respected him and believed everything he said. For, putting aside his laziness and vanity, he was an admirable example of his precept. He urged us to love our enemies, but I cannot remember that he had any enemies to love; I cannot remember anyone ever speaking ill of him or he of anyone else. He was from a 'highbrow', intellectual, agnostic point of view a complete non-entity; but he loved the Lord his God with all his sentimental mind and all his sentimental soul. And apart from and beyond his general moral goodness and kindness he had a certain maleness of attitude which was wholly admirable and right, and which, though it irked me sometimes because he mixed it up with morals and hero-worship and snobbery and emotion, is the thing of all others which, if I can put anything above anything else, I revere and thank him for. A certain 'maleness' I say. And, in short, I mean this: that he saw all things as ends in themselves and nothing simply as a means. He was particularly enthusiastic about sharpening pencils properly, not only about doing it the right way but doing it so as to produce the right result – a well sharpened pencil. Hundreds of times I was shown how to do it or pulled up for carelessness in not doing it properly. This is perhaps a small thing, but it is clear that if a man will make such a molehill into a mountain he must be taking things pretty seriously. And that is the point. There's quite a lot in sharpening pencils and the man who sees more in it than others is not lowering himself to pettiness but raising the job to nobility. My mother was more intellectually combative but my father was male to her female all the same. His whole nature was male. While she worried and fought and sweated, while she worked her fingers to the bone with sewing and washing and mending and cleaning, he, with remarkably little apparent fuss or fume, went on with his sermon writing and his reading of Tennyson and Carlyle and Maurice and Robertson and Farrar and George MacDonald and Kingsley.

These were his heroes, and the children were named after them. Thus: my elder sister, Enid Rose after Tennyson's lady; myself, Arthur Eric Rowton after Dean Farrar's schoolboy hero (but this I always thought was intended as a warning to me as well as a tribute to the beloved author). My brothers: Leslie MacDonald, Stephen Romney Maurice, Evan Robertson, Vernon Kingsley and Kenneth Carlyle. My youngest brother failed to get a Victorian giant for a prop and stay (for that was my father's ingenuous hope: that we should be inspired by our illustrious namesakes), he was called Cecil Ernest Gaspar, Ernest being the name of the Bishop of Chichester (Wilberforce) who received my father into the Church of England just about the time of Cecil's birth. My six sisters, with the exception of Enid, do not seem to have been named with a literary so much as with an aesthetic reference: Cicely Eleanor, Lilian Irene, Madeline Beatrice, Gladys Mary and Margaret Evangeline.

And more impressive than anything else, he went on with his painting! He always said he 'ought to have been an artist rather than a clergyman'; but I'm very glad he wasn't, not because he didn't do very nice paintings — especially in his early days, when he admired Messonier and did sunsets and landscapes in the same nice 'tight' manner, before he got entangled with his artist friends in the vague and woolly business of provincial English 'impressionism' — but because that would have landed us (if indeed we should ever have existed; for he might not then have met our mother) in an altogether sillier and rottener world than that of a non-conformist parson. For though the 'artist' as such and by definition is concerned with ends rather than means, and only with means as leading to ends, and though to man as artist all things are ends and worshipful as such, yet in those days, the 1890's, even more than in these in which I am writing, the 1940's, artists were exceedingly vague as to the nature of the ends for which they worked.

I am not going into this matter of art and life in this part of my book. It will have to come in later, when I try to deal with my own struggles to arrive at the truth of things. The point in this place is this: that if you have to be born into a morass, and that is everybody's fate to-day, it is far better to be born into the family of a poor parson than into any other; for the parson is by profession a dispenser of the truth and even if, as it may come to appear later, his truth is not the whole truth and not nothing but the truth, even so it is the truth he is after and it is such truth as he has that he is minister of. And if you are to be the son of a parson, how much better to be the son of a poor parson than of a rich one. A rich parson is a worldly parson, unless his riches have come to him by accident and even then they are likely to betray him, but a poor parson is helped by his poverty to give himself to true religion — the succouring of the widow and the fatherless in their affliction.

The artist is a minister of truth, and all workmen are artists in so far as they are men and not mere tools, and therefore are ministers of truth; but in those days, as in these, this fact was denied. The artist had become a special class of person — a lap-dog or mountebank, refined or vulgar. He was the flower of a dying civilization, the over-ripe fruit of its rotting tree. His future was downwards to still further decay, in a world doomed to inevitable catastrophe. How clear it seems therefore that those children are blessed and fortunate who find themselves born into a family whose professional concern is not riches, is not 'success', is not 'getting on', is not comfort and convenience, is not fine clothes, is not power and is not even hot-house flowers.

It is of course true that our parents might have rebelled against their circumstances. They might have shown us an example of worldliness in the midst of poverty, of ambition in the midst of failure, of vanity in the midst of the cheap and second-rate. The profession of parson, no more than that of 'artist', will not save a man who is without virtue, or one whose wife sides with the enemy against him. That such was not the case in 'our family', was not only because of our father's profession but also because of our father's and our mother's virtue. Nevertheless to me, and perhaps I may say to us, to me even then, though more dimly than to me now, it was always a matter for congratulation, that I was brought up in a state of life, an atmosphere, a place, where the job mattered because it was in itself a good job and not because it 'paid'. It is matter for congratulation, even though we sometimes thought quite otherwise at the time, that getting new clothes was a rare and marvellous event and that more commonly we were clothed in the much better clothes cast off by our kind and rich relations. We children may have chafed at our poverty when it came to watching our cousins being measured for new suits at expensive tailors while we were given what they discarded. But we were rebuked if we did so. And as to other matters, we were simply unaware of any privation. We did not covet our uncle's big Blüthner; it would have been impossible to imagine it in our small drawing-room whereas it obviously fitted his large one. Moreover no one played the piano in his house, in spite of the Blüthner, so when it came to thinking about music it was mother's playing and mother's singing that we remembered. The riches indeed were ours – and, I fear, some of the pride. And if from time to time we envied our cousins in their big house and magnificence, such envy led to no lasting misery; for it is the way things remain in the memory that really indicates their character and I can only remember that though we revelled in our visits to London, we were infinitely happier at home. And the thing that I am struggling to get clear is that, in spite of the inevitable 'poor-relation complex' resulting from the contrast between our condition and that of our rich cousins and the children of some of the richer members of my father's chapel congregation, a 'complex' I've got still, though now it matters very little because I know about it, and then it mattered not at all because I took poverty for granted, in spite of this and in spite of some real privation and shortage of primary necessities, so that sometimes we really did go hungry and underclothed – as when, with infinite patience and pride in his skill, father would cut one cold sausage into such a large number of thin slices as to give each one of us ten or more children three or four slices each for our breakfast – the essential quality of life in the poor parson's family was one of vocation. He followed his vocation of parson, his wife that of mother, and they both invariably put the good of the work before any other consideration. There was nothing self-conscious about this or priggish or theoretical. I do not think either of them knew anything about the theology of vocation. They never talked about it. I won't say anything about supernatural grace, though doubtless they received it. I am not writing *their* lives and I am only describing these things in so far as they are relevant to my theme which, ashamed though it makes me feel, is my life and not theirs. I will only say that from my point of view and, according to my memory of the point of view I had as a child, this essential quality seemed both good and natural.

So much at this stage for Holy Poverty. There remain Chastity and Obedience. I suppose in respect of chastity we were brought up in the ordinary tradition of middle-class, Victorian non-con-formity. This of course meant complete secrecy as regards sex and, if not secrecy at least complete politeness as regards organs of drainage. We rebelled against neither convention and until the very end of the period of which I am writing I never pene-trated the veil of secrecy. It was, though not frequently indulged in, an enjoyable pastime to stand with my younger brothers in a row on the top of the brick wall which ran along the bottom of the field beside our house and compete to discover which of us was best in aim and which could 'do it' farthest; but we were never caught at this game. We used to visit new public conveniences rather in the manner of little dogs trying a hitherto untried gate post. But I don't remember having at that time anything but a vague interest in any other natural function, except that, as a boy of about twelve years old, I and another boy, while we were 'changing' in the dormitory after football, showed one another our nether eyes. This, though our interest was, without doubt, potentially sexual, was hardly more than curiosity. (Alas! that other boy was killed in Mesopotamia in the war of 1914–18.) And as we didn't talk much about such things it seems to me we cannot have had anything but the commonly approved attitude of mind to the business. And the children of neighbours with whom we played must have been similarly politely brought up; for I haven't any recollection even of conversations on the subject.

But though we knew there was something very remarkable being kept from us, we were, I think by good fortune, not sufficiently precocious and, being, by the care and innocent snobbery of our parents, prevented from making the acquaintance of 'undesirable' children, we sailed gaily through childhood without any painful gnawings of curiosity or any erotic play-makings. Any bad results of the conventions we were brought up in which might be expected to follow did not show in this period. But we emerged from childhood without rational defences. The conventions of politeness with regard to the privy leaves the child entirely unprepared for the discovery, as to which he or she has had only the dimmest premonitions, that organs of drainage are joined to and partly identical with organs of sex, or indeed, that organs of sex, as to which he has formerly hardly suspected the existence, should turn out to be the very organs of drainage which, up to now, he has been so sedulously taught to despise or, at most, to admire only as one may admire the ingenuity of any piece of sanitary engineering. The diaper or napkin is our first article of apparel. Clothes are not primarily for dignity and adornment; they are primarily to provide the first privy – private parts, in fact privy parts. Such is the convention and I say it is a bad preparation for adolescence, with all its budding sexual enthusiasm. It is difficult if not impossible for ordinary vulgar men and women – there is no sin in vulgarity and who would wish everyone to be 'refined'? – to throw off, either suddenly or after a long time, the deeply ingrained habits of thought instilled into them by their parents and nurses and the whole world around them.

One may say this and yet not be blaming either parents or children. The histories of sexual secrecy and privy disgust are about as long as the history of man, and their physical basis is fear, fear almost amounting to panic. We are, as our ancestors were, simply and desperately afraid of what the young things will do. We dare not cultivate a rational attitude towards physical drainage for fear of what games the children will be up to – so we make a great to-do with disgust. We dare not encourage the youthful exercise of sex (the economic aspect of marriage has always been difficult; how much more so the problem of illegitimate and unwanted children) – so we use every dodge of disgust, secrecy and fear to prevent it.

We are now approaching the end of our civilization so it is probably much too late to do anything about it or to hope for any radical change or improvement. In any case it is no part of the scheme of this book to make plans for social or educational reform. I wish to do no more than show what was the mental and spiritual background or foundation of the child of a nonconformist parson in nineteenth-century England. I do not suppose that my experience was in any way remarkable or extraordinary. It was, I imagine, typical of that of millions of children of my generation. I suppose it is the same to-day. The few special schools and the small number of 'enlightened' fathers and mothers can do nothing against the main stream of tradition. I don't mean that I think all 'special' or 'crank' schools are good or all 'enlightened' parents good critics. I'm not judging. I only know that the tradition of politeness and secrecy hides the problem and doesn't solve it. Moreover, though parents and educationalists discuss these matters solemnly at their meetings and conferences, they suffer from the same inhibitions themselves. The privy, and consequently nakedness, is still dirty. The olefactory nerves are still refractory, and town food and sanitation do not make for improvement in this respect. Sex is still a matter of privy parts, and the economics of marriage to-day are even more monstrously difficult than ever they were in past times. Therefore, if we can't or won't tackle the problem of smell and can't or won't tackle the problem of marriage, sex will always be 'dirty' and children always a danger. And chastity and purity will remain what they are to-day – merely negative virtues.

As I have said it was not until I was nearly at the end of my schooldays that I penetrated the veil of secrecy. This was partly by accidental discovery and partly the result of a cousin's information. The information, comically enough, was, in the main point, entirely wrong and therefore innocuous. He told me that the navel was, so to say, the centre of attraction, and the flower of the plant! And as I had always wondered what navels were for (and no one would tell me) this seemed a very reasonable explanation. And as I had for a long time felt very affectionately towards his sister, I thought lovingly and longingly upon her umbilical ornament and basked in this error for several months. But my accidental discoveries caused me black misery for the next seven years. Black misery indeed! but what with prayer and fasting and a not too unreasonable amount of indulgence in between whiles I managed to achieve a sort of accidental balance. But this sort of biography is not a history of adventures and it is not to form an item in the case book of the late Havelock Ellis. I want to discover what things and persons had an influence on me and what opinions I have arrived at in consequence; so both the reader and myself will be spared – moreover I have written about these things elsewhere. The only aspect of this matter which is relevant here is the relation between these things and the rest of life. For that has always been both my difficulty and my enthusiasm – to discover how things are related and to discover a right relation where a wrong one exists. Perhaps it doesn't matter how hair-pins are related to balloons, perhaps there is no relation worth mentioning, but in this business of human sex and its relation to life and work, it is obvious that the relation is both real and important. It must, obviously, make a lot of difference to men and women whether they live lives of puzzledom and repression, false valuations and romantic sentiment, untruth and bad conscience, or whether they escape all such troubles and go through life clear-headed and happy; and it is obvious that, among all the things that are influential in our lives to mar or make our happiness, the instinct of mating is one of the most important.

I have done my best to describe my parents and the environment of my childhood. Such as I am their influence was important and so was that of our chapel, my school, our town and our hills. My judgment of persons and things is neither important nor relevant; I am only concerned to describe them justly. So in this matter if I tell you what I was taught you will know what I had to put up with, and in the matter of sex the only thing I was properly taught as a child was that it was a secret. So when I found out the secret, the last possible thing to be done was to confide in our parents or teachers. We tried doing so, both I and my brothers. We were only told not to do so again and that if we disobeyed in respect of a certain mysterious prohibition, the consequence would be in the first place a thrashing and, if we persisted, 'consumption', madness and death. And this was not at all because my father was a fierce and cruel ogre, for he was precisely the opposite, but simply because he had been brought up that way himself and was not only desperately inhibited but also desperately afraid. So we left it at that and carried on a new and secret life unhelped – and also undeterred. We were given no responsible advice and had access to no reliable reading matter; we were only put off with vagueness and sentimental nonsense about not tampering with sacred things. Why 'sacred' we were never told, for the very things which, up to then, we had been brought up to suppose had no relation to anything but drainage and which were therefore more or less despicable, were now vaguely hinted to be objects of sanctity! So we were undeterred; for when your parents and teachers are quite obviously being unreasonable and even ridiculous they seriously undermine your respect for their admonitions.

But how shall I ever forget the strange, inexplicable rapture of my first experience? What marvellous thing was this that suddenly transformed a mere water tap into a pillar of fire – and water into an elixir of life? I lived henceforth in a strange world of contradiction: something was called filthy which was obviously clean; something was called ridiculous which was obviously solemn and momentous; something was called ugly which was obviously lovely. Strange days and nights of mystery and fear mixed with excitement and wonder – strange days and nights, strange months and years. It was a blessing that this intellectual puzzlement and emotional exaltation was balanced by a good healthy rabelaisianism. Jokes and rhymes took the edge off the parental and pedagogic solemnity and my own.

And in spite of the black misery of bad conscience I was happy. For my conscience was somewhat like the law of gravity; it operated in inverse proportion to distance and in spite of all that we were told (though that was remarkably little and that little was nothing but 'don't'), I saw, more or less clearly that what they called 'unnatural' was natural enough[1] and bound to happen in one way if not in another.

[1] NATURAL: a difficult double-meaning word. It is 'natural' for an acorn to become an oak—it is its *nature* to do so. It is 'natural' for a stone to fall, even if it fall on your toe, but it is not therefore true to say that it is the nature of stones to fall on toes. It is 'natural' for boys (and girls) to be interested in their organs, even before they know anything about sex, and still more so after they have 'found out' or been told. Tumescence is an interesting experience – that cannot be denied, and if, as commonly happens, the boy discovers that it can be induced by manipulation and is accompanied by pleasure, it is 'natural' to repeat the experiment. With or without secular or religious instruction in the matter, most boys, especially among the 'working' or 'country' classes, realize very easily that a pleasure so ecstatic is not a thing to be mastered by, (it would be just the same with intoxicating drink if young boys could afford to buy it), and so masturbation, though indulged in, more or less, by at least ninety per cent of adolescent boys (perhaps (?) a smaller percentage among girls) is only very rarely indulged in to the detriment either of body or mind. It should be noted also that masturbation is by no means unknown among 'animals'. This also indicates a certain 'naturalness' in it. All I am concerned with in this note is to urge that we take a cheerful, open-eyed view of the matter; for frightening people, whether by threats of dire disease or 'hell fire' does not stop it – it only drives it to secrecy and neurosis. The 'natural' remedy is good education, and that is why the 'working' and 'country' classes

The awful thing seems to be the way they try to frighten you. Luckily for me I wasn't a very frightenable subject, and I realized without stating it that the teetotallers had no right to call themselves temperate.

Obedience is an easier matter to talk or write about and, unless my memory is nothing but an apparatus for white-washing the past, it seems to me quite certain that, in the matter of parental authority and childish docility and subordination, things have changed very much for the worse in the last fifty years. I don't claim at all that we were specially good children, or even (though I should like to do so) that our father and mother were specially good parents. But I know that they were very firm in this matter and that we had to do what we were told – 'on the nail'. And we suffered few or no hardships from their strictness.

They may not always have been just. I remember when I first became aware of the possibility of absolute and irreparable injustice. My mother accused me of doing something I had in fact not done. I forget what it was. It was a trivial matter, but the downright monstrosity of the situation, as such and in itself, gave me even at the time, and perhaps more so then because such a possibility had not previously occurred to me, a real shock. I was, so to say, flabbergasted. For if with one's own mother it was impossible to put the thing right and in so small a matter, what frightful things might be possible in the world outside where no sympathy and understanding could be drawn upon.

don't suffer much from excessive masturbation – they know enough about sex not to be excessively curious and imaginative and in such circles there is less unnatural pudicity and puritanism. The 'middle-class' is naturally much more ignorant and therefore much more secretly vicious. 'They order', said I, 'this matter better in France' – I mean in Roman Catholic schools. This may well be so, for in those schools they inculcate at least a true view of 'man's last end', but Catholics, lay and cleric, are, as other people, victims of the society in which they are born and brought up, and in religious houses they are by no means free from 'panic legislation' and the prejudices of the nursery.

This event did not cause me much pain, moreover the affair was so small that I wasn't even punished for it, but it made me think; it seemed so incredible, so impossible, so mentally horrible. It seemed as though the very earth were reeling and insecure. I didn't protest much at the time. I saw that nothing I could say would do any good, for the matter in question was something for which I could prove nothing. So I simply stored it away as a thing to marvel at. And I make no complaint for I have always suffered more from unmerited praise than from undeserved blame, as when, having got it out of a 'crib' I said in a Latin translation at school the Trojan Horse was 'pregnant with arms' and was highly commended for my intelligent choice of words. . . .

My mother, being on the whole more physically worn out than my father, may have demanded more of us and more harshly than he did. He was naturally more easy going and desirous of a quiet life. But the balance of justice must have been kept fairly even; for their general principle: that absolute and instant obedience was the holy duty of children, however unreasonable a particular demand might appear was not accepted by us simply in fear, but also without question. The story of Abraham and Isaac and the altar of sacrifice was a favourite one of my father's. I have a sort of feeling that I remember thinking the story was 'a bit thick', but the principle was all right, I didn't doubt that, and as a consequence I have never succeeded in acquiring the kind of conscience according to which the only sin is being 'found out'. I'm not making myself out a virtuous person, I'm not even saying we were virtuous children. I'm only affirming that we were brought up on virtuous principles and that these principles were put before us in such a way as to win our assent to them — assent both notional and affective. And I think this assent was a consequence of a realization, unexpressed of course, for we were still inarticulate, that, like the centurion in the gospel who, though having soldiers under him, was himself 'subject to authority' our father and mother ministered commandments which were binding on them also and that while they demanded obedience from us they were themselves under obedience.

The modern disease of embarrassment must have been in its early stages in the 1890's. For, though the phrase 'shy-making' had not yet been 'coined', we were already suffering quite painfully from what seemed to us our father's painful lack of restraint.[1] When my father read to us or recited his favourite passages of scripture or poetry or his favourite prayers from the prayer-book he would quite unashamedly put the utmost dramatic expression into it. And when he read the prayers at church he did the same. There is a passage in the Church of England 'Litany' where petition is made for 'all women labouring of child, all sick persons, and young children' and when he came to this he always made a long and tear-making pause after the words 'sick persons' – 'all sick persons . . . and young children'. We discovered in later years that this pause was intended to give the people time to recollect the sick persons known to them, but we children always thought it was meant to give them time to prepare their minds for what was to come – the children. And we were embarrassed accordingly and looked shamefacedly at our boots. What 'labouring of child' might mean we had no idea, unless it meant mother sweating at home mending the children's clothes, but it all seemed to support our explanation of the pause. And we were the more justified in this because, as we well knew, it was just the kind of thing father would do. Young children were one of his special 'lines'.

Another thing that embarrassed us a good deal was a thing he called 'father's eye' – the idea being based on the text 'thou God seest me'. He had a large coloured and very 'natural' representa-

[1] It is an odd thing, one may note in passing, that while the modern art-critics preach the doctrine of personal sensibility and the theory that 'art' in its inmost core is 'self-expression' yet people are becoming more and more shy of mere personal exhibition. They weren't shy in that way when we were children.

tion of an eye – all by itself on a card, without any head or face. He fastened this high on the wall of the breakfast-room so that it stared steadily down on us and followed us all round the room. I don't know that it worried us much, but I suppose it did act as he intended it should and reminded us of his precepts when he was not there. But we thought that was a 'bit thick' too.

But my intention in writing about these things is not in the least to imply that now that I am fifty years away from them I see them as foolish things. Our modern embarrassment is justified because the Victorian tradition, being grown old and become corrupt and the sap of life no longer rising in it, we must necessarily be made 'uncomfortable' by its remains. The remains become superstitions; that is what superstitions are – things 'remaining over' and though dead, valued as though alive. In the 1890's the traditions of parental authority and of the obedience and reverence and subordination of children were still lingering. Now they have gone. It is a disaster, but it was inevitable. It was inevitable because the impressive superstructure of Victorian family life was standing upon an increasingly treacherous and shifting sand. My father and mother were among the last of the old believers, but, as in the case of the cardboard 'eye', it is clear that the old beliefs were inadequately supported. Father's eye is an inadequate substitute for the all seeing eye of God. The substitution has good scriptural warrant; for the father does indeed enjoy a divinely given authority over his children; but when honesty becomes simply a 'best policy' and that policy nothing more than an imperial 'graft', it is clear that the supports have gone.

I look back then to my childhood as one looking back to a different world and the chief thing about that world was this: that, even if we were wrong – and it is easy now to see that there was in reality very little truth in our view – we believed that the world of England was divinely guided, the British Empire a divinely ordained institution, Religion the main spring of political and social structures, Atheism and even agnosticism monstrous perversions very properly indictable at law, and the police the very proper instruments of the practical observance of the ten commandments.

Religion, in the world of our childhood, was the fundamental basis of life. Sunday and going to church, the occasional week-day services (as when a mission preacher would appear from the mysterious outer world and conduct a series of 'revival' services – and on those occasions, instead of sitting up in the gallery as we did, all in a row, on Sundays, we sat down in the church and that added greatly to the solemnity; for we were not then simply 'the children' but part of the great crowd of sinners personally addressed by the preacher. On one such occasion I was actually 'saved' and held up my hand in witness. The church was dark except for a strong light over the preacher, and I see no reason to doubt that I actually was 'saved'. The soldiers in the War to end War, worked up by rum, did, for the time, forget their fears and did actually go 'over the top'. Why should not a small boy, worked up by eloquence, for the time, forget himself and actually go over the top of the mundane watering place in which he lived?), family prayers and our own bedside prayers were obviously and necessarily the basic reference – nothing could claim to be a higher court of appeal or a yet deeper basement. We were not more than ordinarily pious children. We took religion for granted just as we took the roof over our heads, the clothes on our bodies and the certainty of food at meal times – sometimes more, sometimes less, but always some. But taking things for granted doesn't mean you aren't interested in them or that, on occasion, you won't be very interested indeed. As with the house and home, as with clothes, as with food and drink so with our religion. We played at 'houses', we played at 'dressing up', we played at cooking and brewed strange drinks from garden flowers, and we played at religion – dressing up as preachers and reading out the prayers as much as possible in our father's manner. Sometimes we were very hungry for what the larder provided and sometimes we were hungry for what we got in church.[1]

What was this religion of our childhood? Perhaps I must briefly describe the sect known as 'the Countess of Huntingdon's Connection'; for it was at the chapel of that sect, in North Street, Brighton, that our father was the assistant clergyman, or 'curate', as, following the Church of England terminology, the congregation called him. I know very little about the sect – this only: that a certain lady, Selina, Countess of Huntingdon, had some difference of opinion in religious matters with her bishop, and, being of strong character and very much determined to follow her own opinion unhindered, she, with a group of followers, seceded from the Church of England and set up a 'connection' of her own. I don't think they ever numbered more than about a dozen chapels. The main point was that they were free from episcopal interference. They did not repudiate anything officially taught in the Book of Common Prayer and being Church of England people and sharing the common affection for the Church of England Liturgy, they took the Prayer Book with them and conducted their services according to Church of England forms. But they were evangelicals primarily and not sacramentalists, preachers not priests. So the pulpit became the centre-piece of their churches. Though the communion table was still in its old place in the centre of the 'East' end wall, the pulpit was placed in front of it in the middle of the church and the 'curate' read the prayers from a desk below.

The service was read with great care and expression and the

[1] Of course this was not always so and there were times when religious observance seemed very irksome. I recall one Sunday in particular when I was sent to church in the evening though I had already been in the morning. This didn't happen regularly and for some reason I was all alone. I was in a fume of rage and running along the Dyke Road by the Birds' Museum (we always called it that because we thought it belonged to the birds), I threw my Sunday 'bowler' as hard as I could at a lamp-post saying: 'Damn church'. But that outburst sobered and relieved me, and I remember quite enjoying 'church' afterwards.

choir sang at the proper times, but the sermon was the chief thing and, for this, the preacher put on a special black gown, very noble and voluminous. The sermon, always entirely over our heads, lasted forty minutes or an hour, so, with 'Morning Prayer' as well, the whole 'service' lasted a good hour and a half. 'Grief touched us early' therefore. You can imagine the five or six small children in a conspicuous place in the front of the gallery, just over our father's reading desk. We dared not misbehave. Quite apart from our father's displeasure, the publicity would have been unbearable. We scarcely moved; we hardly yawned; we couldn't fall asleep. But, strange as it may seem, we were proud enough of our position and keen critics of father's 'form' and the preacher's mannerisms.

It will not be difficult after this for the reader to guess what sort of religion we learned. They had 'the Communion' once a month and a very large proportion of the congregation took the Bread and Wine. 'Do this in remembrance of Me' – a good and holy and salutary practice. For the rest, it was a kind of combination of Congregationalism (for the congregation was autonomous and elected and paid[1] for its own ministers) and 'Low' Church of England. I haven't the faintest idea what they preached about. The religion we got was out of the Prayer Book and from the lessons and hymns, from the Sunday school and from our father and mother at home. We didn't attempt, at least I didn't, to follow the sermons – that was for the grownups as I supposed.

I think, in view of what followed, both in my father's life and, later still, in my own, that all this is very significant. When we were on our visits to our rich relations near London we were

1 Talking about 'paying': we used to go into the vestry after the service and, sitting quietly in a row (because the preacher was resting after his exertions, on a sofa), watched the deacons count out the 'collection'. We enjoyed that very much – piles and piles of pennies and piles and piles of shillings and other coins – even gold ones. But I don't remember that we ever regarded that money as money to spend. It was church money and its mere quantity removed it from the category of covetable things.

taken as a matter of course to their church, the Congregational church at Blackheath. Here, as children will be, we were highly critical of the proceedings and, though there was a definitely higher standard of comfort (if you've never seen it, you can't imagine the comfort of non-conformist chapels compared with Church of England or Roman Catholic ones) than at North Street, Brighton, and a much bigger 'organ', with a real Doctor of Music to play on it, we were unanimous in preferring the Book of Common Prayer to the eloquent, extempore, though well-prepared prayers of the Congregational minister. We were sufficiently embarrassed, as I have said, by our father's 'self-expression'; much more so by the laborious intimacies and voluptuous servilities which they poured out in prayer at Blackheath.

My father's father was a Congregational minister. He had been a missionary, as also was his brother, my great uncle, in the South Sea Islands and my father was born in the island of Mangaia (Mang-a-í-a).[1] My grandmother and the children came home, via Cape Horn, about the year 1850. A background of missionaries and more or less fabulous stories of the South Sea Islands supplied both mental pabulum and family pride.

The missionary in the South Sea Islands in the 1840's was a very patriarchal personage. Each missionary seems to have had an island to himself and to have been 'God almighty in that place' – with his wife and family and native servants he lived in civilized state in a large bungalow house and dispensed truth and justice and medicines to all. I suspect that in its pious way it was, as we say, 'a pretty good show'. We were told many stories of the life and though they are not very exciting stories, two of them, because they impressed me very much as a child, are relevant here.

On one occasion a native having disgraced himself (I don't remember what he had done but it was something of great offence

[1] Two of my brothers followed the tradition and went as missionaries to New Guinea (Papua) where one of them still is (and a Venerable Archdeacon too), and a sister is a missionary in India.

to Gilliwaini, the missionary's wife) and had fled into 'the bush'. After some days, one morning, in the far distance (for we imagined the garden to be surrounded by a wide undulating plain – such was the impression given by our father's narration) a small dark speck was seen, as it were on the horizon, and this speck was seen to be coming nearer and nearer. At last it was seen to be a man, a native, crawling on hands and knees. Slowly and painfully he came nearer and then it was seen that he was coming to the missionary's house. Who? Why? As he came near he was recognized. It was the fugitive man. He crawled to the garden and up the garden path to the bungalow step. He lay flat on the ground. He grovelled in fear and humble repentance. He said no word but his whole action denoted penance and request for forgiveness. He was forgiven. The awful majesty of the missionary, nay, of an offended God, of the missionary's offended God, was appeased. . . .

And my father enthralled and embarrassed us with the following: He had fallen and cut his forehead open. The bloody wound would not heal; the bleeding would not stop. Nothing my grandfather had in his medicine chest would do it. Everything was tried. The boy was bleeding to death. Even the native remedies suggested by Akaduwaini, the fat native nurse, all dressed up in early Victorian clothes, were tried and found useless. Fear held them all, the child was dying. For days, or was it weeks? the child had been pouring out blood – even spiders' web had been tried. And then my grandmother brought out her box of homoeopathic bottles – and because the situation was so desperate my grandfather at last, after much persuasion, consented to try an arnica bandage. Behold! the bleeding stopped at once! The child lived and told us the awful and touching story. I don't think he actually pointed the moral but he made it quite obvious: Are not Abama and Pharpar, rivers of an allopathic Damascus, good enough? Must we descend to the Jordan of homoeopathy? That was the style of it. But strange to say my father when he grew up was not a homoeopath though my mother was!

All the relations on my father's side of the family were Congregationalists and enthusiastic supporters of the missions, so, even at that date, we were aware of a sort of disgrace. My father had deserted the traditions of his fathers and though he wasn't a member of anything so wrong as the Church of England, he was always regarded as a dangerously independent person. It was playing with fire to use the Book of Common Prayer!

For my father himself had first of all been ordained as a Congregationalist and had been minister of a chapel at Burnley in Lancashire. So his joining with the Countess of Huntingdon's 'connection' was a step in the wrong direction. It is curious to note the occasion of that step. He had preached in his chapel against the doctrine of Hell, and the congregation didn't like it! He had to resign. It was entirely in line with his sentimentalism that he was unable to stomach the notion of eternal punishment, but it was ironical that a man of such mildness and kindness should be forced by his very mildness to place himself in the position of rebel. Our Congregational relations were wise in their generation. They prophesied where it would lead to and they were right. He left the Congregationalists because, in a manner of speaking, he wasn't going to have his pulpit doctrine handed out to him by the congregation of which he was supposed to be the shepherd. He joined the Countess of Huntingdon's because they accepted doctrine handed to them from above – which is the proper place for doctrine to come from – the Book of Common Prayer was the symbol of that. But still things were not right. The judgment of the congregation was still paramount; for though they accepted the Book, they rejected the authority which had brought the Book into existence and was, therefore, the only authority competent to interpret it. The next step was clear and must be taken. He must join the Church of England.

It was not however until 1897 that my father actually took this step and as neither he nor my mother ever talked to us children about it, very nearly all that I am writing about it is

inference. I have often wondered what they thought and said
to one another. It must have been a risky step to take, for from
the money point of view it was going from bad to worse.
£150 a year and eleven children living – the eldest only sixteen –
that was his income at Brighton, supplemented by subscriptions
and clothes from relations and friends. But the income of a
curate in the Church of England might be even less and, as a
fact, in his first curacy at Chichester his income was only £90
a year. Without the help of relations and friends they could not
possibly have existed and there were debts to all the shopkeepers.
It must have been a most tricky business; for by joining the
Church of England they must necessarily alienate the sympathy
of the very people upon whom they relied for help. It is difficult
to understand how anyone could regard their behaviour as that
of people who were anxious to get rich and who put the
acquisition of riches above everything else. Yet some people
did so regard it. I even heard that the Bishop of Chichester
(Durnford) refused to accept my father as a candidate for Holy
Orders on the ground that it was not a genuine case of 'conversion' but simply a move in the direction of better income and
better social status. I am as certain as I can be about anything
that this was a misjudgment but I dare say it could easily appear,
or be made out to appear in that light. The social status of our
family would certainly be raised by the move and my parents
were not innocent of snobbery. Even if my father had been free
from it, it would have been impossible to expect the mother of
thirteen children to be oblivious to the superior advantages of
Church of England society. I don't know what they thought.
I wish I did. I know they were desperately poor and I know
they had their fair share of respect for the social conventions,
for the rich and the great. If they seriously believed that there
was money for them in the Church of England as there was
certainly improvement in social position, then doubtless those
things may and indeed must have been important considerations.
How could it be otherwise? But if such considerations were the

basis of their action, then they must have been woefully disappointed in the event. For when, Bishop Durnford having died, my father was accepted by his successor, Bishop Wilberforce, the grand economic result was a curacy at Chichester with £90 a year, followed by one at Bognor with very little more (I don't know the figure) and then no preferment at all until, in 1913, at the age of sixty-four, he was appointed to the obscure vicarage of West Wittering, near Chichester, with an annual income of a little over two hundred pounds. And that was the grand climax in the career of a man who was said to have joined the Church of England for the sake of money and high society. And I find it pathetic to recall that, when he was over eighty and, owing to his age, had resigned his living, he thought it was a sad 'come down' to be living on a small pension and have only a lodging in my brother's house. If that was a fall, it does not look as though he could have had very grand notions of falling. And indeed he had not. The vicarage and his books, the daily round in the parish, the Sunday services, a new stained glass window in the church, opportunity to read *The Times*, tobacco and a few friends. . . .

As I have said before, I am not writing the history of my parents. It is the various things and persons that influenced me that I am trying to recall and it is in that respect that the affairs and opinions of my father and mother are important and relevant. For though they discussed the matter with us children hardly at all, the conversion was matter for quite a lot of discussion among ourselves — at least among the three or four elder ones — and was in itself, by reason of our move from Brighton to Chichester and all that that implied and involved, an event of 'world-shaking', or more accurately, heaven-shaking importance.

The very first sign that something was about to happen occurred one Sunday morning, in I suppose, the year 1896 (but it may have been earlier). After the service at North Street chapel it was my father's habit to take us along 'the front' for a walk, to get a blow of the sea and, doubtless even more attractive to him, to enjoy the 'church parade'. Sunday morning, between mid-day and lunch time, on the front at Brighton was a remarkable affair in the 1890's. Perhaps it is so still, but, in the days before motor-cars and short skirts, in the days before 'wireless' or cinemas, although it was comparatively innocent it was proud to think itself very worldly and gay. This church parade business was rather a bore to us children. We wanted to get home to dinner and with a mile and a half to walk it seemed absurd to loiter, for the sake of taking 'six deep breaths', down on 'the front'. But on the Sunday morning I am thinking of, my father, instead of taking his usual 'six breaths', took me (I don't know where the other children had got to – gone home to dinner?), in another direction altogether. We went across the old Steyne and up St. James's Street. I had no idea where we were off to. We turned in at an Anglican church near the top, on the left hand side. It was a large place and, by our comfortable chapel standards, arid, bare, and gaunt. There was a general colour of pale bricks and the benches were bare wood – no cushions or carpets, no little lock-up boxes of family prayer books – it was distasteful, but impressive. I didn't know what, if anything, was happening or why we were there. I think there must have been the tail-end of a sermon and my father had come to hear it. Perhaps some preacher he was interested in was there that morning. There was a mystery anyway. Never before had I been in an Anglican church except as a sightseer in a country village. Never before had my father so far as I knew, been in an Anglican church to a 'service', and on a Sunday morning! I don't suppose I thought half so much about it then as I am doing now. I don't remember anything being said about it at the time or from that day to this. I don't know what church it was and I've never been there again. But some strange thing had happened and although I now recall it as being a momentous occasion, I don't think I've ever once spoken of it to anyone. The calm and apparently unchanging and unchangeable current of our life had been suddenly diverted. A strange and uncomfortable, almost disreputable gap had suddenly appeared in our quiet, respectable world of prayerful shop-keepers. For the uncomfortable character of that church was not indicative of mere poverty but of the presence of the poor! It was a place that poor people went to. That was how it struck me. A bare bench is probably much cleaner than a pew uphol-stered with cushions or can more easily be kept so. But you don't have bare benches except in places where people are generally dirty. And who are generally dirty but the poor? I was quite used to poor people as people to be 'visited'. But this was different – this was sitting with them in church! Of course I thought none of this consciously at the time. But looking back to that Sunday morning and trying to dig out the core of that experience I can only see it in that way. I can see, as plainly as though I were sitting there now, not in any detail but in its general shape and quality, that dim and, as it seemed to me, shabby, vast place. I dimly wondered what it meant. I did not find out for many years; but I date the beginning of my adventures from that morning.

And another thing impressed me on that occasion, or by reason of it. Up to that morning the Countess of Huntingdon's chapel had been the unshaken and unshakeable centre of religion. I was of course dimly aware of other churches. My father was very keen on 'architecture' and he often said he would like me to become an architect. I, however, was enthralled by loco-motives and could think of nothing but locomotive engineering as a profession – of this more later; the point here is that my father having his enthusiasm for architecture did not fail to point out the various buildings and especially the various churches we came upon in our walks or when we stayed in the country for holidays. So, as I say, I was well aware that the Countess of Huntingdon's church was not the only church and not even the only kind of church,[1] but other churches didn't concern us.

[1] The only kind of church we never saw, the only kind which was never mentioned, was the Roman Catholic. I can't be sure of this, but I should think

They were places other people went to for reasons which I never bothered about or inquired into. But this visit to the church in St. James's Street was not an architectural visit. That was the momentous thing. It was, in some way unknown to me, a visit of inquiry. It implied that something was lacking in North Street. It was even a kind of disloyalty. I trusted my father completely. I knew without being told (or perhaps I had been told) that there were higher loyalties than those due to employers – even if those employers were ministers and deacons – higher even than those due to king and country. If my father chose thus to imply a doubt as to the complete sufficiency of the North Street chapel, I was ready enough to follow him on his voyage of discovery. It was an adventure anyway and the opening of a door into a mysterious and hitherto unsuspected world. And in spite of the uncomfortableness there was an attraction about it. For though children love the snug fug of the nest they have been brought up in and will defend it with their fists when rich cousins are making sneering remarks, nevertheless they are not by nature addicted to cushions and curtains and fussy old ladies. They don't mind draughts at all. I think they prefer the dining-room to the drawing-room as a place for playing in, and perhaps the kitchen to either and the 'attic' to the kitchen. So, shocked at what seemed to me the place's uncouthness, as if that uncouthness was somewhat unseemly and disrespectful to the practice of religion, at the same time I was a bit awed. And this awe was not the result of any visible loveliness – it didn't seem to me that there was any – it was rather the result of my hardly conscious discovery that the word of God and the worship offered by men was something transcending the comforts of warm air and cushions. I was impressed by that gaunt place; how else can I account for it?

I believe I could fill the rest of this book with probings into

the first R.C. church I ever went into was the big church at Arundel and this must have been about 1898 when I cycled over from Chichester to see the sights.

the quality of that Sunday morning but there are other things to be probed, and I think it must have been very shortly after that Sunday, that the decision was taken, the farewell sermon preached and, the 'hat' having been sent round, the shopkeepers paid. I am happy to record this. They were really pretty generous, considering that the move was in the nature of a defection, and considering that quite a lot of them must have been subscribing to their own bills. But what a mercy! I think we left Brighton without a stain on our family character. I say the 'hat' was sent round, but indeed it was a most solemn proceeding and you can imagine the odd snatches of comment we overheard, as when it transpired that dear Mrs. Taylor, to whose son my father had been tutor and whom we children were taught to look on as one of the high gods, had given the vast sum of twenty pounds – it really was vast in those days, the best part of a hundred now. Then my father, having by now been accepted by the Bishop, went off, with the remains of the 'hat', to be a student at the Chichester Theological College.

There followed a strange period of interlude. We no longer went to the Countess of Huntingdon's church on Sunday mornings. We floated in a sort of heaven of detachment. Religious observance, in spite of all I have said as to our taking it for granted and our pride in our chapel and our father's ministry, had become a little bit of a bore. It was all very well for the grownups; they had what they wanted and what they paid for, and they enjoyed it. But it was beginning to be irksome to us children. We were beginning to take notice of sermons and to be critical of the obtrusion of the personality of the preacher. And, it can't be avoided, my father's painting, my mother's singing, my father's painter friends, his revelling in Tennyson, and many such things, all helped to create an impassable gulf between us and the pious shopkeepers who formed the main body of the North Street congregation. We were a cut above them in appetites and interests. Nice kind old things they were and with what joy we looked forward to the Christmas parties

to which they invited us in the drawing-rooms over their shops!
But, there it was, they and their chapel got more and more
boring. So when my father went off to Chichester it was as
though to herald a new day and we seemed to be like young
birds let out of a cage.

At the north end of Preston Park hidden in the trees is the
old parish church of Preston – just on the outskirts of Brighton.
Here we now went to church. I forget all about the doings
there – whether they were 'High' or 'Low' or, more probably,
'Broad'. I only remember, but this I remember very well, that
it was a treat to go there, as church-going had never been before.
We had always had the Church of England Book of Common
Prayer, and, as I have said, we got religion from it and not at all
or very little from sermons. It would be true therefore to say
that the practice and even the idea of liturgical worship was not
a new thing to us. But, in spite of our inattention to sermons,
the liturgy at North Street was heavily overpowered by worship
of the preacher. The liturgy was there but it was at the foot
of the pulpit, in the lower place, and the table of the Holy
Supper was in the background.

We were too young and too uneducated in religious matters
to know what the great difference was, and perhaps I should now
speak only for myself, but I, at any rate, was aware of a great
change in the idea of religion and, to some extent, I was aware
of the nature of it. For not only was the weight of the personality of the minister lifted off (and if you've never 'sat under'
a minister – what a marvellous phrase and how descriptive of
the oppression! – you cannot understand how great a relief that
was), but you became impersonal yourself, the weight of your
own personality was lifted too, and, though not so obviously,
this was an even greater relief. For the trouble with evangelical
religion as commonly understood is that it is too personal
altogether. There is too much emphasis on the personality of
the minister and too much emphasis on the personal reactions
of those who are ministered to – too exhibitionist on the one

hand and too introspective on the other. There is very little conception of objective, corporate praise, as of the morning stars singing together. 'He prays best', as the hermit St. Anthony said, 'who scarcely knows that he is praying', and what applies to individuals applies also to congregations.

But on the other hand it is essential to keep a balance – as Nietzsche said (paraphrasing someone else); not Apollo, not Dionysos, but Apollo *and* Dionysos. The Gospel is an Evangel, the word must be preached, there must be preachers – and there must be hearers if there are to be doers. 'Faith without works is dead', but so also are works without faith.

Obviously I could not have expressed such views at that date, but I could experience the freshness as of a coming spring. And it is easy to understand our delight in the little old country church with its little coloured windows and its all and sundry congregation, a sort of cross section of the parish, excluding, alas! only the more consciously pious and respectable, for these last formed, I think, the congregation at the Countess of Huntingdon's chapel.

It is easy to overpaint this picture. It is easy to make it appear much more sweet and perfect than it really was. But it is not easy to make it appear more sweet and perfect than it then seemed. How painfully I discovered later that there were flaws in the picture and that much of it was decayed and corrupt and sham. That does not matter. What matters at this point of my book is that we, in some half-blind way, understood our father's conversion; we wholeheartedly approved of it and were, in fact, converts ourselves.

# CHAPTER IV

# CHICHESTER

I LEFT school in 1897 primarily, I suppose, because the family moved to Chichester. It is that momentous event that I must now try to get to the bottom of. And if possible, as all this book is a business of making mountains out of molehills, I want to get the mountains the right shape. For it is the shape of things which chiefly took me by storm at that time. Of course I didn't talk about the shape of things – whether past or 'to come', but I am not concerned in this book to put down what I actually said or thought at this moment or that, but to get at the real quality of my experience, whatever I may or may not have said or thought at the time.

I have said before that from my earliest years I had always been fond of drawing engines and bridges and signals and tunnels. As time went on this enthusiasm was canalized more and more into the drawing of locomotives. Whether or no I was any good at it does not matter. The point is that I was always doing it and with progressively greater and greater attention to the details of structure and the technique of draughtsmanship. I knew little or nothing of mathematical drawing. I used rulers and compasses, but as regards measurements and proportion I went entirely by eye. I was very much concerned with the structure and movement and purposes of locomotives, because you can't make a good drawing of anything unless you know how it works and what it is for. This may be a 'heresy' from the point of pure aesthetics but I wasn't interested in such things then and am only interested in them now in order to repudiate them. But what I was primarily concerned with then was locomotives as such, their character, their meaning. And as this character and meaning were manifest in their shape, it was their shape I was determined to master. I laboured under the

spur of this enthusiasm for ten crowded years. I don't know
how many hundreds of drawings I made. Perhaps it was not
very many; for I could only do them in my spare time in the
evenings and in holidays — on the breakfast-room table when
the things had been cleared away and before the time came for
the next meal to be laid. I suppose I was a pretty good nuisance,
but my parents were proud of the result and encouraged me,
and once or twice my drawings were even exhibited at school.
I supposed I was training myself to be an engineer. I think I
thought that all engineering was like that — an immense enthusiasm for engines — engines as beings. Engines pulled trains; they
belonged to the Railway Company, they did things and served
purposes. Their construction depended upon a vast amount of
mathematical calculation and knowledge of physics. But,
though I saw, though rather dimly, that I should certainly have
to go into all that, it was the shape and character of the locomotive
that really enthralled me.

Some time towards the end of our Brighton period I was
taken by my father to see an engineer acquaintance of his, and
I was put forward by my father as wanting to enter that profession. I remember the occasion very well for, though I didn't
receive a shock, I was certainly appalled. The thing that I had
only seen dimly was suddenly brought into the light. I saw that
engineering wasn't what I had thought it. The engineer friend
didn't seem at all interested in locomotives. He talked about
hydraulics and the planning of reservoirs and he showed us
what, to me, were shapeless diagrams indicating stresses and
strains. I was able to allow for the fact that locomotives weren't
his business, but from his conversation, it was clear that even
railway engineering was 'doings' not 'beings' and that it would
be extremely unlikely that I should ever win through to being a
designer of locomotives. This interview depressed me a lot,
but I think I still thought he might be wrong, and I think it cannot
have been very long after this that the great move to Chichester
was made.

One day in the summer of 1897, while my father was still a student at the Theological College, I bicycled over from Brighton to see him. I have only an intangible recollection of that day but it is not the mere haziness of memory which prevents me from describing it. Nor is it that the vision is not clear and, in some particulars, even precise. It is simply that the thing is beyond words. You must understand that except for that one day I had never, in all my fifteen years, seen anything like it. I had been to London, to Blackheath, to Greenwich. I had been to many of the villages round Brighton, and to Lewes and small towns such as Steyning and New Shoreham, and in all these places I had seen various marvels. What could be more splendid than the walk across Blackheath, along the avenue of Greenwich Park to the Observatory, and then the grand prospect of the Thames and London? . . . What could be more enthralling than the sight from the waterfront by Greenwich Hospital, with the constant procession of ships, great and small, up and down the river? It is no use talking about such things. Such sights cannot be remade by words. Lewes, to my mind, is a lovely town (though I've heard it called 'a dirty old place'), the playing field in the bottom under the Castle and the High Street climbing the hill — Shoreham with its splendid church and the harbour, Steyning and the Ouse River under the Downs, and Patcham and Poynings and Bramber and Beeding, Pyecombe and over the hill to Clayton and Ditchling — in those days, before motor-cars and motor-buses, these places were all unspoiled and untouched. And perhaps before and above and beyond all such things there were the Downs. If you have been a little child brought up in those hills and in those days, you will understand their mortal loveliness. If in your childhood, you have walked over them and in them and under them; if you have seen their sweeping roundness and the mists on them; and the sheep, and the little farmsteads in the bottoms, then you will know what I am talking about — but not otherwise. No one who was not there as a child can know that heaven, no grownup can capture it. Aware, then, of such things, knowing such places and such kindness; filled also with visions of locomotives, a naughty boy too – fond of football and feeding and, for this may have contributed, filled with the new consciousness of adolescence, I arrived at Chichester, on a bicycle, and I had never before seen anything like it.

And, by going to Chichester, I for the first time, saw Brighton. For, however little I put it in words or even into articulate thought at the time, suddenly – and indeed it was quite suddenly, for it happened all in one day – I saw Brighton for what it was – a shapeless mess. Perhaps if we had lived somewhere near the old Aquarium or in one of the superb Regency Squares by the West Pier or on the Marine Parade, I should have been able to think differently of my native town. There are many fine things about Brighton, many dignified old early Victorian houses and squares, and the almost majestic sweep of its long 'parade'. But we lived a long way from these things and we thought of Brighton only from the back and from our suburb above Preston. Brighton was not for me a Regency wateringplace nestling in the junction of downland valleys; it was the Western Road and North Street, the Dyke Road and the Dyke Road Drive. It was Preston Park and the railway viaduct, the Seven Dials and the mass and mess of unplanned slums round Edward Street. All this will be pretty meaningless to the reader who knows not Brighton but that is all to the good, for it is its meaninglessness that I am wanting to convey to him.

I saw Brighton for what it was, and suddenly, almost directly I saw Chichester. It had simply never occurred to me before that day that towns could have a shape and be, like my beloved locomotives, things with character and meaning. If you had been drawing 'engines' for years and were then suddenly taken to such a city, you would instantly see what I mean. I had not been training myself to become an engineer, I had been training myself to see Chichester, the human city, the city of God, the place where life and work and things were all in one and all in harmony. That, without words, was how it seemed to me that day. It was not its picturesqueness; for Chichester is the least picturesque of cathedral cities. It wasn't its antiquity; for I had learned no history and age meant little to me. It was a town, a city, a thing planned and ordered – no mere congeries of more or less sordid streets, growing, like a fungus, wherever the network of railways and sidings and railway sheds would allow. That, I discovered, was mainly what Brighton was to me. A railway, with a sort of nondescript encampment crowding round it. For the railway from London to Brighton had been built in the days when the town was only the Regency watering-place. But since then the population had spread inland up all the valleys and the builders had perforce been obliged to get in where they could, in between the railway lines. And nineteenth-century speculative builders were not concerned with towns or cities, with plan and order, they were only concerned to build houses, as many and as quickly as possible. I did not know the economics of all this then; I only knew that Chichester was what Brighton was not, an end, a thing, a place, the product of reason and love. For love too was visible. Here was no dead product of mathematical calculation, no merely sanitary and convenient arrangement. Here was something as human as home and as lovely as heaven. That was how it seemed to me, and I went back to Brighton on my bicycle in the evening in a glow of excitement.

It must have been very soon after that visit to Chichester that we left Brighton, but before I can embark myself on the voyages on which I set out from that harbour, I must, because it terrified me at the time and influenced my mind very deeply – and, I suppose made a vital difference to my whole life – tell, however briefly, of the truly awful catastrophe which occurred in the January of that year. I know that I am viewing this thing in proper perspective (have I not had forty-three years in which to get over it – if that was all that needed doing?) and yet it is exceedingly difficult not to seem to exaggerate. What human family has not known death? Is not death as common as birth? Animals and flowers die around us every day. By the very fact of living we are acclimatized to death. And if 'in Adam all die' are we not all 'made alive' in Christ? Do we not believe it? Is it only a notion; is it impossible to make the belief affective? If any family had ever been brought up to believe, that family was ours. Sentimentally and dogmatically we had been taught to believe from our infancy. Perhaps, to our realistic young minds, our father had often embarrassed us with his poetical and scriptural eloquences. The miracles of the Gospel story – of Lazarus, of the Centurion's daughter and that other child, of the Resurrection itself – and the stories of the son of the Sunamitess and of the boy raised from death by Elijah – these things we knew almost by heart, yet the death of our sister Cicely was, not only to our father and mother but to me also a more grievous thing than I had ever imagined possible.

'Whereas I was blind . . . now I see.' The simple narrative in John's gospel of the man healed of his blindness – surely the best piece of writing in all the world of books – and all the other stories of the blind receiving sight, owe their effect to the fact that we all know, in our minds, in our hearts, in our imaginations, the awfulness of the contrast between the black world of the blind and the world of those who see. And that a blind man should suddenly see is almost as though the dead should suddenly live. We know there are all the other senses. We know that the deaf are commonly much more cut off from communication with their fellowmen than are the blind and much more self-centred and selfish and suspicious in consequence. We know that the senses of taste and touch and smell commonly gain a compensatory keenness in the blind. We know, even, that the blind are often so much more patient and kind than other people, that blindness almost seems a blessing. In spite of all this we know that to see is to live. And, so conversely, with death – to die and not live. She lived . . . and now she was dead. She was alive in Christ, but she was not alive to us. She was not

here. The most lovely, the best, the most dear – dead – gone
for ever. There was nothing left but a grave in the cemetery
and the cold comfort of a text – ΤΑΛΙΘΑ ΚΥΜΙ. The loveliest
text – but what good is even the loveliest text? What poetry can
bring the dead to life? I wept, I almost screamed with misery.
I dreamed dreams of her return. It was a mercy that the new-
found fields, the new flowers and hills of a medieval city imposed
themselves upon my attention, though for a time even this
delight was spoiled by the thought that we could not share it
and explore it together.

I would not have written these last paragraphs if it were only
to paint a picture of myself and my feelings. The only point of
their inclusion is that I know that the death of my sister was,
because of its lasting influence and impression, one of the things
that must be taken into the account. I had not known death
before, except as a fact of natural history. I had not known
death in the sense in which we may be said to 'know' a lover
('and he went in unto her and *knew* her'). I did not know it
again for exactly forty years, and, admirably enough, I was in
Jerusalem at the time. What things have I known and loved?
What things have I, even in my cold clay, suffered? Of what
things, therefore, am I made?

So we left Brighton. I ought to remember the 'move' in
itself. But I don't. It must have been very impressive – mother
and eleven children all arriving together! I only remember
the first morning after when I and a brother or two went before
breakfast down to the railway station to see the trains. But
the glory had departed – somehow it fell very flat and I don't
think I ever went to the station again except on what you might
call legitimate business.

Now began a new life, a miraculous life, a life as it were in
fairyland. I think it may not be difficult for the reader to understand this. Anyone who has lived for the first ten or fifteen years
of childhood in such a place as suburban Brighton and has then,
almost suddenly been taken, with all the natural enthusiasm of

F

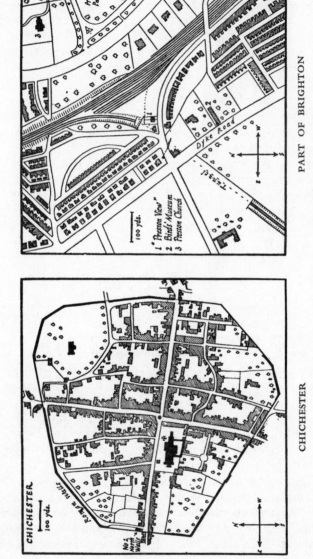

CHICHESTER

PART OF BRIGHTON

In both maps the outside border line represents about ½ mile square.

Drawn by Denis Tegetmeier for E. G., July, 1940

1 "Preston View"
2 Birds' Museum
3 Preston Church

childhood for green fields and pastures new, to live in such a truly noble town as Chichester will understand; and I think even those who have not had such an experience will see that the contrast must have been almost frightening in its violence. For even if a Brighton suburb is not more than usually shapeless, not more shapeless than all such nineteenth-century towns are and must naturally be – for they are the product of nothing nobler than the speculative builder's appetite for money – on the other hand the 'ancient and loyal' city of Chichester is more than usually serene and orderly. And it owes its quality not merely to the civil and religious exuberance of the medieval world but, more fundamentally, to the military and civic order of Rome. For the sake of my own amusement and in the hope that it may even convey something of the contrast I am writing of, I have made the diagram here inserted. Though not at all mathematically symmetrical the plan of Chichester is clear and clean and rational – a thing of beauty having unity, proportion and clarity. The small modern growth of the town outside the walls was, forty years ago, almost negligible. Over more than half the length of the Roman wall (a great part of which is thick enough to form a broad footpath along the top) you could look straight out into the green fields. A town, a city, of ten thousand persons, with the Cathedral, the Bishop's and canons' houses, ten parish churches and twice as many 'public' houses – four straight, wide main streets dividing the city into nearly equal quarters and the residential south-eastern quarter similarly again divided by four small streets and these almost completely filled with seventeenth- and eighteenth-century houses[1] – and all this almost immediately obvious and clear.

[1] I cannot refrain, for the benefit of the reader who has never seen it, from mentioning especially the East Pallant. This is not the best kind of building in the world – nothing of such a period could be – but of its kind (Queen Anne and Early Georgian) there is, I suppose, nothing more perfect in England than the five or six houses on the south side of this street. They are not big and grand, like the one ascribed to C. Wren at the corner, but little and perfect. I trust they are still there.

But Brighton, as we knew it, the suburban development of Brighton between what used to be called Cliftonville and Preston, for that was Brighton to us, the square mile or two of which our house in 'Dyke Road Drive' was the centre, well, there is simply nothing to be said about it. And I think it is significant that when we thought of Brighton, our 'home town', it was of a place of which the centre was our home – the 'semi-detached' house called 'Preston View' – there was no other. But when we lived in Chichester our home, though no less a home, became less the centre of things. The centre of Chichester was not No. 2 North Walls but the Market Cross. This may have been unfair to Brighton, but it signifies a change and, I think, a change for the better. We gained not only a civic sense but a sense of ordered relations generally. Brighton wasn't a place at all. As I have said, we didn't mind, for we knew nothing else. It never occurred to me that any other sort of town could exist. The idea of a *civitas*, of a town as a complete and self-sufficing entity was never put before us. Brighton in its beginnings must have been a most lovely village, a fishing village at the foot of the Downs – the bare Downs above and behind – and the Regency squares, in spite of the monstrous incongruity of the Prince Regent's 'Pavilion' in the middle, must have made the Brighton of William the Fourth a very dignified and delightful resort. As to the 'Pavilion', I don't want to say much about that, but, at the risk of being accused of mere local patriotism, I must say that, though it is a ridiculous affair, and all the more so where it is or rather, where it was (for it is no more ridiculous now or out of place than nine-tenths of the buildings around it), it is actually, in itself, a very good piece of work. Compare the late Victorian additions with the original building. The difference is the difference between pre-industrial England and the dead England of commercialism. The stones cry out. For all its fantasy there is a subtlety and refinement about the work of the Prince Regent which is entirely absent in the additions of the pig-witted town councillors.

But the Brighton of the Regency was not the Brighton I knew, and therefore Chichester was a revelation. Perhaps I was, unless I deceive myself, ready for it. I was, I suppose, just the right age. I was mentally bursting like a bud and physically too. The door of the sexual world had been opened to my mind but not into the actual world of the flesh. (It seemed incredible that real union, physical union was a thing that a real woman would actually consent to. One side of my mind knew that it must certainly be true and another side refused to believe it. It seemed too good to be true that women could want men as men want women.) So in those years I lived in a state of romantical imagination. Moreover I had just come from a period of intense concentration upon the particular form of a particular thing. For now I will use the word 'form' rather than the word 'shape'. Form, though of course I didn't know it for many years later, is a much bigger word than shape. Shape is only the visible aspect of form. The soul of a thing is its form. And though I knew nothing about it, and no one ever talked to me in such terms – though perhaps, nay, certainly, the hard core of my father's sentimentality was that very thing, even if he didn't know it himself – that was, in fact, the thing I had really been concerned with during all those years of 'engine' drawing. And what I had put into drawing locomotives I now put into drawing churches, and doorways and towers – and with this advantage: that now I was, for a time, released from any consideration of earning a living. When I drew locomotives people said: Oh, you're going to be an engineer; you'll 'get on', you'll make money. But when they saw me drawing churches, they didn't worry me like that. They didn't see any use in it. In the ecclesiastical world of Chichester there was no money in 'art'. They liked the drawings and were entertained; but they saw no future in it save that of a 'poor artist'. This was all to the good. It was a disinterested activity as far as I was concerned and no one thought of it otherwise. So for the next few months (it seemed much longer – but months are years to the young) I drew the cathedral, from every point of view, and all its doors and windows and pillars. I cycled about all round the countryside, going home in the dusk of the evening with my bag of catches. And churches had shapes, because they had forms. The form was what mattered, though I knew it not.

I made no measured drawings at that time. If I might have wandered away into mere romanticism I was, I think, saved by my interest in perspective. My father had always been keen to drill me in that subject and it satisfied whatever orderly appetites I had to respond to his teaching. To draw a thing accurately in perspective is as good a discipline as to do it with footrule and measuring rod. To see a thing accurately and to draw it thus is as good as measuring it up. And that was all I thought I was doing, making good records. I wasn't interested in sculptures or carvings; I was only interested in buildings – how they stood up on the land, their shape, yes, but also their character and meaning – the meaning of buildings as buildings and also of buildings as churches or houses or barns or windmills – for I drew these things too – but chiefly as churches. I don't mean their ecclesiastical meaning. I think the nearest I can get to it is by saying it was their 'liturgical' meaning, that concerned me. This may be misleading, for I didn't know the word and our family was only in a very vague sort of way 'high church', whatever my father may have been, and he didn't take a very definite line in the matter or say anything to us about it. Nevertheless it was certainly as being in some way manifestations of public worship, a sort of architectural *ikons* that I looked at and drew church buildings. They quite clearly took the place of locomotives and were a 'whole time' enthusiasm.

Then, after a while, I suppose they thought I had had enough freedom and ought to be doing something regularly and definitely. My memory of that time is of a constant activity of drawing, but I expect the truth is that I spent a lot of time idling about and being a nuisance. It must have been so because although, I fear, I have given a picture of myself as an industrious young prig, I was not that at all. I was seething with adolescent enthusiasm and exuberance and not at all a pure-minded young angel.

How well I remember the day when, as the result of being shown a photograph, I discovered that the adult human female has a bush of hair on its belly! This knowledge pervaded my mind, filled all the nooks and crannies of thought, both day and night, for several months – and added a lot of fuel to the fire. The student of such matters must consider whether the complete ignorance of my first fourteen and a half years – an ignorance not only of function but also of things as things to be seen – was a good thing or a bad. I was certainly not blasé but, on the other hand, I was entirely unprepared and I find it difficult to describe the intensity of my interest in the matter. I dare say other boys, and girls too, are the same, but some kind of pudicity prevented me from talking much to my brothers or even doing anything in a bold manner – a furtive peep through a crack in a wall, a secret searching of dictionaries – and lewd conversation with other boys or young men rather shocked me although it allured me too. And although it allured me it disgusted me – not morally but intellectually. They didn't seem to me to put the right value on it. Rowlandson is all very well, and I enjoy both his draughtsmanship and his pig-sty robustiousness, but they weren't Rowlandsons. So the intensity of my exuberance was a rather secret affair and probably no healthier in consequence. I think I had periods of moody selfishness and gaucheness. I don't think I was any help at home. I was being spoilt – the budding 'artist' to whom the other children must look up and for whom 'allowances' must be made. So my father took me round one evening to see the master of the Art School and told him that I wanted 'to embrace a career of art'. The phrase embarrassed me, but I certainly wanted to do something definite and was very glad to be taken on as a whole-day student at the Chichester Technical and Art School.

Then began a period almost equally divided between rapture

and rebellion. I worshipped the art master.[1] Everything he said was right, and everything he did. He represented the good and the true and the beautiful. I hung on his words and followed him about like a dog. On Sunday afternoons he took me for walks in the country. He pointed out all the beauties of nature and taught me all about the styles of medieval architecture and how to tell the dates of buildings and he quoted Tennyson's *In Memoriam* at every turn, so that I became a great student of that poem and learnt great patches by heart.

> As year by year the labourer tills
>    His wonted glebe, and lops the glades;
>    So year by year our memory fades
> From all the circle of the hills.

I learnt it then; I know it now. I am sitting up in the Welsh mountains, at Capel-y-ffin. The hills are all round. I am looking across a broad valley and the rill of the water fills my ears – the trees, lopped by the hard winter and not by the labourer, the little farms. It is not the Sussex above Chichester; it is much less genteel and much less prosperous, but I recapture the same mood of love for the life of the earth and especially for the earth that man has loved, for his daily work and the pathos of his plight. And then we went back to tea in his little Queen Anne house – Sunday afternoon tea and toast, the glow of firelight and the glow of spiritual fires.

And I worshipped at the art school too. But there things after a time became difficult. The art master made me go in for 'exams', and I had to prepare great sheets of drawing – plant life drawn with extreme accuracy, and meticulously 'shaded' drawings of cubes and blocks and other art-school 'properties', examinations in 'perspective'. And it gradually transpired that I was destined to be an 'art-master' and that all these examinations were to that end. I worshipped my teacher but somehow or other my acquiescence in his plans became less and less enthusi-

[1] George Herbert Catt.

astic. I didn't see myself like that. It was all very well to get medals and prizes (I never got a medal but I did get a thing called a 'Queen's Prize' — that was in the days of Queen Victoria — for perspective drawing) but it was quite a different matter to spend your life in the 'South Kensington' art-school world. I began to like the prospect less and less.

Meanwhile, in addition to the art-master, I had made another friend and found another angel of enlightenment — or, more accurately, I had been befriended by him and taken under his wings. For, though the drawing and 'sketching'[1] and art-school classes may be said to have occupied all my time, there grew up in the interstices a great enthusiasm for church music, for going to the Cathedral services and sitting in the choir stalls. I suppose I did this almost every day, I was as regular as any canon and much more regular than any lay person except the usual Cathedral lunatic. I made friends with all the choir boys (and played football with them) and the lay vicars, and then a great day came when I was asked to tea by one of the Prebendaries. I was already very great friends with the head verger or sacristan and under his instruction I learnt all the odd gossipy history which is the mainstay of that profession. But he was a truly grand old man, his deep loving-kindness to young boys and old stones made him as much more than a mere 'cathedral guide' as a bishop is more than a man and a priest — he was more than a guide, he was also counsellor and friend, and he seemed to have been in some way consecrated. He allowed me to have the keys of the doors and I got to know the cathedral in its very bones — all the mysterious circular staircases and dark places over the vaulting — I climbed the spire and walked all the clerestories and galleries. I knew my way about as well as the masons and much better than any of the clergy. I haven't got much of a head for high places but I dared myself to a lot of dangerous and very silly adventures and I made drawings in all

[1] Odd though it is to remember, my great exemplar at this time was Herbert Railton!

sorts of odd places and listened to the music through holes in the bosses of the vaulting.

And then I went to tea with the Prebendary. I don't really remember the first occasion, but it was the first of many. He lived in a little house just outside the cloisters and I had only to wait for him as he came out after the evening service – he was sure to ask me to tea. He was a Doctor of Divinity and had been a missionary in Melanesia. He was great on heraldry and medieval architectural archaeology. He supplemented what I learnt at the art-school so that what might have been simply a matter of beauty became also a matter of goodness and truth. He gently ridiculed the enthusiasm of the 'restorers' and though he would have been horrified at the suggestion that anything but 'Gothic' was suitable for the cathedral, he laughed at the idea that modern Gothic should look like the old. This, at that date and in those countrified circles, was true enlightenment and, whatever I might and did come to think later, it was a good foundation and made it clear that the accepted opinion was not necessarily the right one. The old Doctor probably never imagined that he was at all revolutionary, still less that he was training a rebel, but in his quiet way, and a way of boundless benignity, he was a keen critic and he smiled to scorn the foibles and foolishness of our little ecclesiastical society and its snobberies and pretences.

So I had two admirable guides and at least one rock of ages to lean upon and shelter against. And as I am seeking to recollect all those things and persons which or who influenced me and to which or to whom I am grateful, I must also mention the assistant organist of the cathedral. He was a good friend because, though he was a man and I was only a boy, he never condescended to me, but welcomed me as a 'pal' and an equal. Perhaps, in his innocence he thought my talents as a draughtsman were equal to his as a musician; but it never seemed so to me and I basked and, I might almost say, wallowed in his musical enthusiasm and genius. When we arrived in Chichester I was still at the stage of thinking that Mendelssohn's *Lieder ohne Worte* were the most beautiful music in the world and, though I hadn't heard the pretty story at that date, I should have thoroughly agreed with the American gentleman who said that there was one thing about Classical music which it was a great comfort to know and that was that 'it was much better than it sounded'. Our mother played Chopin's *Nocturnes* and such things and I liked them very much, but I was an innocent child of the period and heard nothing amiss in Stanford and Goss and Dykes – and Mendelssohn. But now I was hauled over the coals. It was lucky for me that I was 'easily led', for I discarded the old favourites without any pangs, and though a lot of the stuff I so eagerly accepted then has since had to be discarded in its turn, the world of music, represented by Beethoven and Mozart and Handel and Bach and Corelli and Purcell and the early English composers of church Services, was as new and exciting and almost as unexpected as the city of Chichester after a childhood in Brighton.

And then I went and fell in love – oh delightful and desperate and unrequited love! And the girl was a fellow student at the art school. I suppose there is nothing unusual about this, but it had the awful result of estranging me from the art-master. For, in spite of all I have said, and I might say much more and still fail to convey a faithful picture of my sinful nature, I was, in respect of that love affair, as innocent and guileless as the most puritan person could have wished. I loved her completely and every inch of her body. I desperately wanted to kiss her, but I never once did so or even thought such a thing possible. Moreover I don't think she responded, for though I used to call on her at her home and was introduced to her family, we never got as far as talking about love. There is not much point in writing about this. I am not writing a history of such things. The point here is only this: that one of the effects of the affair was to make the art-master angry with me and the effect of that was to destroy my abject worship of him. He thought I was bringing the school into bad repute. I was innocent and he did not seem to believe it, and that was monstrous. Perhaps he was already less hopeful of me because I wasn't taking too kindly to the career he had mapped out for me. Schoolmasters, it seems, are like that. However that may be, the spell was broken and through the kindness and extraordinary generosity of my friend the Prebendary and some friends of his I was found a place in the office of the architect to the Ecclesiastical Commissioners in London and a specially reduced premium paid. My father was more pleased than annoyed by my desertion of the art-master career. As I have said, he had always wanted me to be an architect and I had come round to the conclusion that architecture was a real job and no mere schoolmastering.

So my two years of Chichester came to an end but not before I had 'got over' the art-school love affair and had really and truly fallen in love with the daughter of my old friend the sacristan and, on the strength of the grand future which loomed up before me as a London architect, had actually proposed marriage and been accepted.

But I can't leave Chichester and go to London and not say a something about one other enthusiasm; for this one was really of great importance, at least in this story. That enthusiasm was the enthusiasm for lettering. This had begun in Brighton; for locomotives have names, and these are painted on them with great care and artistry. If you are keen on engines, you collect engine names (at our school it was as popular a hobby as 'stamps') and if you draw engines you cannot leave out their names. But at Brighton this lettering enthusiasm had hardly won a specific recognition. I don't think I ever did lettering separately or, if I did, it was only as practice for doing it properly on engines. I was very keen on handwriting too, and, as an example of my ambition to get all things to go together (one reform leads to another), I remember writing to my father, when he was away in Chichester as a student, and beginning my letter with the plain word 'father' without any 'dear' or 'my dear'. But I had to give this up because he was much offended. This was an early example of the impossibility of getting people to be reasonable. I think it made me register a silent vow 'never to take offence', never.

But at Chichester, under the influence of the art-master I discovered that letters were something special in themselves and, urged by his enthusiasm I became expert in inventing what seemed to me later the most monstrous perversions and eccentricities in the way of 'new art' lettering. I could almost wish I had that freedom now. And yet we weren't really free; for we laboured under the tyranny of art-school fashion — a harder master because more capricious than any 'tradition' or than any such rational notion as that the primary business of lettering is to be legible. Lettering was a part of art-school 'art'; its primary business was to be what they called and still call 'decorative'. But though I am ashamed of it now, I was jolly proud of it then, and my prowess was highly esteemed and earned me much undeserved praise. The 'really important' thing, however, is this: that I was, in a not too inaccurate manner of speaking 'mad' on lettering, and this, though I never dreamed of it at that time, led to a complete change in all my ambitions and the wrecking of all the castles in Spain built for me by my kind friends and relations.

My departure to London almost coincided with our family's departure to Bognor where my father had been appointed curate with, I hope, a better stipend than he got at Chichester. I was only a short time at that remarkable place (truly remarkable because it's so difficult to know why it exists — except for its sands and the amazing number of hair-pins which, in those days, were to be counted on the promenade) and so never properly succumbed to its influence. I was in fact most thoroughly miserable there. I was at a bad dissatisfied age — my future was unknown. My new love affair was no more approved at home than the former had been. I was in disgrace at the art-school and, instead of the high visions of a heavenly Jerusalem which Chichester had meant to me when we came there from Brighton, my whole world seemed to be crumbling. Shapelessness and disintegration! We seemed to be falling back into chaos. Moreover the new-found sanctuary of religion, the august and unshakeable castle which the Church of England had seemed in comparison with the Countess of Huntingdon's chapel, seemed now less venerable – not venerable at all, less holy – good kind clergymen but many asses as well – no force, no sharp edge, no burning fire of Christ's word, no apostolate, no martyrdom – no power to bind or loose, no strength to hold even me, still less to hold all men.

A different light filled the sky and just as the little church at Preston had seemed more perfect than it was, so I was, without being able to say why or how, beginning to realize that Chichester was not only 'no abiding city' but one in which I was no longer able to abide. I was very miserable and dissatisfied. I was hateful at home and hated being there. The only hope was the new life and work offered by my London apprenticeship. The world must be built anew and I myself must be rebuilt. Fortunately I did not see this rebuilding in grandiose terms. I did not think of myself building palaces and cathedrals. By some grace of humility – or perhaps I only cut my cheek to spite my face – I saw myself simply as a builder of cottages. Odd though it seems, I went to London with that ambition filling my mind. I was 'fed up' with the vague 'career of art' and, in mere self-defence (like a person who, beaten by Beethoven, says to himself: well, I will at least play my 'scales' decently), I thought of my future in the solidest and most tangible terms I could imagine. It was a sort of talisman. I referred everything back to that – the cottage, the little house – four square, with doors and windows and a roof.

And though few things could be more at variance in mood with the state of mind in which, as it seems to me in recollection, I then was, I am reminded of what, to me now, is surely one of the best rhymes that can have ever been written:

## CHICHESTER

He that is down needs fear no fall;
He that is low no pride.
He that is humble ever shall
Have God to be his guide.

My mood in 1899 was far from that. There was no spiritual humility in me (or was there? I don't know), it was a mood of desperation, even a sort of rationalism. I would begin at the bottom — not out of any humility but because there seemed to be no firm ground anywhere else. It was a long time before I realized that rationalism and humility and poverty were all in the same boat and longer still before I realized what that boat was. I do not blame myself for this, for I suppose nothing on earth is more completely and efficiently camouflaged than Peter's 'barque', which, from a short distance, looks exactly like the Ritz Palace Hotel.

# CHAPTER V

# IN AN ARCHITECT'S OFFICE

Now began a period of all-round iconoclasm. I can think of nothing which escaped attack and nothing which, for a time at least, escaped destruction. Architecture was the first thing to suffer; but as I was in an architect's office the attack was, to start with, indirect. I was not immediately told that architecture was 'a rotten job'; but I was led gradually and surely to discover that fact and very largely by my own rationality. Naturally the boss didn't tell me so, and most if not all the draughtsmen in his office, and there were sometimes nearly twenty people working in it counting clerks and office boy, took it for granted that the profession itself was all right – provided you were able to keep the first principle of it – 'getting the job'.

I don't really know which item in the outfit of beliefs and prejudices with which I went to London was the first to receive direct attack. You see I was a fairly perfect specimen of the earnest and enthusiastic boy from the provinces. The Church of England, the family, the Conservative structure of English society (for you may guess that on joining the Church of England, my father and therefore all the family had abandoned Gladstonian Liberalism and embraced Liberal Unionism – Joseph Chamberlain was the great man then and the Boer War was in full swing – if you can call it 'swing'), my notions of 'art' and drawing, my 'morals' (which were a common mixture of puritanism, secret prurience and romanticism), my notions of good lettering, all these things, separately or simultaneously, were subject to more or less ribald scorn from one or other of the draughtsmen or my fellow pupils. The 'office' was on two floors and we were like two separate camps. Throughout all my three years I was on the basement floor, I hardly saw the men in the upper office and seldom spoke to them except as passing strangers. They had no influence on me; we weren't intimate enough. But in the basement office which, in spite of the name, was the chief place and the chief draughtsman was its ruler, we were a sort of family and knew one another very well indeed. Pupils and assistants might come and go. 'Improvers' might come and stay a few months, or draughtsmen working on some special job. Occasional foreigners would appear and stay a month or more, a Norwegian, a Swede, a man from Glasgow, but there was a sort of permanent family, a paternal centre and one or two elder brothers, which remained stable. It was from or through this family nucleus that my notions received attack. I saw the boss very rarely. He had no time to teach his pupils and least of all the sons of poor clergymen who paid reduced premiums. I don't say this in malice – in this kind of world, it must be so. After all it was my privilege to be allowed to work in his office and under the instruction of competent draughtsmen. An enormous practice, hundreds of jobs on at once, and a large office cannot be conducted on personal lines. We had our little family in the basement office and that was good enough. So, as I say, I hardly ever saw the boss. In fact the only times I ever saw him were when, having made a drawing or tracing under the direction of the head draughtsman, I took it up to him to be signed. Sometimes he might make a correction or alteration and say a word or two – but he was too rushed with affairs to take any personal interest in me. This may seem a hardship. As a matter of fact it was exactly the opposite. For if the boss had been friendly, if he had personally interested himself in my affairs and development, I might have been impressed by him and influenced by his notions. I might have become an architect of the same kind myself. I might have thought an entirely different set of thoughts from those which I came to think. I say this was no hardship and this sounds extremely arrogant. I am sorry for this, but, as I hope to show (for I think the development of my ideas is the main line of this book and so I must risk the appearance of egotism), the ideas of architecture as held by the architect to the Ecclesiastical Commissioners in 1900 were appallingly wrong and bad and therefore it was a mercy not to be constrained to accept them by personal and human considerations, by affection or by intellectual force. I was free from that, and our basement family was so mixed and so intellectually free; moreover it was itself so unconstrained by any affection or respect for the boss, that if you thought anything at all you thought it as the result of your own mental development or through personal friendships with your equals. Perhaps this also sounds bad; it may sound too much like a mere melting pot. It may sound like a den of licence and indiscipline. But it wasn't simply that, though there was a lot of that about it, because the head draughtsman,[1] though coercing no one and himself a sort of pious agnostic, was a man of such firm goodness and kindness of character, that the whole office was as it were cemented together. That was how it seemed to me. I was often, in my first year or two appalled by what I heard. My whole world was disintegrated. But, though appalled, I wasn't frightened. I clung inwardly and outwardly to the guardianship of the head draughtsman and felt safe. I don't think he influenced my opinions much one way or the other. He was disillusioned and tolerant but kind and guileless. What luck! For, in the turmoil of iconoclasms, I might easily have been led into dissolute ways if it had not been for the restraining power of his fatherly presence. And there were other restraining influences too – my non-conformist conscience, my 'poor relation complex' (this was most influential for it had the effect of making me mean and careful about spending money – and I had very little to spend – ten shillings a week to include all bus fares and lunches), my consciousness of my unfashionable appearance (I never could bother to dress smartly or care about doing so), my lack of interest in any girls but one and my hatred of 'parties' and dances. I never could dance (on the one

[1] Colin Campbell Wilson.

or two occasions when I tried, I felt a fool and did it so badly that I realized it was not my affair) and I hate gatherings of people who don't know one another. So in spite of being 'easily led' I managed to live a reasonably innocent life and to keep off the things and ways which, though they allured me, frightened me. Moreover, I am physically and morally a cowardly person. Physically – I don't mind a 'scrap' once I'm in it and have lost my temper, but until that blessed moment I'm all for keeping out of it. Nothing seems to me so typically alarming as a half-drunk man in a pub who, having received my polite remarks as an insult, begins to remove his coat. I am all for backing away towards the door. We did a bit of boxing at school and I wasn't too bad at it, but I don't rush to it . . . And morally – well, I never was one of those noble fellows who stand up with folded arms and say: no, I won't do it, it's wrong. I manage to find some way of backing out before it's too late. I despise myself a lot for this cowardice and very often it really has been despicable. But I can claim, on the other side, that it's partly the defect of a virtue; for there's always a good many sides to a question and, for example (and it's the kind of example which typifies a lot of other things) even pornographic photographs are generally photographs of things very good in themselves.

I mean: what's wrong with a naked girl that you shouldn't look at a photograph of one? What's wrong with sexual intercourse that a picture of it should be considered damnable? You deceive yourself, I used to say to myself – you're just pretending; you only want such things to gloat on them. No, but honestly, I used to reply to myself, it's true, it's true, it's true – those things *are* good things and suppose I am gloating, well, what's wrong with gloating if it comes to that? Can't I do a bit of gloating without going to the devil? So argument went to and fro, and though at the age of which I am writing, nineteen to twenty, I took a lot of risks and played with fire and burnt my fingers too, and though, at that age, I was compelled to solve my own problems, for I lived in a world which was almost entirely without moral certainties – the world of most young men in London – I somehow managed to keep a sort of balance on the tight-rope of life.

All the foregoing is by way of making a picture of the sort of life I was plunged into on coming to London. It was in that life that I had to pick and choose my leaders and to discover what line I would take. I have also been leading up to the first great influence in my London life. This was George Christopher Carter, my fellow pupil though several years my senior. If my sister Cicely was perfect, so was he. He had all the virtues and all the gifts. The other chaps trained me by laughter and scorn but he took me in hand as a friend. And just as in my Chichester days I was befriended by the art-master and went for walks with him and sat at his feet and hung on his words and basked in his smile, so it was with George Carter. A few months (or it may have been weeks – time is long in a new prison house) after I arrived at the office, he suggested my coming with him to Westminster Abbey during our lunch hour. It was an event of the first importance. I might be and doubtless was as bad and foolish as I thought myself, but henceforth I had a leader. He was the first person I had ever met in the world who had moral and intellectual integrity.

Integrity! The word in its common usage means little more than truthful – at the most when we say a man is 'a man of integrity' we mean that his obvious veracity is not belied by his actions. But the word means much more than that and is perhaps one of the most important words in the world. They say that the result of Original Sin, in its proper theological definition, is precisely loss of integrity. That doesn't mean that Adam and Eve immediately became untruthful. In our familiar arithmetic a certain kind of number is called an 'integer' or an integral number. That can hardly suggest to our mind that other kinds of numbers are in any way morally reprehensible. In fact the rather exclusively 'moral' tang which the word has in our modern English speech must be unwarranted by the word itself. It is perhaps like the very word 'moral' – a word which qualifies a whole range of activities but which, owing to a strange but common aberration of the English mind, has come to qualify only one special and restricted set. A stock-broker who sells what he has not got for a sum of money larger, and perhaps much larger, than what he has promised to pay for it, thus by cunning obtaining something for nothing and thus, of necessity, robbing someone who does not happen to have his inside knowledge – such a man is not considered 'immoral'. A man who, without taking any part in the enter-prise, invests his money in it with the sole object of obtaining a share of the profits, is considered to be rendering service to his fellows. To invent a new machine-gun or a more efficient poison-gas is held to be more meritorious still. If you buy a newspaper and, by pandering to the lowest common denominator of taste and intelligence, succeed in selling several millions of copies daily, you will hardly escape being made a 'peer of the Realm'. You may blaspheme your God, dishonour your parents, rob your neighbour, kill your enemies and covet all things; you will very likely be thought wicked but you will not commonly be called immoral. Your morals will be judged solely by your behaviour with women. This is what the psycho boys call a 'defence mechanism'. So it is with the word 'integrity'. By its unnatural confinement within the narrow bounds of veracity, we are able to escape from its wider implications. It is as though we presented ourselves at the bar of heaven and claimed all the rewards of morality because we had never committed adultery or coveted our neighbour's wife; it is as though we claimed that the British Empire must be wholly good because its graft is honesty.

Perhaps the shame of 'our first parents' gives a clearer indi-cation of the real nature of their sin, for a just punishment always fits the crime. But without going into that question at this point, and I can't say at this moment whether it will seem necessary to go into it at all in this book, it is clear that it is their shame that is significant, they were deprived of something proper to them, they were in some way disfigured and deformed. This disfigurement and deformity was not immediately apparent in their bodies, though it was of their nakedness that they were ashamed. It was a disfigurement and deformity and derangement and disorder of the mind – it was in one word a disintegration. A oneness had become diffuse, a thing firmly knit had come unstuck, a clear thing clouded, a sweet thing soured. Henceforward there would be war where there should be and had been peace. The Lion in their members would refuse to lie down with the Lamb. The flesh would lust against the spirit, the will against the reason. This is disintegration; it is a kind of death – By sin came death.

This is a long preface to the description of a friendship – but that's the kind of book this is. It's more concerned with meanings than events. It is the meaning of that friendship that matters and though, as must be obvious, it is only in later years that I have been able to formulate or guess the meanings, it is also obvious that whether we think about them or not when we are young, the meanings were as present then as when in our old age we discover them. Well then, the point is that George Carter was the first person in my experience who had integrity and, indeed, he was the first man I had ever met who was unashamed – physically, morally, mentally unashamed. His mind was clear, his body beautiful (which is the same thing, for though beauty consist in unity and due proportion, it is clarity by which we know it), his manner cheerful and gay. For the first time, I met a person whose opinions were not the product of prejudice or school teaching or wayward ratiocination, but of simple right mindedness, an infallible rectitude of will and imagination and intelligence. It is not surprising that I should have worshipped.

I have tried to explain what a revelation of order and seemliness the city of Chichester had been to the boy from Brighton.

In the same way George Carter was a revelation. And just as I had seen little wrong with Brighton until I saw Chichester, so I had seen little wrong with anyone but myself until I met George Carter. He was a new kind of being, a kind hitherto unsuspected. It is very difficult to express this clearly and perhaps I am foolish to attempt it. I must do so if I can, because the revelation made a sort of watershed in my mental and spiritual life. Whereas I had been bond now I was free, or to put it less bumptiously, whereas I was aware of bondage now I was aware of the possibility of freedom. Conscience, however frequently disobeyed, had always been the acknowledged arbiter of my deeds, but it had been a kind of slavery. Now for the first time I saw a person for whom the dictates of conscience were also the dictates of good sense and good will. It was on the one hand a release from the arbitrary and, on the other, from fear. Of course this did not happen immediately – it has not completely happened yet. Baptism doesn't alter psychology and revelation does not alter behaviour. But what I see now I also saw forty years ago – an upright man, a man unprejudiced, a man without guile, moreover a lovable man, a man of genius, and a man both humorous and kind.

So we went to Westminster Abbey and to other places, and there was the daily life at the office. And one by one my Cicestrian sentimentalities were gently or otherwise knocked off. Architecture ceased to be a matter of style and became *building*. The constant presence of our boss's 'sham Gothic' and his almost complete lack of any interest in anything but theatrical effect (apart from his personal ambition to get all the jobs there were, and in that respect he was the most perfect exemplar of 'the first principle of architecture' that I ever heard of, though I dare say some eminent Royal Academicians were equally good), the pervading atmosphere mixed of drainage plans and full-size details of irrelevant and generally excessive and meaningless 'ornament', these things instead of being, as they might have been, so many incitements to an immoral life

(I mean, of course, architectural immorality), were no more than constant reminders of evil to be avoided and object lessons in what not to do. As far as I was concerned, architecture in that office was almost completely 'debunked'. My ideal cottage, four square, three or more up and one down (i.e. one big living-room and lots of little snug bedrooms in a high roof), faded into the background. I still clung to it as to a talisman but I saw that it was nothing to do with 'architecture', still less with a London architect's office. Architecture in such a place was (once you'd got the job) simply a business of 'designing' and, with the aid of building contractors, getting somehow erected, striking visual effects. Truly houses are places to live in and churches are places to pray and preach and play organs in, but that's only the necessary and more or less humdrum condition of human life. Architecture begins where that sort of thing leaves off! That the way you live or pray in any radical sense determines the very existence of architecture is an idea, or it was in the 1900's, unheard of in any but revolutionary circles.

Of course there are lots of sides to everything and it is only fair to say that we have the architecture, and everything else, that we deserve. The client who pays is also to blame. I said 'the way you live determines the existence of architecture'. So it does, to be sure, and nothing could be clearer than that the manner of living in Victorian or Georgian England determined the existence of Victorian or Georgian architecture. Pretentious architecture fitted a pretentious age. The architecture of the 1920's is no less appropriate to its period. And behind the 'architecture', which is, as it were, the shop window display, there is in all periods the equally appropriate mass of building done by mere contractors for people who can't afford to pay architects. The sham Gothic church, scholarly or otherwise, may affront you with its pretentious nonsense; but you've no business to be thus affronted unless you are equally affronted by the whole civilization which it so admirably portrays and advertises and shows up. Good taste, as understood by the genteel, is no remedy for corruption. The Bank of England and the Royal Exchange and hosts of other such places, and Town Halls and St. Paul's Cathedral are all built with pillars and porticos copied from Greek and Roman temples and thousands of little dwelling houses followed the fashion. The whole thing is just play-acting. But that, without knowing it, is exactly what the architects and their customers wanted to do. Perhaps very often the play-acting was very good. It is quite possible to find it very pleasing and amusing. It was very pleasing and amusing while it was young and fresh and gay. It was pleasing, if not amusing, even when it got elderly and pompous and solemn, and very likely, in their natural kindness of heart, the poor were as much pleased by it as the rich – after all they enjoyed the display as much as their betters and if your idea of architecture is something to be seen from the street then 'the man in the street' can see it as much as anyone else. But there does come a time when new life is required and then you have to forget your beloved romancing and get down to reality. Theatrical banks and fancy-dress churches won't do any longer.

All this or a great deal of it was clear enough to the rebels in our architect's office and some of the implications too. The connection between building and politics and religion was not stated as I'm stating it here. But it is certainly true to say that most of those who rebelled against the Victorian tradition of architecture were also rebels against Victorian political and religious mug-wumpery. In fact religious rebellion came first and then political revolution and the reform of the building trade came last. This was as it should be, and it was my anglicanism that had to receive the first sneers and jibes.

I can't remember the arguments we had when we were supposed to be drawing plans, or details of Gothic tracery. They took up a lot of time and it is a comfort to know that the time could not have been better spent. And lest anyone should think that the paid draughtsmen were, in effect, robbing their employer, I might reply that 'in effect' they were only raising their wages without putting him to the pain of agreeing to do so – the Bedaux system had not then been invented. And our arguments, perhaps they were seldom worthy of the name, were always very disjointed and frequently interrupted by the ominous sound of the boss's door opening and sometimes, very often in fact, they were brought to an untimely close by a remonstrance from the head-man, if he didn't happen to be mixed up in it himself. Of course the office was that of the architect to the Ecclesiastical Commissioners and perhaps that accounts for the preponderance of discussion on religion, and as none of us was aware of any visible connection between the practice of religion and the building of churches, still less between the practice of the virtue of intellectual sincerity and the architectural service of the Ecclesiastical Commissioners, it is perhaps not surprising that the general tone of those arguments was that of discussions among sceptics. It is saying too much that *no* man is a hero to his valet, but the implication is good enough, and I should think two or three years behind the ecclesiastical scenes could hardly fail to knock the stuffing out of the youthful romance of any young man 'up' from the cathedral city.

The gulf between precept and practice was I think the main cause of scepticism – it prepared the ground. Destroy respect and veneration for pastors and masters and disbelief in their teaching will generally follow. It is not a logical sequence but a natural one. There's no reason why a rich man shouldn't know and speak the truth about holy poverty, but somehow people are inclined to doubt him, and among the young and foolish this is I should think inevitable. There is no need to enlarge on this. It must be a commonplace of our experience that the widespread scepticism of our time is as much the consequence of loss of respect for the preachers of Christ as it is of the writings and teachings of unbelievers, and that that loss of respect is a necessary preliminary.

All the time we had lived at Brighton and Chichester I had

lived in more or less romantic worlds. Towards the end of my time in Chichester I had become discontented, but I still lived in romance. This was not difficult during childhood; for as I have tried to show, our parents were, both in general and in particular, honest exemplars of what they taught us, and to my young mind, the idea that there was or should be any connection between the 'shape' of Brighton (its streets, its people, its Esplanade, its 'West Pier', its Railways and its Preston Park) and the religion taught or preached in its churches and chapels did not occur to me and was never pointed out. The only thing that remains in my memory in that connection is an overheard conversation between our parents in which they complained about the indecency (in a social sense) of the building of a Music Hall in the same street with the Theatre Royal. I gathered that Music Halls were extremely reprehensible places and when, at school, some of the older boys told me that they had actually visited the place I had a feeling that they must be living secret lives of great depravity. As I have said, my father was 'curate' at the chapel of the Countess of Huntingdon's Connection. But that the word 'connection' was, in that context, comic, and that the only connection meant was that between a dozen or so obscure chapels and was therefore symptomatic of the general divorce of religion from the life of our times, was an idea absolutely outside my education. And when we migrated to Chichester the romantic bliss remained undisturbed. That migration was incalculably important to me. In a physical sense it was a migration from chaos to order, from ugliness (i.e. disorder) to beauty, and for the reasons I have stated earlier in this book, the parish worship of the Church of England seemed an emancipation and release from the stifling personal, all-too-personal religion of the non-conformist chapel. I did not perceive the decay. It all seemed stable and beautiful. The well ordered city, the cathedral and the village churches, the cathedral music, the lovely and neighbourly countryside – how was I to know that the city was but a museum piece slowly decaying before the impact of 'Timothy Whites' and 'The Home and Colonial', that the cathedral was not only a museum piece but itself a museum — "Christ! what a peep-show" — that the village churches were only attended by a smug handful of the parishioners and their parsons asleep, that the beloved music was little or nothing to do with religion and was to a very large extent only a polite form of sensual entertainment and very second-rate at that? How was I to know that the countryside was in the last stages of technical neglect and economic despair? I couldn't know such things. Who was to tell me? They wouldn't tell you such things in such a place even now. It was necessary to go to London to find out things like that; and I very soon did so. I'm not that sort of loyal person who says 'my England right or wrong', and I don't think my lewd and sceptical pals at the office had much difficulty with me. Moreover London, in spite of its multifarious attractions . . .

When I was staying at my aunt's in Blackheath (this was before I became an architect's pupil) I used occasionally to be allowed to go up to London for the day — all by myself. I went several times like this but I can't remember anything I did except go to Westminster Abbey and St. Paul's Cathedral — and especially to the latter. I wish I could recapture the romantic bliss in which I bathed and basked on those occasions. Everything seemed perfect. The building was perfect. The music was perfect. The vergers were revered and privileged beings. The foggy mist in the dome was perfect. And indeed what could be more surprisingly wonderful to someone young and small and burning with virginal enthusiasm than a building so large that it seems to contain the very sky (what a thing it must have been to the Londoners of 1700!) — the clouds, the mists! But what impressed me most of all — in the sense that I have remembered it best and most clearly — was the noise of London outside. But that was in the days before motor cars, the days of horses and hansom-cabs and in those days the noise of London was very mysterious and undefined, a sort of everlasting noise, an eternal noise, a noise untainted by any earthly thing that you could put a name to, not menacing or horrible but a sound of fearful power. I used to go there sometimes only to hear it. It was like the noise you seem to hear in a big sea-shell, but vaster. It was not the sound as of the sea-shore at your feet; rather it seemed to be the distant sound of all the oceans of the world. It must be gone by now as is the London that made it.

And another thing I specially returned again and again to see was the view from the transept of Westminster Abbey looking up the south choir aisle into the eastern ambulatory — the groining of vaulting, and the windows, so nearly perfect, made just at the moment when windows were still thought of as spaces of light, before they started getting clever about tracery and became more interested in patterns of lines.

I don't know what kind of influence those things had on me. Perhaps they didn't influence me at all. Perhaps old Walt Whitman was at least partly right when he said 'architecture is what you do to a building when you look at it'. But he was only partly right; for after all there must be a building for you to do something to and it must be such that it can bear what you do to it. And if he was only partly right, what about the other part? When I went to Westminster Abbey I endowed it with something I brought with me, but not being omniscient I must have seen things in it that I had never seen before and perhaps not thought of or imagined. Moreover such buildings are not merely mechanical contrivances exhibiting man's technical ability, though they do exhibit it; they are also the vehicles of spiritual communications and he who submits himself to receive such cannot but be made in some way spiritually pregnant and thereby changed for better or for worse. . . .

I was about to say London, in spite of its multifarious attractions, is an even more shapeless mess than the provincial watering-place, in which I was born. Such order and decency as it has is but the pathetic dregs of a past age, and even its past was never particularly orderly. A shapeless mess, and a monstrously dull mess too. For the first two years of my apprenticeship I lodged in Clapham and every morning and evening I made the journey along the Wandsworth Road in a horse-tram or, for variety, by bus (horse also) over the old spider-web suspension bridge to Victoria — and sometimes I walked it; it took exactly one hour and not much less by tram. I was fairly happy at the office; I was fairly happy in my lodging (I even repapered my sitting-room with brown paper — and silver paper ornaments) and I didn't mind the journey; but any romantic view I might have had as to the loveliness of London was soon dispelled. If you wanted to create something dreary and wretched, it would be difficult to create anything more dreary or more wretched, than Clapham — the Clapham of the Junction and the miles of silly little dirty houses between the Wandsworth Road and Battersea. I lodged at the Church Club next door to the Church of St. Saviour. I was therefore, so my parents supposed, in the safe atmosphere of ecclesiastical respectability. It was respectable but it didn't save me. For the first year or thereabouts I went regularly to the church on Sundays (a frightful church with a brazen new organ, a brazen choir and a smart young parson) but, without any violent break, I gradually gave it up. I do think this is rather shameful. Surely it is clear from what I have said that I was not at all indifferent to the appeal of the religion in which I had been brought up; nor had I become so. But religion in St. Saviour's, Clapham, and irreligion in the architect's office were unequally matched. Nothing in the out- ward show of that Christianity could possibly hold me — the frightful church, the frightful music, the apparently empty con- ventionality of the congregation. And nothing that the parson ever said seemed to imply any realization that the Church of England was in any way responsible for the intellectual and moral and physical state of London. At the office, on the other hand, the implications were clear enough. Impious and lewd we often were, and intellectually half-baked or even absolutely raw, but scornful of the sham piety of the sham medieval by which we earned our livings, and scornful of the smugness and hypocrisy of an ecclesiastical world which taught the people a lot of palpable nonsense about the nature of things and did nothing whatever to defend them from the rapacity of landlords and commercial magnates, or to oppose the ugliness and filth and disorder of the world around.

The Church of England, or any other church, was, it seemed, just like a professional football club. It owned its playing ground and its pavilion, it kept its paid players and it lived on the gate-money. If you enjoyed the entertainment you paid your money; if you didn't enjoy it you didn't go. The Church of England was just one of a number of other more or less similar clubs. And just as only a very small proportion of the population of the country goes to football matches on Saturday, so only a very small, indeed a very much smaller proportion of the population goes to church on Sunday. They are two different kinds of entertainment – many people enjoy both, but a much larger number enjoy neither. And it doesn't make any difference; the banks will still open and so will the shops. The railways and buses will still run and the food shops will still have food to sell whether it comes from our own countryside or from Australia and South America. Free Trade or Protection? that was the really important question.

And with regard to such questions as that, it was becoming obvious that politicians also were smug and hypocritical. Politicians were no more devoted to the common good than professional footballers or the clergy. Their job was not to renew the face of the earth, to withstand injustice and the power of the rich over the poor. Their job was simply to maintain the sacred rights of capital. The fight between the party in power and 'the Opposition' was more or less a sham fight, and politics, just like professional football or the Church of England, was simply one of the accepted forms of entertainment. Parliament did not really represent the people nor did it really enact laws. Parliament really represented business and laws were really enacted in board-rooms and counting-houses. Thinking and saying such things, I became more and more sceptical about the value of the Bible as a general scientific text-book, and of the Church of England as guide, counsellor and friend. And as you never can talk to parsons as man to man (at least I can't), they never got a chance of answering back. I suppose there were books I might have read, but I never heard of them and the sceptics had it all their own way. H. G. Wells was the rising god. Omar Khayám, a herald of the dawn – a sort of cheerful, cynical but kindly prison-warder, who took pleasure in letting out the prisoners. Stevenson – not anti-Christian but not a buttress to Anglicanism either. Thomas Carlyle – *Sartor Resartus* (which occupied my breakfast times at Clapham for many months) and *Past and Present* – I cherished the memory of the moment when I first read the words: 'and him of the shovel hat, oh heavens! what shall we say of *him*?'

But books, after all, only provided confirmation in words of what was everywhere visible to the naked eye. Christ as a sort of Buddha or Confucius was generally approved and applauded in our office – it was the Christian Church and particularly the Church of England which was the joke. Very little was said of the Church of Rome, and nonconformity was more or less unknown in an ecclesiastical architect's office. Except for one or two young gentlemen pupils, comers and goers of no architectural or artistic staying-power, and one or two obstinately loyal adherents of Anglicanism, we were all more concerned about social affairs than about religion. It might have been otherwise. I might have found myself in a group of high-church Christians. I am not saying that it was inevitable that in going to London I should find myself in a ribald and sceptical society. I am only saying that that was the kind of society I did find myself in and that, in such a society, it was inevitable, that I, being 'easily led', should shed my religion and piety without difficulty and without loss of time.

So I became an agnostic and in a vague unattached way a

socialist. I took to reading the sixpenny booklets of the Rationalist Press Association and Fabian Tracts and of course I read Ruskin (especially *The Seven Lamps* of which I had a first edition) and William Morris. We had always been poor but we had never been destitute, never really underfed or badly clothed or housed, never wage-slaves, so my socialism was from the beginning a revolt against the intellectual degradation of the factory hands and the damned ugliness of all that capitalist-industrialism produced, and it was not primarily a revolt against the cruelty and injustice of the possessing classes or against the misery of the poor. It was not so much the working *class* that concerned me as the working *man* — not so much what he got *from* working as what he did *by* working. (See Note, p. 277.)

But at that date I did not tabulate things thus. I thought myself a socialist like any other and indeed the only difference between my kind of socialism, the kind inspired by Ruskin and Morris, and that of the socialist clubs and parties was that I and my friends, or my friends and I (for I was never the leader), added something which we considered vital but which they had never heard of or thought of no importance compared with the winning of the political and economic battle. We accepted their economics and only asked that they should accept our humanity. But at that date these things did not transpire. I have said enough to indicate the kind of influence the architect's office had on me.

And now having turned agnostic and socialist, having made the religious rebellion and turned towards political revolution, there remained the reform of the building trade. It would require a very cynical person to be an agnostic and at the same time an ecclesiastical architect. It would require even more than cynicism to be a socialist and take the pay of the ecclesiastical commissioners. It would require either a sort of dishonesty or a detachment of mind of which I was never capable, and it would mean an acceptance of that lack of integrity, that lack of *integralness*, which was coming to seem to be the main disease of all diseases, the master disease, the generalissimo and chief field-marshal of diseases. And to go on turning out plans and details for buildings in a way which took it for granted that the workman was either a complete fool or a knave and probably both, seemed more and more contemptible.

You can't imagine, unless you've been in such places yourself, the madness of the procedure. It is assumed in the first place that the architect is not a builder, but a gentleman. It is assumed in the second place that the builder is not an architect, but a man of business. In the third place it is assumed that the builder's workman is incapable of intellectual responsibility and that, though he is often 'a grand chap' and often of great technical experience, you can't and mustn't trust him to do anything without measured and precise directions and drawings. You can generally assume the workman's loyalty and the builder's honesty, but you mustn't act on those assumptions. So you must not only supply drawings of everything, including full-size drawings of every detail, but you must supply a specification of the works to be done which shall describe precisely everything you can think of, and many things you never would have thought of in any other kind of world, as to the nature and quality and amount of all the materials to be used. Finally you must have a legally drawn up contract with your builder, thus making it clear from the start that it is chiefly as a man of business, a contractor, that you are dealing with him and that, as long as he doesn't depart from your drawings or specification, you don't care a damn whether he likes building or not, still less whether he likes the building he's going to build for you. The whole thing is completely inhuman. And the result is what anyone might expect but few people see — a world in which buildings are not only dead but damned.[1]

Of course the agnostical socialist cannot see further than death.

[1] I must not enlarge on this matter here, for better or worse I have done so in many other places – e.g. *Art Nonsense* (Cassels, 1929), and *Beauty looks after Herself* (Sheed & Ward, 1931).

That holiness rather than happiness is the criterion of judgment was a thought beyond our grasp at that date. It was sufficient for us at that time to hold fast to William Morris's saying that every man ought to have joy in his labour[1] and that therefore not only the whole factory system but the architectural profession too are monstrous perversions. It does not follow that all architects are knaves. If we live in a world in which builders have in fact ceased to be anything but men of business and cannot therefore without assistance put up buildings worth looking at or living in, you must have someone to do the assisting. That is the architect's function: to protect his customer from the artistic degradation of the contractor and his possible or probable dishonesty. And if the contractor's workmen have also become degraded to 'a subhuman condition of intellectual irresponsibility' then someone must tell them very precisely what to do. If indeed that is the world we live in, and indeed it is, then there must be architects. But there are limits, both in theory and practice, to what he can do. In so far as a thing is patient of exact measurement, then you can supply a measured drawing of it. In so far as a thing is patient of dialectical exposition then you can dialectically expose it. But you can't sit in an office and make twiddles on paper and expect a workman somewhere else to turn your twiddlings into lively sculptured ornament. The result is both ridiculous and nauseating and for two reasons: first, because you, in your office, cannot have more than an amateurish museum student's knowledge of what sculptured ornament ought to be and second, because the architectural idea of ornament is in itself a false one – to make the building look 'beautiful'. There is properly no such thing as ornament in that sense. Ornament is simply furniture; it is as much furniture as office chairs. Of course a well-furnished office is a beautiful place, but that's not what architects mean, at least they didn't in 1900.

[1] I don't know if he knew it, but the same thing is said in the book of Ecclesiastes, chap. 3, v. 22.

So the architect's pupil began to feel very uncomfortable and rebellious. It was hateful to be employed drawing carvings and mouldings and ironwork for other people to make – other people who ought in the nature of things to be able to do it much better without our drawings (I even had to draw the two sides of an iron gateway different from one another, in order to insure that the smith didn't make them exactly the same and thus give away the fact that he was scarcely human . . . thus we preserved or sought to preserve an appearance of humanity where humanity no longer existed . . . ) and it was hateful to be drawing things which meant nothing at all in themselves and only existed to flatter the vanity of the architect and his customer.

And this dissatisfaction didn't only arise from the false notions of ornament or from the inhuman treatment of the workman, but also from the fundamentally false notion of architectural style and of the false notion of the very business of building itself. The whole thing was play-acting and the building of 'follies'. Architecture didn't represent the needs of the people; it didn't represent the necessities of organic construction. It represented nothing but the vanities of the rich merchant classes which had usurped the rule of the world. In what other kind of world could you possibly have had what we call the Renaissance? How could we possibly have had 'the Gothic revival' in the nineteenth century if architecture had been the product of the people and the expression of their real needs and their real beliefs? I am not saying that no good buildings have been built in these last centuries. I am only saying that they are all in the nature of 'follies'. In the first years of the period good quality was not so difficult to get. The industrial degradation of men had not proceeded so far; the complete victory of the banks had not yet been won. But by the year 1900 the process was obviously nearing its term.

And I hadn't any money – and no prospects of customers. I could see myself as an architect producing absolutely plain buildings – a sort of engineering in brick or stone (and a grand prospect too!) but I couldn't see any people wanting such buildings and I couldn't afford to wait for them. Moreover there was always the gnawing at my heart, so to say. Even the grand conception of architecture as a sort of humanized engineering depended upon the acceptance of the present degradation of the workman and the regarding of him as a person existing only to do what he was told. I would rather be a workman myself and start my rebellion from that end. I would be a workman and demand a workman's rights, the right to design what he made; and a workman's duties, the duty to make what he designed. And that plan didn't need any money – if only I could find work that was wanted and work that I could do.

But I didn't have to look for either. By absolutely providential good fortune there was work ready to my hand and by the guidance of the same Providence I had learned how to do it! And it is in this connection that my friendship with George Carter was particularly important. How, but for him should I ever have come to think the sort of thoughts I have been trying to recollect and epitomize? And the consequence was, among other things, that instead of going to lectures about architecture I went to a technical school to learn masonry and to a craft school to learn about lettering.[1] And the combined consequence of those was that after a few months of masonry I took to cutting letters in stone so that when an eminent painter came to the lettering class to ask if there was anyone among the students who could cut an inscription on a tombstone for him, I was named. So it was the lettering enthusiasm, begun in connection with Engine Names, and continued at the Art School at Chichester, which gave me the opportunity. Already at the architect's office I'd got a sort of reputation as a letterer and used to do a lot of lettering on the drawings; so I began to awake to the possibility of doing lettering for a living. And one thing led to another. The tombstone inscription took me about three

[1] The Westminster Technical Institute and the L.C.C. Central School of Arts and Crafts, in Regent Street.

months of evenings and I got five pounds for it. Then the
eminent painter, being quite unnecessarily satisfied with my
exceedingly amateurish letter-cutting, recommended me to an
eminent architect and I did a small inscription on a church by
Sloane Square – and from that day to this I've never been out
of a job.[1]

At first these inscription jobs had to be done in the evenings;
for I was at the office all day. Then by a roundabout turn of
events I got the offer of a big job of letter cutting at Cambridge,
big at least for me. It happened thus: there is, as is well known,
a very remarkable market cross at Chichester and some fatuous
people were proposing to have it removed from the centre of
the city where, they said, it was 'a menace to the traffic . . .'
Letters appeared in the Chichester *Observer* and George Carter
helped me to concoct a sarcastic reply making fun of the proposal. This was published, and brought in support a letter from
Edward Prior, the architect, who at that time lived at Chichester.
This was an enormous event from my point of view – I, the
young architect's pupil publicly supported and commended by
one of the few among architects then living who accepted and
acted upon the ideas and principles I had come to accept and
uphold. I suppose anyone can imagine and forgive the pride
which inflated me, and when, on my next week-end visit to
Chichester, I, having previously written to thank him for his
commendation, went, by his invitation to Sunday afternoon
tea, my good fortune was complete. Soon after that he offered
me the job of cutting some inscriptions on the new Medical
Schools which he was then building at Cambridge. My acceptance of this job depended upon my being able to leave the
architect's office. A decision had to be made. It was no use
consulting anyone but myself. My parents would naturally have

[1] But, I should like to record, my absolutely first job was not this inscription
but the drawing of Portfield Church (near Chichester) for the cover of the
Parish Magazine, which I did while I was a pupil at the Chichester Art School,
and mighty proud I was.

been horrified at the suggestion of my giving up architecture and thus apparently, as they would suppose, wasting all my apprenticeship and all the money kind friends had expended to pay my premiums. The boss could hardly be expected to advise such a course just at the time when I was beginning to be useful as a draughtsman, and in any case he wasn't the sort of man to share my opinions about architecture and therefore my discontent in his office. So I had to decide for myself and that wasn't difficult. It's not at all that I'm rash and adventurous; but I know a good thing when I see it. And this was a superlatively good thing. A real job of work and no more sitting on an office stool drawing things for other people to do. So I went off to Cambridge. I just went; and I wrote to the boss saying I was very sorry to behave in what must seem a most improper manner, asking him to forgive me, but making it quite clear that I wasn't going back. I must say he treated me most kindly and generously. He went so far as to give me my articles, endorsing them with a certificate of my three years' service and even promising me work in the lettering line, foundation stones and so forth, if ever he had anything of the sort for me to do. I think this was a very great kindness. I didn't deserve it in the least. I had been a most unsatisfactory pupil, consistently despising my master and sneering at his work and working no harder or more conscientiously than I was obliged. But lack of deserts is no reason for refusing a gift and I accepted my freedom gratefully. After all it was necessary for me to earn my living and there was no chance of doing that as an articled apprentice. My parents could no longer afford to keep me, I must somehow find a living for myself. All these things worked together, and henceforward I gave up all idea of being an architect and became a letter-cutter and monumental mason.

But, as I have said, it was providential good fortune that I was able to do letter-cutting. I managed to hit on something which no one else was doing and which quite a lot of people wanted. On the one hand architects were often wanting inscriptions cut and were glad to employ someone who could save them the trouble of making full-size drawings and not charge them any more than the 'trade'. And ordinary lay folks of the more cultured circles were wanting to escape from the deadly corruption of the trade monumental mason. So one job led to another and if you do all the work yourself and think two shillings or half a crown an hour jolly high pay (that's one advantage of being one of thirteen children – you have pretty low standards), then, as some jobs may take a week and others a month or more, it is clear that you don't want a very large number of jobs in a year. In my first year I made about seventy-five pounds and work was coming in well. It was enough to marry on, and marry we did. Oh, what sport; oh, what bliss! We had a workman's flat in Battersea, in the County Council 'dwellings', and lived happily ever after.

I have made a big leap and got further than I intended to in this chapter. It is necessary that I should go back a little. I have done my best to do honour to the name of George Carter. It would be both disgraceful and ungracious, much as I wish to avoid exploiting great names, if I were to omit mention of my debt to Edward Johnston. It was through George Carter that I went to Edward Johnston's class of writing and lettering at the Central School. It was through Edward Johnston that I finally threw off the art nonsense of the Chichester art-school and got away, though of course not immediately, from the amateurishness of my efforts as an architect's pupil – if indeed, not having been brought up 'in the trade', I can ever be anything but an amateur. But this event was much more than that. I won't say that I owe everything I know about lettering to him – not that that is very much, for I'm no sort of learned person and have never been much of a student of anything – but I owe everything to the foundation which he laid. And his influence was much more than that of a teacher of lettering. He profoundly altered the whole course of my life and all my ways of thinking. Just as 'art nonsense' couldn't stand against him, so also 'thought nonsense' was toppled over. He was a man miraculously deliberate of speech and equally deliberate in thought, and I was just the opposite. I don't mean that I was quick of speech or thought, but I was hasty and careless and ready to jump to conclusions and make rash generalizations. I was 'easily led', and as easily led by my own exuberance as by anyone else's. And Edward Johnston was like a perpetual brake on all such rashness. This might have been only a bore, and lots of other people have found it so. But other people weren't 'mad' on lettering! And as a writer with the pen, a calligrapher – it will have to be sufficient if I say that the first time I saw him writing, and saw the writing that came as he wrote, I had that thrill and tremble of the heart which otherwise I can only remember having had when first I touched her body or saw her hair down for the first time (Lord! what the young men have lost since women bobbed their hair!), or when I first heard the plain-chant of the Church (as they sang it at Louvain in the Abbey of Mont Cèsar) or when I first entered the church of San Clemente in Rome, or first saw the North Transept of Chartres from the little alley between the houses. Many other things, a million, million other things are equally good. I am only saying that these are, for me, the things that stand out. On those occasions I was caught unprepared. I did not know such beauties could exist. I was struck as by lightning, as by a sort of enlightenment. There are indeed many other things as good; there are many occasions when, in a manner of speaking, you seem to pierce the cloud of unknowing and for a brief second seem to know even as God knows – sometimes, when you are drawing the human body, even the turn of a shoulder or the firmness of a waist, it seems to shine with the radiance of righteousness. But these more sudden enlightenments are rare events, never forgotten, never overlaid. On that evening I was thus rapt. It was no mere dexterity, that transported me; it was as though a secret of heaven were being revealed.

So I went regularly to learn writing and to learn about the Roman alphabet. And I fell in love with Edward Johnston and physically trembled at the thought of seeing him. But he kept me severely in my place and I trembled under his rebukes. I fell in love with him – but don't make any mistake as to my meaning. I fell in love with him as I might, and indeed did, with Socrates. It was a joyful passage. Life was full of physical excitement and the excitement was as of the intelligence discovering the good. It is very well to know the logical truth, but fancy knowing the truth and finding it desirable! More and more desirable and more and more the truth! And lettering has this very great advantage over other arts; at its very base, conjoined and inseparable, are the fair and the fit – most obviously useful and depending for its beauty upon nothing but man's musical sense. The shapes of letters do not derive their beauty from any sensual or sentimental reminiscence. No one can say that the o's roundness appeals to us only because it is like that of an apple or of a girl's breast or of the full moon. We like the circle because such liking is connatural to the human mind. And no one can say lettering is not a useful trade by which you can honestly serve your fellow men and earn an honest living. Of what other trade or art are these things so palpably true? Moreover it is a precise art. You don't draw an A and then stand back and say: there, that gives you a good idea of an A as seen through an autumn mist, or: that's not a real A but gives you a good effect of one. Letters are things, not pictures of things. And I remember how annoyed I was when I had once to paint some letters on a portrait by an eminent portrait painter and he insisted on my painting the lettering to look as though it were part of the furniture of the room in which the subject of the portrait was sitting. I submitted, because I respected the painter – and besides you can't fully know how wrong a thing is until you've done it – and it was a 'job', but it was a bad business and contrary to all intelligence. Lettering is a precise art and strictly subject to tradition. The 'New Art' notion that you can make letters whatever shapes you like, is as foolish as the notion, if anyone has such a notion, that you can make houses any shapes you like. You can't, unless you live all by yourself on a desert island – and die there.

So for a year or more I went to Edward Johnston's writing class. Towards the end of that time I did that tombstone inscription of which I have spoken. I was still lodging at Clapham and it was about that time that I first 'went' with a woman. This is not a history of doings but of the influences to which I have submitted or succumbed, so it is not to the point to describe such experiences. The sexual appetite may be a great influence in a person's life and as such must be dealt with in mine. But this or that adventure, pleasant or otherwise as it may have been at the time – charming and illuminating, disappointing or disgusting – was not influential in my life but only wayward boiling-over. There were men at the architect's office whose main theme of conversation was sexual adventure – not bad fellows but frivolous asses. My physiological ignorance and my erotical exuberance combined to make me a ready listener. I would not say that they influenced me to follow their example; the most that can be said is that dormant fires were fanned to flame by the things I heard. A moment came which was a sort of breaking point. How well I remember the moment – one evening in the lodging of Clapham – when the chain of fear snapped, and I stifled whatever was left of my prejudices, and all reasoning, for or against. The final cause, as I thought then and as I think even now, was not so much sensuality as curiosity, the desire to *know* even more than the desire to experience – to know rather than to feel. And the curiosity aroused by the ignorance which I have disclosed on an earlier page in the matter of human hair, strange as it may seem to some readers, was by now a *burning* curiosity. Let psychologists and moralists decide. I can only say that that curiosity finally broke the chain. Had I not been under the spell of a deep love for my Sacristan's daughter and been thereby assuaged (for young lovers can find ways of satisfying one another) I should, without doubt, have gone further than I did on the barren and destructive road. But my love affair was not approved of by my parents – it had no worldly advantage that they could see, and I was not yet of age – so while I burned with desire I also burned with a passion of faithfulness, and the more my parents objected so much the more loyal was I determined to be, and thus the mutual dalliance which we enjoyed whenever we could contrive a meeting, became the symbol of the marriage for which we both yearned and of which lechery would only have been a betrayal.

But, if I am recording influences, surely it would be altogether absurd to omit the influence of erotic appetite. We know what Renoir said, naming the tool with which he painted his pictures. Let his confession suffice for me. Lettering, masonry – these are not trades for eunuchs, they are different sorts of priesthood. And thus, almost consciously and very nearly in so many words, for ten years I pursued them. You may name such and such a book or such and such a person as one whose influence must be acknowledged. But there are other sorts of influence. Our move from Brighton to Chichester and the quality of that Roman and medieval city were a great influence on my life. The non-conformist background of my childhood was a great influence; so was the pervading beauty of the South Downs. And there were many others of which I have written or have yet to write. And doubtless accompanying all, changing all and pervading all there was and is the perpetual seethe of tumescence. I suppose most men would, if they had occasion, admit the same, and I suppose even in business, even in accountancy or shop-keeping, even if you were only a lift-man in 'the tube' or a poor victim 'on the belt' at Cowley, the exuberance of nature is a factor of paramount importance. But there are some trades and professions in which it counts for more than in others, in which indeed it is decisive. It can make little if any difference to the work of a man doomed to the factory whether he be amorous or no. Such an inclination, and all other such, must of necessity be relegated to the time when he is not working. But for the architect, the draughtsman, the stone carver, 'the exuberance of nature' is a determining influence and the quality of the man is evident in his work. It either flows forward in a rich stream of enthusiasm or meanders in emasculate hesitancy. The urine of the stallion fertilizes the fields more than all the chemicals of science. So, under Divine Providence, the excess of amorous nature fertilizes the spiritual field.

I do not think I have exaggerated the importance for me ('such as I am' being understood throughout this book) of our family move to Chichester. I must now record another move which made a sort of water-shed in my affairs. This time it was not a family move but only a change of lodgings. For, in spite of all I have said, the move to Chichester, revolutionary as it was did not effect any revolution in my way of living. We lived a suburban life at Brighton; at Chichester we did the same. 'Preston View' was replaced by '2, North Walls', and it was an improvement, because that little squashy house was at least free from the modern improvements and conveniences of 'desirable' residences. It was a distinct lowering of our standard of living. There was no bathroom; there were innumerable black beetles in the kitchen. There was no 'tradesman's entrance'. Our bedroom window looked onto the neighbour's backyard. The front door (which was also the back door) opened straight on to the pavement, and you went down two steps into the entrance passage. There were no 'bay' windows. Domestically, we were pretty well crowded in – but it was an improvement on 'Preston View' and it was sufficient for me that we lived in Chichester. I wouldn't have minded where or how we lived, provided we lived there. I see now that it was only by Providential mercy that things were thus. Our parents might have got a house in one of the new beginnings of suburbs to the north or south-east of the city. Perhaps the house in North Walls was cheap – it certainly ought to have been – and they certainly had to look at every penny. But if we had lived in the suburbs I dare say my life at Chichester would have been completely different; it would have had a quite different soul. We should not have been living in the city. We should not have been part of its very body. It makes a difference infinitely important whether you step out of your house into a noble town or only into the blasted smugness contrived by a speculative builder who can, by the terms of his occupation, only pander to your lowest tastes and your worst snobberies. God be praised, we were saved from that. There was very little good about the house in North Walls; I should think it would only just escape the condemnation of sanitary authorities, but it was spiritually decent and unadorned.

Our family left Chichester and plunged straight back into the suburbia of Bognor, villadom and all. Fortunately for me I very soon went to London, though, by so doing, I did not escape the suburbs. I went to live at Clapham, and this might well seem a descent into a far worse abyss. Victoria Road, Clapham! If you could walk up it with your eyes open you would certainly think you were in the lowest part of hell – the dullest, the most God-forsaken, the furthest removed from any heavenly light. But my eyes were shut. I had escaped from that awful period of youth when the future is a blank and your own part in it unknown. I had joined up, so to say, with the great army of people with work to do and a clear vision of a possible future. It was amply sufficient for me that I had lodgings and food; there was no need to worry about the street I lived in or even the lodging itself. You can be happy anywhere, if only you are undisturbed and haven't got to endure other people's pictures or knick-knacks – of course if you like them, then they cease to be other people's, they become your own. So it was in my Clapham lodging and for the first year or more I was very happy there. Lord! what kindness I received. The cost was entirely borne by the brother of my old friend the Prebendary. And what ingratitude I showed when, as far as I can remember, with the minimum of thanks and no repayment whatever, I ran away from Clapham, ran away from architecture and all the bright prospects those kind people had been paying to open to me, ran away from the church and the religion I had been brought up in and, with sneers and ribaldry, spurned all their culture and all the world that made it. How glad I am that they are all dead and can no longer suffer. But, on the other hand, kind friends do make things difficult. The obligation of gratitude may easily become a kind of trap, and the young are often caught and maimed in it. How could a boy of twenty hope to convince his parents and his benefactors, twenty, thirty, forty years older than himself, that his actions were better than theirs? What could they know about things so foreign to their world; how could they see his visions? Doubtless he was often wrong and always crude; but at least they couldn't say that he had deserted architecture to go on the stock-exchange. Doubtless to become a letter-cutter and a monu-mental mason was a big 'come down' – it was, in effect, to cease to be a gentleman. From their point of view the prospects of my some day building another St. Paul's Cathedral were not improved; but they could not say I was moved solely by concu-piscence and the desire of inordinate riches.

I was not too miserable in my Clapham lodging and sometimes one or other of my friends at the office would come back to supper with me (one of these it was who helped me to repaper the sitting-room with the then artistically fashionable brown paper – with silver ornaments – and I had a photograph of Rossetti's *Blessed Damozel* and a coloured reproduction of Queen Wilhelmina as a young girl and a print of Nicholson's *Queen Victoria* – so you can see), and sometimes I would go home with one of them in return. I think it was thus that I first got hold of the notion that a good life wasn't only a matter of good politics and good buildings and well-ordered towns and justice in economic relations. I began to see that domesticity itself must also be brought under the same rule of justice – that men and women were not just rabbits snuggling down into comfortable little fuggeries when their day's work was done. Indeed I began to see that my precious little cottage, 'foursquare', was an empty notion unless the life inside it, the life it was built to shelter and enshrine were foursquare also.

But whatever notions I may have begun to develop in this matter I was entirely unprepared for what happened. One evening at the Lettering Class (I don't know where else it could have been, nor do I understand how such a proposal could have been made in those circumstances), Edward Johnston told me that he had rooms in Lincoln's Inn and that under certain circumstances (such as my being able to pay a share and my willingness to keep quiet and not spread myself over the whole place) he would be willing for me to share the rooms with him. From Clapham to Lincoln's Inn, from paltry rooms in a scabrous Victorian street to a room with a vaulted ceiling looking out on to a noble square, from a suburb an hour's bus journey away right into the city itself, from the kindly but entirely misunderstanding company of the Church Club to the society of him whom I most honoured . . . Of course I accepted his offer and, with the least possible delay and, as I have said, a disgracefully small show of gratitude to my kind patrons at Clapham, I moved my scanty belongings to my new abode. 'Light's abode, celestial Salem' — I know it must seem absurd, but it was no less than heaven to me.

All enlightenments are, it seems, the same enlightenment. Different things are illuminated, but it is the same light. If you become a Buddhist and then a Plymouth Brother, if you are truly converted, it can really be only one conversion. Presently, later on in this book I will try and write of these religious matters. At this moment what I am trying to expose is the fact that all good is one and that the good things of my childhood in Brighton were not brought to naught and shown to be of no account because the evil thing that is Brighton, the Brighton of the drunks from Hammersmith or of the empty-heads from Kensington, was shown up for the evil thing it was by the order and decency of Chichester; that the rationality which is engineering is not contradicted by the rationality which is or was medieval stone building; that the personal piety of non-conformists is not reduced to absurdity by the parish piety of the Church of England. So my little move from Clapham to Lincoln's Inn, momentous though it was for me, more than a release from evil and actually an entry into good, did not involve any denial and, so to say, right-about-face to the things and thoughts I had accepted before; it was simply a realization of them, an incarnation, a real touch of the flesh and a fleshly touch of the real. What I experienced at Lincoln's Inn must have been very much like what, as I imagine it, a new undergraduate might feel when he begins life in his college rooms (though, in reality, undergraduates being seldom more than overgrown schoolboys, this must be very rare). It must have been like the experience of the novice entering religious life – but the comparison fails because few monasteries have any decency or dignity comparable to that of the old lawyers' Inns, and unless you were nearly blind, you would suffer unbearable offence from the fripperies of ecclesiastical worship. Nevertheless both these comparisons have justification. As in a college or monastery, we were bound by the rules and regulations of the house. The gates were shut at a certain hour every evening; boundary walls secluded us from the frivolities of the streets. There was a tacit agreement understood and accepted by all tenants of the Inn to conform to a certain unwritten but recognizable rule of dignity and decorum. It was in fact a community life and, as in all schools and colleges and religious houses, the rules were only irksome to those who didn't want to obey them. Edward Johnston was simply a tenant of the Inn and not a member, so of course we only lived there by courtesy. We usually went out to dinner in the evening – not for us to dine in hall with master and brethren – but we enjoyed the amenities of the collegiate life all the same, and you can see easily enough that it was a very different sort of life from that of my Clapham streets.

I suppose the life in all the old London squares – especially the smaller ones such as Woburn Square or Gordon Square — had some of the collegiate dignity of the Inns, and there were some residential streets which being all one property and having a porter's lodge at each end, were able to preserve a sort of free communal living. To-day this communal dignity has almost departed from London (and everywhere else); it only remains among the poor. The modern blocks of rich men's flats with their restaurants and swimming pools might be thought to be aiming at something of the sort, but rich men are incapable of dignity (I mean rich *business* men; but the qualification is hardly necessary for there are few others) and places so obviously built as money-making investments are damned from their conception. But workmen's dwellings are not thus handicapped. Whatever may be the bribery and corruption among town and city councillors (and we may assume that there is very little else), such things have nothing to do with the men and women who pay the rents which provide the commissions and 'rake-offs' and what-nots. In many parts of London, in the centre more than in the suburbs, you will find these great blocks of 'dwellings' with their courtyards and playgrounds. There is asphalt instead of grass and bushes. There are no smart nursemaids with babies in perambulators, but there are hundreds of children and a real fellowship between their mothers. And when eventually I had to leave Lincoln's Inn (because in those days they did not allow married people to live there), we were lucky enough to be able, by claiming my rights as a working man and no gentleman, a letter-cutter in fact, to get our 'dwelling' in Battersea. Thus by a merciful providence we were able to begin married life in a dignified manner.

Just as at Brighton I had never experienced anything that could be called communal planning, so at Chichester and Clapham I had never experienced anything that could be called communal living. Oxford and Cambridge meant very little, if anything, more than 'the boat race'. I had never visited either sanctuary, and I was even less acquainted with monasteries.

That there could be any other sort of living than the individualist domesticity in which I had been brought up did not occur to me and I never heard such things mentioned. We were still in the grand era of Victorian self-satisfaction and complacency. When we were children it seemed perfectly natural, and not in the least funny or mad, that each householder should choose what colour he or his wife liked best to paint the outside of the house with, and that in consequence it was not uncommon for two adjacent houses of the same identical 'stucco' terrace to be painted at different times with different colours and thus one-half of the front gate post might be new paint and the other half old — one half new chocolate colour and the other a dirty yellow. I don't say there is anything very bad in this; it's only funny and a bit mad; but it was typical of the period and typical of its individualism.

I suppose if I had been older when we moved from Brighton I might have thought differently. Perhaps there were many things known to our father and mother which made Chichester society very different from that of Brighton. 'Things that no fellow should do' in one place might be quite all right in the other. But I didn't notice anything different and nothing was mentioned that I can remember. So it was not until I got to Lincoln's Inn that I realized, almost all of a sudden, that neighbourliness need not mean only loving-kindness and readiness to lend a hand or a hammer; it might also mean *unanimity*, an agreement in the mind as to the good and the true and the beautiful and a common practice founded thereon. It was clear that such things had existed — Lincoln's Inn was the proof. Not only might builders and architects get together and agree to work harmoniously, but even the inhabitants might be of one mind and not strangers to one another. But I think this can only be thus when they are bound to one another by spiritual ties. Among the poor, poverty is thus a bond of peace, and workers are bound by a common understanding. Among the tenants of Lincoln's Inn there was not the bond of poverty, but there was undoubtedly the bond of work. Whether lawyer or architect or writer it was generally understood that neither riches nor social advancement – the things which chiefly interest middle-class women and wreck all chances of communal living in middle-class society – were the most important things. In fact it was not a society of men of business and therefore it could agree about good living.

All this has now passed away. More and more of the old 'chambers' are let to commercial firms and they have now admitted married couples – i.e. middle-class women.

I gained two things of inestimable value by going to Lincoln's Inn. I gained the experience of the good life – and I gained the experience of good life shared with good friends. In my last years of childhood, my last years at home and in my first two years in London I had no integrated life. Many things and many persons were good, but they were not knit together. Many of them had been masters of my soul – George Herbert Catt the art master, and Dr. Robert Codrington the prebendary at Chichester, and his brother Oliver at Clapham, George Carter, Colin Wilson the headman, and Tom Bridson my fellow pupil at the office – but in body and soul I was all at sixes and sevens. George Carter represented the integrated man, at Lincoln's Inn for the first time I experienced the integrated life. All things worked together for good. Breakfast time was as good as the beautiful room we had it in. Work and argument and the green trees of the square all went together. And argument ceased to be what so often it had been in those last years at home or at the office – the airing of irrational prejudices and predilections. Above all I enjoyed the privilege of living under the influence of Edward Johnston's subtle, painstaking, precise and original mind.

Two years this lasted and then he got married, and I became the tenant of the holy place. In this new phase I was joined by my younger brother, MacDonald, and until I also got married, a year later, he and I lived there together. I only hope that he found the same enlightenment that I had found.

# CHAPTER VI

# THE MONUMENTAL MASON AND LETTERCUTTER

WE entered the enchanted garden of Christian marriage in the year 1904 when I was twenty-two years old. I suppose few young men can have been more fortunate. I had enough work to bring in a modest living and evidence of an unfailing supply. I had £15 in hand, a bed, a table, some chairs and a few knives and forks and the top hat I was married in. I also had a wife and we had a home . . . (on our marriage night we woke from the sleep of bliss to find the room full of smoke, and glowing with red light. The timber yard next door was on fire. We spent the next few hours watching the blaze and then returned to bed. In the morning, we had bacon and eggs for breakfast and then returned to bed again. In the afternoon we paraded in Battersea Park, with all the other married couples, and found ourselves completed.)

And among the first of my good fortunes was, as I have said, the fact that living in workmen's dwellings we were able to start our new life in communal dignity. 'Once aboard the lugger and the girl is mine' and that is true, but just *any* lugger won't do. And getting married isn't just having a girl to keep, and 'for keeps'; it is also having a home. And having a home isn't only having a roof over your head, and taxes on your chest; it is also having a dwelling in suitable association with your neighbours. This suitable association can be achieved in a thousand different ways, but there is one way in which it can't be done. It can't be done in the suburban streets of modern England. Madly as I wanted to be married, I would have postponed my marriage for ever rather than live in such a place. Fortunately such continence was not imposed on me and thus we were not only able to marry young (though not so young as would have been better) but also, and this is the point here, I was subjected to the influence of marriage without the complications of suburban snobbery and domestic indignity — marriage unalloyed, marriage, as one may suppose, as it was meant to be. 'Always ready and willing' was our motto with respect to love making and 'let 'em all come' was our motto in respect of babies. 'Never buy what you can make' was as much the rule in the house as in the workshop, and, though at that date I didn't profess belief in any Lord, I had an unwavering conviction that the Lord would provide. This wasn't blind piety but the product of health and strength and a quite rational knowledge that the kind of work I could do would always be wanted — provided I did it as much as possible myself and didn't entangle myself in any damn-fool capitalistic scheme for making chickens lay more eggs than they had inside them. For that's what all capitalism really is. In the hope of increasing your product beyond human limits, you borrow money (from some robber) and employ some wage slaves. Then you have not only to pay their wages, and your own salary for looking after them (and naturally they won't want to do more work than they can help), but also interest on the money you've borrowed (or a share of your takings). You can only go on doing this as long as the people who buy whatever it is you turn out or produce (you can't call it 'making') do not see that your eggs, for example, are becoming more and more sterile and diseased and, in fact, are not really there at all, but only a more or less fraudulent imitation.

Thinking thus, or in that direction, we started married life and thought neither of future nor past. The work was enough for me, why should I think about the future? And, as I say, I had enough work to do. When it came to pawning some of the more preposterous of our wedding presents we certainly thought ourselves 'hard up', but such doings, though casting a gloom on the proceedings, did not actually sink the ship. Thus we were able to meet the baby problem. The babies came. They

were neither a problem nor a disaster; they were the consequence of marriage. Marriage meant babies – if it weren't for
babies there wouldn't be marriage; there wouldn't even be sex.
And the union of the sexes, however little or not at all you
think about it at the time, is fraught with the possibility and
even the probability of babies. Before you are married you say
'won't it be nice when we can do it properly' – meaning won't
it be nice when we shall be able to do it without worrying
about babies. And as marriage means babies, it means that
babies will be welcome – otherwise there's no point in marrying.

I gather that times have changed. I understand that people
don't want babies now-a-days and marriage is simply a 'hangover'.
All this is both understandable and forgiveable – up to a point,
for who would wish to bring children into the world of 1940?
I'm not going into this matter here, the point here is that in
those far-off times we took the coming of babies for granted
and themselves as welcome and that thereby your whole life
was altered and transformed.

It must be so. You can't become father and mother, with
three or four young children and not find your life fundamentally
different from that of the childless. You become a society with
claims and duties outside itself – claims and duties imposed by
social necessity and not by conscience. If you live all by yourself,
or even with a lover, and interfere with nobody, nobody need
interfere with you. 'I care for nobody, no not I, and nobody
cares for me' and that's all right. If your conscience doesn't
prick you into works of mercy or usefulness, nothing else can.
But you can't bring children into the world and still maintain
a life of independence. If starving or otherwise maltreating
your children doesn't revolt your conscience it will revolt the
conscience of your neighbours. There's no need to argue
whether this be right or wrong; it is simply a fact and most
parents accept the fact gladly.

But the consequences are momentous. You are no longer
simply concerned to discover what conditions are best for your

work (that which you do for your living – i.e. in return for the bread and butter you eat) and what conditions are best for your comfort, you are concerned to discover what conditions are best for a growing family . . . And admirable as was our life in our Battersea dwelling and in the lane in Hammersmith[1] it became increasingly irksome to be told to 'keep off the grass' and 'don't pick the flowers'. Looking after children is a mug's game when such a large part of it consists in seeing that they don't do things which their every natural instinct prompts them to do. Oh, Hell! I said and I think she more or less said the same, and as we both regarded our native hills as our natural home and London an increasingly unnatural prison house, we suddenly packed up and went to Ditchling in Sussex, where we managed to get an old house with an entrance hall that wasn't a mere passage, and that makes a big difference to your whole domesticity, and a great big kitchen big enough to have family meals in. Here life at once became good again. For a year or more I kept on the workshop at Hammersmith and then, my work not being very local, I was able to shift the whole show, faithful apprentice and all, to Ditchling.

This move was not prompted by any notion of liking the country for its own sake, but simply because London seemed an impossible place for children. That was the beginning of it; it would not have happened otherwise. But one thing leads to another and very soon did – chickens, a pony and trap, an acre or two of land, a cow, a pig (and that means fourteen more every now and then). It meant the discovery of genuine exponents of genuine domestic traditions – old Mrs. Bourne, a farm labourer's wife, and Miss Collins the policeman's daughter, who taught the mistress and the girls all about bread-baking in brick ovens and all about the insides of pigs and a host of other domestic doings such as our great-grandmothers knew about but which

[1] To which we moved because I couldn't get a workshop in Battersea. I had a 'studio' in Chelsea for some months, but I had to leave it because I was surrounded by 'artists' and the noise of stone working disturbed their meditations.

our labour-saving gadget-mongers and dead-food-purveyors have destroyed. But the mistress had an itch to learn about such things and the children naturally revelled in it. I hadn't any theory about all this domestic and farmyard development. In a general way it frightened me and I put a brake on it. But it was entirely in tune with all our other notions of life and work, so I couldn't but see that it was good. And if they had the courage, which I lacked, I was thankful, and not a little proud.

Meanwhile the lettering business was developing in several directions. Lettering in stone was the chief thing but this led to others – drawing lettering for books (title-pages and such) and that led to engraving in wood (because the photographic line-block is essentially an inferior article); painted lettering, and that led to quite a brisk trade in shop-facia writing, and me going up and down the country as a sign-writer, and even to Paris, and there was more work than I could do all by myself. I had an apprentice in the stone shop and a pupil assistant in the sign-writing and sometimes I had a mason in, or two masons, to help with the tomb-stones. But my work was all lettering, and until about 1909 I don't think I so much as dreamed of doing anything else. Of course on a tomb-stone or memorial tablet there would occasionally be a shield with heraldic emblems, and there would be simple mouldings and perhaps occasional flowery borders, but carvings of the 'human figure' whether naturalistically represented or otherwise, seemed to me another trade and not mine. I never was any good at naturalistic drawing. As a child I was a little jealous of those who had the knack or talent for getting, with a few lines or dots or dashes, an effect of reality. But I didn't take it very seriously, and if ever it happened that a customer ordered a cherub to be carved on a stone I used to call in a sculptor friend to do that part of the job. I do think this is rather odd, because it wasn't as though I were unacquainted with or unappreciative of ancient stone carvings, and I ought to have realized that there was no difference whatever in principle or technique between, for example, medieval English carvings of angels or saints and the floral or heraldic carvings of the same period. I accepted the latter as being within my potentialities, but the former I assumed to depend upon knowledge and skill I neither possessed nor could attain. I shall have to return to this later; at the moment I have to try and explain the influences which moved me in the lettering business.

These influences were mainly two, and were matters of conviction as to the end of the work and the means to be employed. What kind of lettering was good lettering, the right kind to be done, and what technique and social conditions were suitable for its production? I have explained at some length the line of thought provoked by three years in an architect's office, and the revolt against the common architectural method of providing measured drawings of everything — even full-size drawings of carving. Obviously I did not become a lettercutter and monumental mason in order to become one of the hack carvers who follow architect's 'details'. My chief claim to support was that I could relieve the architect of the necessity of supplying drawings in connection with one craft at least. But such a claim depended upon my ability to give them something better than they could get otherwise. Therefore I had to profess to 'know' — and to know better than they did themselves. That was where I was lucky; for I came along just at the moment when the work done by William Morris was bearing fruit in the minds of architects and the influence of Edward Johnston, supported by that of W. R. Lethaby (who shall measure the greatness of this man — one of the few men of the nineteenth century whose minds were enlightened directly by the Holy Spirit?), was making it clear that fine printing was only one of a thousand forms of fine lettering. And what *was* fine lettering? It was in the first place rational lettering; it was exactly the opposite of 'fancy' lettering. That was the new idea, the explosive notion, and, you might say, the *secret*. For the world thinks that art and reason are poles asunder, that the artist is the irrational person and all his works the product of caprice and emotional temperament. It has been brought up to think so — art dealers, art critics and artists themselves have more or less consciously conspired to preserve the fiction. Thus art becomes mysterious and a false glamour surrounds it — and better prices. And what applied to the 'fine' arts applied to all the others. Directly a thing was given the title of 'artistic' it was supposed to be a work of fancy, and irrational. Artistic lettering meant lettering in which legibility was sacrificed to something called beauty — beauty, the beautiful, that which tickles your fancy.

Well, following Morris, following Ruskin, following the universal practice of the world, except in eccentric periods such as that induced by our irreligious commercialism and the insubordinations which made that commercialism possible, we were in revolt against the whole conception of art as being irrational. Without knowing it we were Thomistic and Aristotelian. I say 'we'; but the word gives a false suggestion. It was a movement but it had no creeds or formularies. It was, if you like, a reaction against Victorianism and at the same time, a flowering of Victorian rationalism — an application of that rationalism in spheres in which the Victorians had never applied it. The Victorian period was a capitalist period. The one test under capitalism is: does it pay? and saleability is the one criterion of good. 'Rationalism' in Religion was a paying proposition in the nineteenth century, for it helped to destroy the oppositions to rationalism in scientific research. Scientific research was a paying proposition because it made possible the application of science to industry, and that was the most paying proposition the world had ever known. Rationalism, scientific research, the application of science to industry — these things are good things; but the point here is that the only reason for their success in the reign of the Great White Queen was that they helped to build up innumerable bank balances. But with the arts it worked exactly the other way round. The application of science to industry which, in a world conformed to charity and consequently to justice, would have been wholly good, became simply the instrument for the complete degradation of men and the destruction of all the trades by which normally men serve one another – that is to say all the trades which were patient of mechanization, all the so-called 'useful' arts. But the others, not so patient, the 'fine' arts, were thus isolated. They became 'hot-house' arts; and as one of the most conspicuous effects of mechanization was to reduce the workman to an impersonal instrumentality, an exaggerated importance came to be attached to the exhibition of personality fostered in the hot house. Personal, all too personal, and eventually only to be judged by irrational and even anti-rational standards of aestheticism. 'All art is useless', said Oscar Wilde, and, as Dali now adds, 'All art is meaningless'. Poor Oscar Wilde! what he had at the back of his mind was quite true – that art, in any human sense of the word, has nothing whatever to do with the monstrous filthiness of the man of business and his mechanized world. But the said man of business only laughed; for he knew that nothing Oscar Wilde could say would upset his factories and, on the other hand, a much more profitable business could be done in 'fine art' if you could persuade the public to forget all about *meaning*. It's beauty that pays, not doctrine. A Raphael Madonna may fetch a hundred thousand pounds if you can prove it's by Raphael and forget it's a Madonna – for if you don't forget it's a Madonna, it will seem a monstrous sacrilege to put it up for auction and then stick it up in the National Gallery. It's beauty that pays – because beauty is dope and in their kind of world it's dope we need. But doctrine, if only there were priests courageous enough to preach it, would bring that world down like a – well, 'like a house built on sand'.

So there we were, and there I was. What is good lettering? That was the job before me. And at every point a justification must be found in reason. Of course we weren't teetotallers about fancy work, but it must be kept subordinate and even fancy work should grow out of legitimate occasion. What is decoration but that which is seemly and appropriate? And having made some beginnings in the job of discovering a reasonable basis for lettering, the next thing was to discover the basis of a reasonable workshop life, a reasonable life for workmen.

In this matter you obviously can't get far without getting entangled in political theory. And as the socialists, of whatever party, were all agreed in antipathy to the control of the world by men of business, whether industrialists or landlords, I, in company with so many others, became a socialist. This is natural, inevitable, and eminently right and proper; and the results would almost certainly be all that could be desired if the socialist parties and societies were in the main or to any large extent led and controlled by persons as humane and as saintly, or even as human and as disinterested as William Morris and John Ruskin. But though there are many such persons in the socialist movement, it is, in spite of the noble minds and the noble ideas of many of its supporters, simply a revolt and a reaction against the widespread tyrannies and injustices and cruelties of those who possess property. According to my experience of it during the years 1900 to 1910 it was not moved or led, still less could it be said to be inspired, by any ideas of man or of man's life or of man's work other than those of the capitalist world against whose injustices and cruelties it was in revolt. The capitalist world had produced the England of Queen Victoria and, for the most part, both capitalists and their victims were equally and shamelessly proud of it. Take for example, the ordinary process of factory 'mass-production', and take the ordinary products of that process. Both capitalists and victims were convinced, as they still are, that mass-production is the solution of the problem of poverty. Both were and both are still convinced that there is nothing wrong with the products. From the socialist point of view there is only one trouble and that is mal-distribution. Some people get too much and the majority too little. That there is anything wrong with the method of production or anything wrong with the things produced did not and, as far as I can learn, does not, occur to anyone – either to slave-master or slave. Socialism, therefore, as a political movement is hardly more than an attempt to re-order the distribution of factory products and factory profits. Thus not only will there be plenty for all but there will be proper provision for health and, as is supposed, happiness.

In the circumstances of our world it was, as I have said, natural that young craftsmen and architects and all such should become socialists. The general detestation of the man of business and his unnatural and abominable stranglehold on everything, could not but unite them with the masses of the robbed and the dispossessed and the maimed. The interests, the political interests of the craftsman could not but seem identical with those of the trade-unionists. The iniquity of landlordism could seem neither less nor different from that of the industrialist – slum owning (and therefore slum profiteering) and factory owning (and therefore industrial profiteering) were simply different forms of the same evil and both seemed to derive from the legalization of absolute ownership which the breakdown of feudalism had made possible. Therefore the main principle of socialist politics – the nationalization of the means of production, distribution and exchange – seemed both natural and just. And it did not seem less natural or less just when it was observed that the main opposition to this principle came from the persons and classes who profited from the opposing practice of capitalism – that production, distribution and exchange (the land and the factories, transport and banking) should all be conducted by private persons for their private profit. It was true that the full development of the inhuman practices of capitalism had been prevented. Trade-unionists, after the spilling of much blood and tears (hangings, transportations, imprisonments), had won recognition for the justice of their claims. The spectacle of so much blood and misery and the threat of even worse things and even more dangerous eventualities (widespread disease and pestilence in the slums and factory towns) had both shamed and alarmed the possessing classes. Elegant persons like Benjamin Disraeli were moved to write books about it. No more eloquent description of the hell which our high-minded and self-righteous mine-owners and industrialists had made and drawn profit from could be written than occurs, for example, in his novel called *Sybil*. Noble lords, like him of Shaftesbury, were thus able to gain a hearing which otherwise would certainly have been denied them. Thereafter the principle was established that the common man and the common man's wife and children, the proletarians, the dispossessed, the working classes and, in general, the 'poor', could not legitimately be tortured for profit. This was an entirely new principle in industrial England and there were not wanting many who feared the worse consequences from its embodiment in legislation. For not only would the costs of production be increased beyond all calculation, but if kindness to workers, or even decency, was to become compulsory, it was difficult to avoid the conclusion that the workers would become more difficult to control; they would be getting it into their heads that they had rights as human beings whereas it had hitherto seemed to be universally admitted that they only had duties as animals. These fears were to a large extent justified and had it not been for the spur which trade-unionism gave to human inventiveness and the consequent development of machinery it would very certainly have been necessary either to repeal the Factory Acts, and all Acts designed to protect the animal classes, or else to abandon the ambition of being a first-class multiple-store and shop-keeping nation.

The wickedness, the material wickedness (for of course one cannot suppose that they were intelligent enough to be fully responsible for their deeds), of the possessing classes in the half-century immediately following 'the industrial revolution' was so monstrous and so devilish that it would be impossible to exaggerate it. We are accustomed to the emotion of bewilderment which we suffer when we read of the tortures inflicted upon one another by the American Indians, or by Christians upon one another, or by pagan Romans upon Christians; for it seems impossible to recreate in ourselves the state of mind in which such things are possible. The America of the Hurons and Mohawks and Algonquins, the Europe of the Inquisition or the Reformation, the Rome of the Caesars are too remote for our comprehension. In the same way for many people (even though perhaps a minority of the population) there is the same emotion of bewilderment when attempting to reconstruct the frame of mind of the 1820's. It is difficult to understand how such things could be possible. It is not only difficult, it is impossible to understand how the police and the soldiery could have found their oaths of obedience so binding upon them as to make them the instruments for the perpetuation of so much and so obscene cruelty to their own parents and brothers and sisters. And it is equally difficult to understand how such things could either be borne by the victims, acquiesced in by the general public or approved of by those who profited by them. But, in order to make some approach to understanding, it is only necessary to consider our own times. There are things being done to-day, whether by the military under the guise of what they still call 'war', or by the police in preservation of what is still called 'peace', whether by industrial magnates in the name of 'trade and commerce' or by ordinary men of business simply for the sake of gain, that will be no less difficult to understand and forgive in the years to come. The factory system itself is in itself so inhuman, subhuman and anti-human an institution for the production of things for the use of human beings that, were we not so used to it, had we not been born in it, did not so many of us derive profits or wages from it, we should, as we some day shall, find it impossible to understand the frame of mind of the nations that endure it or the writers and politicians who applaud it, and of the Christian clergy who seek every excuse to avoid condemning it. And the same difficulty of comprehension is found when we consider the product of our industrialism as when we consider the monstrous inhumanity of its method. How any individuals, and still more, how whole populations, whether cultivated or simple, can be so obsessed by the merely quantitative advantages of machine production as to be able to endure the food, clothing, furniture and buildings of industrial England, France, Germany, America and all other industrialized countries will, to our posterity, be a problem as insoluble as our own in relation to the cruelties of the past. Yet we build and fill up with great pride, and perhaps even greater expense, vast buildings called museums and art galleries for the preservation of enormous collections of the very things which, by our industrial practice, we prevent the making of. Could madness go further? Could malice do more?

Yet surprise is sometimes expressed at the hatred which the poor, and the wage-working people generally, have for the rich and for the Church of England. People have forgotten the monstrous cruelties inflicted upon the poor in the past and they think it wicked that the poor should not have forgotten also. They have so thoroughly forgotten that they can hardly believe such things ever happened and they are so convinced that all reforms were brought about by themselves that they think the poor are simply ungrateful wretches. For they have not only forgotten the sins of their ancestors but they have also forgotten that the reforms in the poor law, factory acts, etc., were only wrung out of them after much shedding of blood. Let the doubter read, for instance, *The Village Labourer* and *The Town Labourer* by J. L. and B. Hammond. He will find a record of cruelties so great and so vile that his only surprise will be that men and women could endure them. What hope then is there for the future if the present is thus poisoned by memory? There can be no forgiveness until there be contrition and of that there has not yet been the slightest sign. On the contrary there is every evidence that it is only fear which prevents the rich and powerful from falling back into the same cruelties. Even now the injustices and cruelties have only been mitigated; they have not been removed. Still less have they been repented. Even now there is little reason to suppose that the clergy of a State Church are capable of turning against their paymasters, or that the rich will not always exercise a preponderating influence over the clerical mind.

Even now, though its failure is evident on all sides, there is no sign that the root principle upon which our capitalism is built is not still the ruling principle in the minds and hearts of our people – the principle of production for profit. What right have we to condemn the banks and big financiers for their exclusive attention to money-making while investors and all men of business, large or small, pursue their affairs upon the same principle? Moreover they are in a net of accountancy from which they cannot escape. The balance sheet is the final judge, 'double-entry' has them in thrall. I know my words will seem those of a person either ignorant or mad, but I say with certainty that there cannot be any hope for the revival of either good life or good work until double-entry book-keeping is abandoned by all the producing and distributing trades. It is no use talking about forgiveness and repentance – such terms are totally irrelevant in a world run for profit and ruled by accountants. . . .

Thinking such thoughts, spurred on by such angers and exasperations, filled with such hatred of the world we were compelled to inhabit – for even emigration was out of the question, seeing that men of business had laid their evil and blighting hands on every country of the earth – it was inevitable that we should seem to find in the socialist parties the only hope of reform. Having no experience of actual political life and therefore unaware of its meanness and corruption, its fraudulence and hypocrisy, we still hoped for salvation through parliamentary action. If we were blissfully ignorant of the corruption and career-hunting of Trade Union secretaries, we were even more blissfully ignorant of the same vices among Labour Members of Parliament. 'All things are possible to those who vote' might have been our bedroom text. And this mood, as of victims ground under the heel of cruel over-lords, was in my own mind still further fomented by an incident which occurred one Saturday afternoon somewhere about the year 1906 (earlier or later, I cannot remember) in Whitehall.

With a thousand or more other people I had attended a meeting in Trafalgar Square. Among the speakers was Cunninghame Graham and the occasion was some action of the British Government in connection with happenings in Russia (I think that was why Cunninghame Graham was speaking – for he was well known as a traveller in Russia and a supporter of the down-trodden people of that country). I don't remember exactly what the occasion was, nor does it now matter, but I remember standing in the crowd of socialists and labourites just under one of the silly lions and cheering with the rest. At the end of the speeches there was a conference among the speakers and it was presently announced that a procession would form and march four abreast down Whitehall to Downing Street to present a petition of protest at a certain person's house in that street. It was announced that the police were agreeable to this procession if it proceeded in a quiet and orderly manner and to that end it would be led by a mounted policeman and there would be mounted police on each side. Without much delay the procession started. I saw the policeman on his horse high up in front. Cunninghame Graham and others led the demonstration and I, having been quite near the front of the audience was also quite near the head of the procession. We marched, according to plan, down the middle of Whitehall. The horseman in front was well in view and other horsemen were on each side. There was no noise. There were no banners or flags, for this procession was not an advertised part of the afternoon's proceedings. As far as I knew it had not been expected by anyone, but the whole thing was very quiet and orderly and it was led, guided and controlled by the police themselves. It must have taken half an hour or more to get down to the Inigo Jones palace. Then suddenly, just before we got to Downing Street, and without the slightest warning, out of Old Scotland Yard and Whitehall Place, out of Whitehall Gardens and up from Parliament Street and New Scotland Yard hundreds of policemen rushed. We had been deliberately led into an ambush! There for the first time I knew the bitterness of treachery and the panic cowardice of the armed confronted by the mob. For the first time also I experienced the police tactics for breaking up the cohesion of a procession, and very illuminating it was. On such occasions, it seems, you don't come out and meet the procession and say to its leaders: 'Sirs, we regret our mistake in allowing you to come thus far, but we must ask you to stop here and disperse. Moreover we cannot allow the presentation for which, without due thought, we gave permission. We trust you will accept our apologies and believe that we are only acting thus by reason of orders from above. We must add, though with much regret, that, should your followers prove recalcitrant, we shall be compelled to disperse them by force. We will, however, give them ten minutes in which to disperse peacefully after which . . .' etc. No, such is not the method employed. Doubtless they know better than to suppose that such 'tripe' would be believed. What they actually do is less wasteful of breath and more expeditious. They don't meet the procession 'head on', so to say and drive it back. They don't merely put up a barrier of armed men and announce to the leaders that the procession must disperse, telling them to pass the word back rank by rank. They have no training by which they can distinguish between a procession of political enthusiasts and one of angry or starving unemployed. Their training only informs them that 'the poor in a loomp is bad' (as Queen Victoria's friend Tennyson expressed it through the mouth of his Northern farmer[1]) and that all criticism of and

[1] I can't recall who it was that first pointed out this poem of Tennyson's to me. It can't have been my father, though he was the great Tennyson exponent in my youth. It can't have been the Chichester art master – it wasn't up *his* street. I think it must have been either George Carter or Tom Bridson at the

opposition to the existing regime is an offence against the King's Majesty upon which they depend for their pay. So they don't take any risks and, having led the silly sheep well into the ambush (led by themselves, mark you, and with a great show of doing so to give the said sheep full confidence, a false sense of security), they then rush out upon them, and knock, push, shove, and if necessary kick them in all directions. In *all* directions, that is the secret of it. I was, with the gentle suasion of a policeman's hand on my neck, shoved in one direction, my neighbour in the opposite. If you ran in one way you found yourself confronted by a bobby who instantly pushed you violently the other way. The amiable result was almost instant disintegration and confusion and if, in the course of a few minutes, you found yourself somewhere near one of the side streets you were made very clearly to understand that for such swine as you a hasty dash up it was your only chance of avoiding 'jug'. Any momentary hesitation on your part, whether intentional or the consequence of your confusion, was simply the occasion for more dirty words from the nearest policeman and more neck-handling, and if you fell it would be a good thing to get up quickly without the assistance of a large size in boots. I can plainly feel the hand of 'the law' on my neck as I write and I can as plainly feel the impotent bitterness of my disappointment.

I have met some nice bobbies in my time and even had drinks with them in the back parlours of pubs after closing time (in fact our local policeman at Ditchling was a regular inhabitant of the bar parlour after the farm labourers had been shut out). I have only on very few occasions had similar experiences to that

office. Anyway the phrase stuck in my mind and I hated the old boy for it quite unjustly. I hope he now forgets or forgives. I could not forgive in those days. I had not yet come to see either the irony of Tennyson's poem (it's a grand piece of work in its kind) or the wisdom of the remark, attributed to Dr. Johnson, that 'a man is never so honourably employed as when he is making money'. But did he say 'making' or did he say '*earning*'? or did he say 'making' and mean 'earning'? Apart from all that, the quotation from Tennyson made me see red, and the red flag among other things.

one in Whitehall. (One of these was a very nasty one but there is no point in recounting it.) The whole point of my attempt to recall the pitiful story of the Whitehall 'riot' (as it was called in the next morning's papers) is that it had a great influence on my mind and showed me the futility of placing any reliance on what is called 'peaceful demonstration'. There isn't such a thing – because those in power cannot afford to let there be. If there is no riot, a riot must be provoked, or the semblance of one created. Power, as Lord Acton remarked, is always corrupting, whether among princes or churchmen, soldiers or police or men of business, but particularly and above all among politicians. And the corrupt are not to be trusted. You have heard them talk about 'the British love of fair-play'; you have heard them on the subject of their honour and patriotism; you have heard them bragging about their services to their fellow-men. Do not believe a word of it. And, particularly, do not believe politicians. By the nature of their trade they have no professional pride and can have none. The phrase 'professional politician' has brought the very notion of professionalism to dirt. It means only money-making. 'Religion is politics and politics is brotherhood,' said William Blake, but what has parliamentarism to do with either? And what qualifications for government can be claimed by those whose parliamentary existence depends solely upon their ability to catch votes – when catching votes depends solely upon the ability to make plausible promises which, even if he genuinely intended to do so the vote-catcher has no power to honour.

We were not thus completely disillusioned as to parliamentary plutocracy in the year 1906 but we were moving in that direction and my experience in Whitehall, foolish though it may seem to the reader, did a great deal towards establishing a different frame of mind with regard to the powers of those in power and the possibility of an unscrupulous use of them. It began to be clear that the hateful world of the man of business and its hateful cruelties would never be abolished by those who profited by them and that 'the mother of parliaments' was not an institution for righting wrongs (after all, it never had been) but one for the promotion and preservation of whatever seemed most profitable to owners of capital. And foreign politics was nothing but an extension of home politics on the same general principle. As for the redressing of the wrongs of the poor, of course no one could object to this being done, but in the first place it must be made clear that such wrongs really existed and were not merely figments in the brains of paid agitators, and, in the second, nothing must be done to jeopardize the sacred rights of capital or the stability of 'the City' and the empire founded upon it. These things being understood and agreed, everyone was only too anxious to display kindness to animals, and to prevent cruelty to children.

I say these things began to be clear and the hope of reform by parliamentary means began to recede proportionately. And this clarification brought another and even more fundamental one in its train. For I was not so simple as to suppose that physical cruelty and economic injustice were either the only or even the chief evils of capitalist commercialism. At the most such evils were only symptomatic, and the deep wickedness of which they were symptoms was a dirtiness of soul. And though to those who suffer them, cruelty and injustice must seem the only evils of any importance, there are others which, though not so frantically crying to heaven for immediate vengeance, are symptomatic of even deeper blasphemy. The physical conditions of the women chain-makers at Cradley and Cradley Heath were, until a very few years ago, as cruel as those of the women hauliers in the mines of 1840. The injustices perpetrated in the name of 'sound finance' are as great to-day as at any time. But it is easily possible to abolish such cruelty and such injustice and still have the civic centre at Cardiff, the central square at Leeds, Piccadilly Circus and Leicester Square. And it is possible not only to have such things but to be proud of them! That is the incredible proposition. The mutilation of small children's bodies, the misery of the poor everywhere, in contrast with the paunchy luxury of the city business man with his gold chain across his fat belly – such things are causes for curses and tears, God knows!, and not less so when the gold chain and the fat belly are only metaphorical. And curses and tears are not without effect. The fattest belly is sensitive to pain and, indeed, few things can be more difficult to bear than the indigestion of the rich. There is therefore a bond, the bond of pain, between rich and poor and the kind hearts which beat beneath coronets have been known to beat so loudly as to cause doubts even of the simple faith which rules the Monty Norman blood – in other words, the belted earls who grace the boards of directors, though admitting no more than a limited liability, have often headed the lists of subscribers to 'charity', and the conservative party, the party of owners, has often led in policies of social reform. But what avail are tears and curses when you find yourself in the central square at Leeds, or in any other modern city? It must very soon be obvious, it was soon obvious to me, that no merely political or economic rearrangement of the world was going to be effective to remove such horrors. For though it was easily demonstrable that the spiritual degradation of men – as far as modern Europe was concerned – dated from the rise to power of the man of business out of medieval feudalism, nevertheless that demonstration still left two things to be explained. It did not explain why such a rise was tolerated – why many should prefer the rule of the money-lender, most despicable of creatures, to that of princes, the most admired, or to that of ecclesiastics, of all men the most feared. And it did not explain why both the governors and the governed should find the results so pleasing. The groans of the poor in their pains and miseries might reach the ears of the Lord of Sabaoth and might be made to penetrate, though with much difficulty, even the ears of the rich. Even the rich are not too happy and, as I have said, even though the rich do not suffer the pangs of hunger they suffer the similar and equally painful pains of indigestion. But pain is not the worst evil in the world and the pain of having too little is no worse than that of having too much, though there be many more that suffer it. And though I could not say what that worse evil was, I knew it was something for which neither the Fabian nor any other Socialist society had a remedy. All I knew was that this evil arose somewhere in the sphere of what they called religion. I had cut myself off from the religion of my fathers and from the religion of my childhood. The complete detachment of the Church of England as I knew it, and of the various non-conformist bodies, from any concern in the problems which thus vexed me, precluded or seemed to preclude any possibility that Christianity might turn out to be the cure to the world's sickness of soul. The churches seemed to be concerned solely with their sectarian games – they hardly seemed to be interested even in feeding the hungry. And if you couldn't count on the parsons to help to redress even common cruelties and injustices, how much less could you count on them in deeper matters? For that was how it struck me, and that was why eventually I had to leave the Fabian Society also, for I could not believe that charity was the flowering of justice but, on the contrary it seemed to me, all inarticulate though I was and quite utterly unable to express the matter, that justice was the flowering of Charity!

'Abu ben Adhem, may his tribe increase. . . .' No, no, no, no. There was something wrong with Abu ben Adhem, and quite apart from his insupportable self-appraisement, he was wrong, and Mr. Clough was a liar and a false prophet. You couldn't profess to love your fellow-men and know no more. It was damned impudence to start with – Damned Pharisaism too. I give tithes of all I possess; I give alms – see, boys, in short, how I love my fellow-men. That was not at all what was meant when it was said: how can you love God whom you have not seen, if you do not love your neighbour whom you have seen. It means that you must *start* by loving God and, in the light of that love, in that light of love – for God *is* love – and as its necessary and inevitable fruit you must love your neighbour. But you must love God first. Otherwise your neighbour-love would be a wrong kind of love; it would turn out to be no love at all or simply self-love.

How to get all this right? that was the trouble. For I was outside the churches, God's official mouthpieces! How could I be inside them? They seemed to be doing precisely what was forbidden – professing to love God whom they had not seen and yet bearing no fruit in the love of neighbours. Their God-love was suspect. Their God himself was suspect. But, on the other hand, my friends, the socialists, were in no better case. Like Abu ben Adhem they professed to love their fellow-men and, according to their lights, I did not doubt that they did so. But they did not profess to love God. On the contrary, like myself, they professed ignorance of God's existence. Then how was anyone to know that their neighbour-love was well-founded? Justice and equity and fair dealing between man and man, between man and woman, between parents and children, what is the ground of such justice and equity? The greatest good of the greatest number. Plenty of food, clothing and shelter for all. Higher wages and shorter hours. Sanitation and so many cubic feet of air for every child. Book-learning for all and privilege for none. You could easily make a sort of Army and Navy Store's catalogue of all the goods a socialistic state would provide and, in a world ruled by selfish men, how right and proper it seems thus to make a sort of 'soup kitchen' of it. And who was against it? Who but the selfish men themselves. By whose arrangement was it that some should be too well fed and many should starve; that some should live in Park Lane and many in slums; that a few should enjoy the amenities of country estates and the majority work in miserable drudgery in crowded and airless and dangerous factories. 'Oh yes, we admit', as the head of the big insurance company said, 'that some readjustments must be made. There is certainly a dead weight of undernourished poverty which must be dealt with and of course, the housing problem . . . but much has already been done to bring Art to the masses. . . .' Nevertheless the opposition to the Socialist 'soup-kitchen world' was not made on the ground of its godlessness – though that was a very good line in the newspapers – but solely by reason of the curtailment of profits which it involved. The rich were against the poor and poor were against the rich, and naturally I was on the side of the poor.

But still the problem remained. Plenty of food, clothing and shelter for all! In the semi-starving world which our men of business had fostered even if they didn't invent it, such a political programme of first aid to the wounded must of course gain the approval of all generous young men. But it is impossible to stop there. Mere plenty is not enough after the first pangs of hunger are appeased. Inferior bread is better than none but provision must be made at least in the mind, for the time when everyone being fed, it shall be possible to consider giving good bread rather than bad. And when you start to consider such questions you find, almost at once, that the question: what is good bread? is actually the first one to be asked. For ultimately (and what is 'ultimately' but firstly? For ultimately doesn't mean last in time, but that which remains after all extraneous and irrelevant matters have been eliminated) only good bread is worthy of the name of bread! And this is true of all goodness. A good house is simply a house; a bad house is hardly a house at all. And the less a thing is good the less it is anything. The more you deprive a thing of what is proper to it, the more you deprive it of being. So that it becomes obvious that you can't say: let's give these chaps some bread and after we've done that, we'll consider whether we can give them some *better* bread. That is, it turns out, simply impious nonsense.

And what applies to bread, applies, as I have said, to all things. You can't just demand justice for the poor, and leave it at that. You must find out who are the poor and what is 'who', and what is justice that the poor should be given it.

So you cannot stay calmly in the socialist ranks and agitate for justice as though everyone knew what it was. You can't go on arguing about the rights and wrongs of municipal trading and municipal trams and leave unanswered all questions, all ultimate questions, about man and the universe, as though the answers to such questions could wait until all men were fed and all men were clothed and given houses. What is man that he should be fed? And what is food for *man*? What is man that he should be clothed? And what are suitable clothes for such a being? Is it conceivable that he is a temple of the Holy Ghost? But what the devil is that? and what kind of housing can possibly be his suitable shrine?

It may not matter whether Mr. Einstein be right or wrong. Indeed that is quite obviously a matter of very relative importance. But what is man? is a very different order of question and the answer makes all the difference between good politics and bad. In fact, applying my previous argument, there is no such thing as politics except the politics which are good. Any other politics are no politics, and therefore unless we are on the right track as to the nature of man we must keep out of politics altogether. So there I found myself – religion the first thing necessary and I without religion!

Well! well! If religion is the first thing necessary – and, of course, by religion, I mean an answer to the primary and ultimate questions; what is man and why? – and I hadn't got one, then, obviously I must get a ready-made religion or make one up. Naturally I took the latter course. But this doesn't mean that I had to invent a reason for the existence of the universe, as though no such reason existed, but simply that I must discover it for myself, and it sounds as presumptuous as it was. But there again, there was plenty of good excuse. Was it not obvious that the world, even the world as a whole, and particularly the world of England, was in a shocking and disgusting mess? And was it not equally obvious that such religious bodies as existed were either doing nothing whatever about it, or aiding and abetting it in its confusion? If you see a man with a broken leg in a ditch and a so-called doctor is binding his leg up crooked, you naturally assume that either the doctor doesn't want the man to get well or else that he's got a rotten idea of well; for, you see, we do all know, by an almost infallible instinct, what is straight and what is crooked in the matter of human anatomy. We know a deformity immediately. (And how often my relations have told me that my sculptures are out of proportion! *They* know.) And if you see your country going to the devil and the churches battening on the profits, you assume that either they approve of the country's direction or they don't know of a better one. And in that case you don't either join the choir or listen to the sermon. You may be wrong about the doctor's ideas. He may be simply lazy or he may have forgotten all his training. You may be wrong about the churches — the clergy may have got into a rut and forgotten all about Christ. But, being young and foolish and full of zeal and enthusiasm, you may be forgiven for your hasty conclusions. You are right in your facts. The world *is* in a mess and the churches don't *seem* to be doing anything about it; on the contrary they do *seem* to be rather enjoying it and, how they do hate the socialists!

So I invented a new religion — and then discovered it was an old one. This must be explained, but, before attempting to do so another factor in the situation and one of growing importance (please forgive me — I know very well that none of this stuff is of any importance whatever except to me) must be mentioned. From the year 1903, when I got my first inscription job, to the year 1909 I had done nothing whatever in the way of earning my living except by lettering and, as I have explained, it did not occur to me to do otherwise. Apart from work actually done for money (i.e. bread and butter) I did a certain amount of architectural drawing. I spent a week at Chartres in 1907 and again in 1909 and drew the cathedral, and I'm proud to say that a large drawing of the north transept is now in the Victoria and Albert Museum – a very good place for painstaking efforts of that sort – not a 'picture' of the cathedral but as nearly as my eye could make it, a stone for stone record of its structure.[1] And at odd times and places I did sketches and drawings of buildings and landscapes – close-ups of flowers and trees and what not. But one thing I never did and that was drawings or carvings of animals or humans. I don't know why I kept 'the life', animal or human, in such a completely water-tight compartment. I can't imagine why I was so frightened of it. I found naturalistic drawing of flowers or landscape equally terrifying and equally outside my powers. But in the case of inanimate nature my inability didn't worry me or put me off. If I couldn't draw flowers as they *appeared* – in light and shade and with all their proper colours altered and, as it seemed to me, a mess of irrelevancies and accidents, well, why draw them as they appear? Why not draw them, or try to draw them as they more or less *are*. Other people might be very clever at drawing the appearances of things and I appreciated their talent without coveting it. But the sort of flower drawing you find in ancient Herbals or eighteenth-century coloured prints was the kind I really liked and the kind I really wanted to do. And it can be done. It's a matter of time and trouble – that's all. To give

[1] In passing I should like to say that, except for the week I spent in Paris in 1903 when I was painting the lettering on W. H. Smith & Son's new shop in the Rue de Rivoli, the only time I had ever been in a foreign country before was when, in the spring of 1906, not ever having had a honeymoon (and I think that was one of the good things about our marriage – that we started off in our very own bed in our very own home), we thought it would be a good idea to expend a £20 prize I had won from the L.C.C. Central School for a certain inscribed slab, on two tickets to Rome. We went on a Cook's Tour – and I learnt about women from 'er, in a manner of speaking. Although the mistress came with me, it was a strictly professional visit and I spent the brief six days of our stay carefully looking at inscriptions ancient and modern – from a lettercutter's and signwriter's point of view. On Easter Sunday morning we went to St. Peter's High Mass – but we weren't interested in that, and the place was bung full and we couldn't see a thing, so we came out again . . . and went to Tivoli, where we didn't see the waterfall.

enough time and to take enough trouble means of course that you've got to have an overmastering appetite for the job; but it was not necessary to possess some special and peculiar talent, such as you have to possess to draw naturalistically. In fact if you *want* to draw heraldically, so to call it by way of distinction, *there is nothing to stop you.* You've got to *understand* the thing you are drawing, its physical structure and proportion, and your drawing is a communication of that understanding, a communication and a monument or memorial. The other people aren't so much drawing *things*, still less are they *making* things, they are drawing the effects of things – putting on paper or canvas and in between the four walls of a picture frame, a record of emotion, of the effects things have on them. Well, let them. They don't hinder me from drawing my herbals or my architectural records, so why worry? But why not take the same happy and carefree line of argument in the matter of animals and humans? What absurd reverence for naturalism prevented me in one case and not in the other? Why did I not even try?

I suppose the explanation is easy enough to find. The water-tight compartment is not merely an art school convention, though it is very strong in that place. In fact the art school only reflects and reinforces the conventions existing outside. The sentimental, emotional, naturalistic, selfish view of life drawing which prevails in the art school is only the counterpart of the sentimental, emotional, naturalistic, selfish view of life itself which prevails in the world outside. I had been brought up in that view of life, and had come to repudiate it, as I have tried to show; but I did not immediately see all the implications of that repudiation. I wanted to achieve an integration of all things but had not yet come to see that man was not only not integrated in himself but was not integrated with the world he lived in. Chichester, the integral city! Lincoln's Inn, the integral life! George Carter, the integral man! But what about cats and dogs and mountains and mud and worms and grass and gas? Do you get me, Stephen?

This is all very difficult and if my job in this book were to place before the reader a convincing philosophy or theology, I should somehow have to set to and arrange my arguments in proper order, and I should have to begin at the beginning. But that would be a quite different book and one I am not in the least competent to write. Fortunately my job, though difficult enough, is not so difficult as that. I have only got to place in more or less correct order the various phases of my emergence from complete sleep to partial awakeness and to describe the nature of the successive shocks which aroused me. So it is, fortunately, not necessary to make any attempt to convert the reader; I have not got to argue with him but only to tell him. And the thing to be told at this place is that by reason of an apparently irrelevant happening I broke through the inhibition and started a stone carving of a young woman. The irrelevant happening was the comparative continence caused by the approaching birth of our youngest daughter. In the absurd refinement of our puritanical civilization these things aren't talked about, so I have very little idea as to what goes on in the minds or bodies of my fellow-men, and practically none at all as to what goes on in the minds of those whom I may call my fellow-women, but this book, though necessarily more or less absurd, need not be refined. So I am at liberty to say that as I couldn't have all I wanted in one way I determined to see what I could do about it in another — I fashioned a woman of *stone*. Up to that time, I had never made what is called an 'erotic' drawing of any sort and least of all in so laborious a medium as stone. And so, just as on the first occasion when, with immense planning and scheming, I touched my lover's lovely body, I insisted on seeing her completely naked (no peeping between the uncut pages, so to say), so my first erotic drawing was not on the back of an envelope but a week or so's work on a decent piece of hard stone. I say this seems praiseworthy, and so it is.

But I give God the praise and am as duly thankful as a self-conscious human being can be. I don't think it was a very good carving and in spite of all I have said, no one would guess the fervours which conditioned its making. But there it was; it was a carving of a naked young woman and if I hadn't very much wanted a naked young woman, I don't think I should ever have done it. Lord, how exciting! – and not merely touching and seeing but actually making her. I was responsible for her very existence and her every form came straight out of my heart. A new world opened before me. My Lord! can't you see it? Lettercutting – a grand job, and as grand as ever – the grandest job in the world. What could be better? If you've never cut letters in a good piece of stone, with hammer and chisel, you can't know. And this new job was the same job, only the letters were different ones. A new alphabet – the word was made flesh.

I showed the stone carving to a friend in London – my dear Count Kessler, who had been my friend and patron for some years in the lettering business, and he showed it to another friend and patron, the equally dear Roger Fry. To my innocent astonishment they took it extremely seriously and what I, in spite of the enthusiasm which I had put into it, thought a very amateurish piece of work, they instantly hailed as a sort of baby angel announcing a new incarnation. All this was right over my head. I didn't know what they were talking about. I wasn't an art critic or an art connoisseur. I knew nothing about the art movements of Europe. In my own opinion I wasn't even an artist. I was a lettercutter with a mission for propagating good news about lettering and craftsmanship. And the letter-cutter had made an experiment in stone carving and what more was there than that? I didn't see any more, but the result of their enthusiasm was that instead of being shut up, as I might have been, and rather expected to be, and told to go home and not do it again, I went home very much 'bucked' and determined to do it again as often as possible.

Now, in view of what I have said above about my inability to draw naturalistically, and in view of the fact that my little stone woman was, to my eye very unlike nature — in spite of the fact that all the time I was carving her I was trying exceedingly hard to get her as 'correct' as possible, the approval of my London friends seemed to me somewhat inexplicable. If she was as bad as I thought, how could she be as good as they seemed to think? I trusted their opinion (after all they were eminent critics, so they ought to know) and I also trusted my own. How could the contradiction be reconciled? It took me a long time to find the answer, but I found it in the end. I discovered that my inability to draw naturalistically was, instead of a drawback, no less than my salvation. It compelled me, quite against my will and without my knowledge, to concentrate upon something other than the superficial delights of fleshly appearance. It compelled me to consider the significance of things rather than their charm. One might have made the same concentration in the medium of pencil or paint, but I couldn't do that because a thousand thousand people were making drawings and I couldn't, as it seemed to me, hope to emulate their successes. But, and this was my extraordinary luck, not one single person was doing stone carving! This sounds incredible but it is a fact, and therefore there was nothing with which to compare my amateurish efforts and therefore nothing to put me to shame! No one was doing stone carving — no body except the trade stone carvers and they, sad to say, didn't count. They didn't count because they were only poor hacks copying Gothic or Classic or Chinese, or whatever they were paid to copy (and damned expert they were) and they weren't making it up out of their heads, still less out of their hearts and even less out of their loins. No one was doing stone carving — except a few arts and crafts people and they seemed content to do arts and crafts flowers and arts, and crafts animals . . . and except that really good old man Stirling Lee and he wasn't really a stone carver but a Royal Academy *modeller* who refrained from employing a 'pointing

machine'.¹ For stone carving properly speaking isn't just doing
things in stone or turning things into stone, a sort of petrifying
process; stone carving is *conceiving* things in stone and conceiving them as made by *carving*. They are not only born but
conceived in stone; they are of stone in their inmost being as
well as their outermost existence. That's where I was lucky.
I'd only been doing masonry and letter-cutting. I had no ideas

¹ But what a generous old boy and what a good story he told me about the
wood-engravers of the 1860's. That it be not lost for ever, I must try to record
it here. When I was a young man, he said, I used to have business with the
illustrators and engravers and one day I was sent on some errand or other up to
St. John's Wood. I didn't know my way to the house I was to go to and I found
myself at the end of a lane going up between the bottoms of the gardens of the
houses – one of which I wanted to get to. As I stood hesitating, I saw, a hundred
yards or so up the lane, one of the back garden gates open and a man came out
with a long coaching-horn. He raised it to his mouth and looking in my
direction, blew a great blast on it. It couldn't be a summons to *me*, so I looked
behind me and there was a public-house with a doorway facing up the lane,
and as I looked the door opened and a man with a green baize apron on came
out and made a sign of recognition to the man with the horn, and then went
back into the pub. I went up to the man with the horn and asked my way and
he told me the house I wanted was the very one whose garden he had come out
of. So I followed him in and up the garden path to a veranda at the back of the
house and up the veranda steps into the back drawing-room. There were the
people I wanted to see. The room was empty of furniture but the floor was
more or less covered with piles of wood blocks for engraving. There were no
tables or chairs and the two or three engravers who were there working, were
working on tables made out of piles of wood blocks. Standing at their work
with no apparatus but their gravers, their sand bags and their eye-glasses.
Hundreds of wood blocks, hundreds of engravings – and on the floor hundreds
of empty bottles – and as I stood there and discussed my business, the garden
gate opened and in walked my man with the green baize apron carrying a tray
with bottles of beer. He left them and departed. My business took a long
time and presently down the garden again goes the man with the horn and
again blows his blast. Soon again appears the man from the pub – and more
bottles of beer. So, apparently it went on all day long and into the night.
A St. John's Wood garden in the 1860's, engraving demanding drink, drink
stimulating engraving – wood blocks and beer – an endless supply of both . . .
until the photographer and the chemist destroyed the whole thing, took away
their trade and destroyed the trade itself.

about the human figure save those discovered in bed or in the bedroom. I had no real idea what things *looked* like; I only knew what I loved in them. And I was quite competent with hammer and chisel. So instead of being like an art student and knowing a hell of a lot about what things look like and precious little about making anything, I knew practically nothing about appearances, a decent lot about loving, and enough about making. Well, that's fine!

So all without knowing it I was making a little revolution. I was reuniting what should never have been separated: the artist as man of imagination and the artist as workman. And, as I say, I had the great advantage of having no art school training. I really was like the child who said 'first I think and then I draw my think' — in contrast with the art student who must say: 'first I look and then I draw my look'. Of course the art critics didn't believe it. How could they? They thought I was just putting up a stunt — being archaic on purpose. Whereas the real and complete truth was that I was completely ignorant of all their art stuff and was childishly doing my utmost to copy accurately in stone what I saw in my head — with reference from time to time to the mirror (if I couldn't remember how many toes I had, or what happened to your shoulder if you held your arms up and such like conundrums) or to my friends and relations or whoever was willing to take his or her clothes off. But I didn't do much of that and very little life drawing — and, in fact, none at all in the sense understood in art schools, except once and once only, when I hired a model for a day in the room in Lincoln's Inn which I still shared with my brother so as to have a place of call in London. But that one occasion, though I enjoyed looking at the girl, was enough to show the futility of life drawing as a means to stone carving. The girl was too full of irrelevancies, too many charming and seductive accidents of fleshly by-play, dimples and what-nots. Such things tend to obliterate and overcharge the simple notion which is the *raison d'être* of the work to be done — at least of the work I wanted to do. This wasn't any moral virtue on my part, but quite the contrary – a refusal to be way-laid by irrelevancies, and therefore a sheer panic and running away from what seemed an alarming vista of uncontrollable complications.

Anyway, there it was. Without any theory about it I just wanted to make in solid stone, round and smooth and lovely images of the round and smooth and lovely things which filled my mind. But two enormous difficulties almost immediately presented themselves, both of them inseparable from and growing out of the general confusion of our age – our industrial-capitalist society, our irreligious commercialism. In the first place our whole industrialism was inimical to the craftsman world in which alone a healthy production of 'goods for use' could be effected (for capitalist-industrialism means the majority of men reduced to imbecility and the remaining few turned into hot-house plants) and in the second place, our irreligious commercialism had destroyed the religious basis of society and made all ritual and mythology and hagiography seem ridiculous. On the one hand there was no *place* for human work, on the other there was no *reason* for it. And whereas the socialist movement of revolt against capitalism and money-rule might seem to promise the reconstruction of a human world, a world of production for use rather than for profit, yet it offered nothing in the way of divine inspiration, nothing beyond the ideal of a world in which all should be hygienically and warmly clad – with a sort of B.B.C. 'culture park' looming in the background, as though to say: when we've properly got going with the love of our fellow-men, then we'll see what we can do about culture and, well, you know, religion and art and stuff.

This state of stupid mediocrity hadn't worried me much all the time I was just carrying on as a lettercutter and specialist in lettering. But as soon as I got all het up with things in three dimensions (which is both factual and figurative) the situation wasn't good enough. The ultimate questions of why and wherefore emerged from the dark corners and started stalking about demanding to know: what about it? Hi! young feller, what's it all bloomin' well for? Who d'you think you are, anyway? What d'you know about that?

My sculpturing experiments were, after all, only an extension of my lettercutting into another sphere — but it was a sphere into which the arts and crafts movement of William Morris and his followers had not only never extended, but had fought shy of and turned away from. My friends in the arts and crafts circles rather looked askance at me. I seemed to be deserting their homely fireside and going into brothels and dance-halls. They really are like that; they're terribly strait-laced and prim. They're mostly agnostics, just as I was, and, it stands to reason, if you're not going to have any truck with gods you must take excessively good care or you'll find yourself caught by the devil. They say there are more Roman Catholics in gaol than any other kind of person; but, in a manner of speaking, they can afford to be. Other people can't afford to take risks and if you've got no 'rock of ages' to hang on to when shipwrecked, you'd better take care to keep off the rocks; be a teetotaller at least and certainly beware of women. As I say, that prim line of life was all very well so long as you stuck to what one may call the useful crafts, and if you kept off religion as well as the drink, no one would notice it — though it's really noticeable enough or would be in a world less corrupted by men of business; for there was something very emasculate and lacking in guts as well as other appurtenances about most of the products of the arts and crafts movement. You can *see* the boys don't drink; you can *see* they're not on speaking terms with the devil.

I've been trying to get to this point for pages and pages — or rather, back to it. I said I invented a new religion. Well, I had to do so. It had become obvious that the first need of the world was religion, and at the same time it was obvious that all the existing religions and churches were fighting against one another. Nobody could tell you what was the meaning of the universe because everyone told you something different. And if twenty people give you twenty different answers to the same question you must either abandon the hope of an answer or answer it yourself. And this is not so mad or so bad as it sounds. For it seems difficult and even impossible to escape the conclusion that there is a creature whom we call man and that though all men are different they are nevertheless all men. Therefore the twenty different answers which twenty different men give you to the same question must really be only twenty different ways of expressing the same thing. And therefore instead of abandoning hope of an answer to your question all you've got to do is to make a synthesis of the twenty answers. Twenty different men, yes, and I was a twenty-first. But I was a man too and therefore must have some common ground with all the others. What was that common ground? What was the binding truth which, because we were men, bound us all together? It might be very presumptuous for me to attempt to state this truth; but I must make the attempt – for my own sake, because I could not go on without it. Religion was not only the world's first need, but *my* first need. The lettercutter might procrastinate; the sculptor couldn't afford to.

I say I invented a new religion and discovered it to be an old one. But really it wasn't a religion but a metaphysic, a preamble to religion. And it was a very good one, a very good preamble; for it was all acceptances and repudiated all denials. 'Yes yes and not not', as Edward Johnston used to insist. 'Man is the consciousness of God' – that was the primary truth – i.e. that the universe arrived at consciousness by arriving at man, and the universe being a creation and therefore manifestation of God, the primary act of consciousness was consciousness of God. God was conscious in the universe by means of man, who, as it were, bounced the ball back to him. Man, physiologically speaking is a pretty comic contraption – a curious bag of tricks, marvellously intricate and subtle and complicated and sensitive, but none the less comic. Fancy Julius Caesar having a pimple on the tip of his Roman nose. But as Chesterton, with his usual profundity remarked: 'it's funnier to have a nose than a Roman nose' and in the same way it's funnier to have a nose than a pimple on it. And fancy the great screw manufacturer, Mr. Neville Chamberlain, having twenty-five feet of intestines and a heart going pit-a-pat all the time. Fancy the Pope of Rome having to use a pocket handkerchief like anyone else . . . you can't say that, physiologically speaking, man isn't comic – and it keeps him humble. But no, in spite of everything, it doesn't do that. Isn't that marvellous? You'd think he would never forget. But he forgets all the time and struts about as though he were a pure metaphysical entity. But that's the point! He *is* a metaphysical entity, even though not pure, and that's the most obvious thing about him. For in spite of all the naturalists, and the astronomers and microscopists, the first thing we know about ourselves and about one another is that we are persons. We know (though very little), we will (though very feebly) and we love – O God, we do!

I can't recall all the tenets of this 'new religion', nor is it important to do so now.[1] What interested and excited me in those years was the discovery, a very slow and gradual discovery, that the religion I was inventing was really Roman Catholicism. Though I did not think so to start with. In fact I thought I was doing quite the opposite. I thought the Christianity of the churches was dead and finished, and surely one can be forgiven for thinking so. The effect of Christianity in the world seemed non-existent and I knew of Roman Catholicism only by repute. I did not know any Roman Catholics and I hardly ever went into any Roman Catholic churches or even read Roman Catholic books, moreover what little I knew of Roman Catholicism from outward appearances was, in a general way, revolting. The point was this: I had arrived at the general position that the first need,

---

[1] Anybody interested could look up some early numbers of *The Highway*, the organ of the Workers' Educational Association, viz., Nov. 1910 to Feb. 1911, wherein in an embarrassingly verbose manner, my ideas were displayed, by the great patience of the editor.

my first need and the world's first need was religion – 'for only he' (as I was very fond of quoting from Nietzsche, whose *Zarathustra* was one of my most cherished books) 'who knoweth whither he saileth, knoweth which is fair wind and which is a foul wind'. And religion means rule, and therefore God-rule. It seemed obvious that a world without God was a silly notion. You might be an agnostic and claim not to know whether there was a God or not, but I don't think I ever met anyone who seriously thought or even said that it would be a jolly good thing if there wasn't. I only speak for myself, but it seemed to me as soon as I got over the excitement of what seemed like a release from prison – the prison of the anglicanism I had been brought up in – that Heraclitus, as quoted by both Nietzsche and H. G. Wells, was only stating one half of the truth when he made his famous remark ΠΑΝΤΑ ΡΕΙ, all things flow, and that, however exciting it was to read when you first read it and however much it had the effect of opening the windows, Nietzsche was carrying the idea to quite unwarranted lengths when he said 'there is no being behind doing, acting, becoming. The being is a fictitious addition to the doing; the doing is all'. ΠΑΝΤΑ ΡΕΙ – that is so true, so obviously true, and therefore, at first sight, it does seem to follow that the being is a fictitious addition. And yet (I write as a fool and an amateur fool) there is, at least in the mind, a being that flows not, and therefore, as it seemed to me, there must be a source of being, a fountain head of being – Being itself. And, in spite of anything that philosophers may say, one does seem to know oneself as a being. Some people tell you that they are quite different beings from those whom they were when they were children. But my own experience didn't support that view. In fact this being or no-being problem seemed to me analogous to several others commonly met with. The problem of free-will for instance. If you inquire into things you can often find what appear to be adequate causes for their existence or occurrence. In fact the notion that everything has a cause seems an eminently reasonable one. And if you apply this to things of the mind why should not the same laws hold? We know that many of our thoughts and feelings are caused by this or that antecedent thought or feeling. The whole notion of a science of psychology depends, like that of any other science, on the notion of an unbroken chain of cause and effect. Then where does free will come in? Well, it doesn't, you may be tempted to say. And I suppose there are a lot of similar problems. But in spite of the philosophical difficulties we don't let these things worry us when it comes to the actual business of living. We know ourselves as beings and responsible beings and we don't let any philosophical doubts get in the way of action. We may think personality and responsibility are illusions, but we don't act as though they were. So it seemed to me rash and ridiculous to deny a palpable reality just because it seemed to clash with another palpable reality. It would be less rash and less ridiculous to accept both. And why not? The absence of an explanation does not prove that there isn't one.

Religion was the first necessity, and that meant the rule of God. If then there be God, it is obviously foolish to go against his rule. If there be God, the whole world must be ruled in his name. If there be a religion it must be a world religion, a catholicism. In so far as my religion were true it must be catholic. In so far as the Catholic religion were catholic it must be true! The Catholic Church professed to rule the whole world in the name of God – so far as I could see or imagine, it was the only institution that professed to do so. That fact in itself seemed conclusive, conclusive and sufficient. That was the impressive fact that gradually impressed me. That was the thing that caused me to reconsider my judgment as to the Church's vitality. Of course if the Catholic Church were simply an arrogant upstart institution, with no roots and no history and, more important to the innocent person, no fruits by which you might know her – no good fruits, nourishing and delectable – then there would obviously be no point in considering her. But this was clearly not so; there was fruit in plenty, and, in my mind very good fruit, even though they seemed to be fruits of the past. I could not but believe that the way of life and work represented by the remains of medieval Europe was mainly a product of the influence of the Catholic Church, and I could not but believe that that way of life and work was not only Christian but normal and human. The way of life and work in the world of modern Europe was obviously neither human nor normal nor Christian, therefore it could not be said that modern Europe was a product either of Christianity or catholicism. Moreover the modern way had only come into existence subsequently to the decay or defeat of the power of the church to influence men's minds, and the modern way flourished in inverse proportion to the degree of catholic influence. The typically capitalist and industrialized countries were the typically non-catholic ones.

I exaggerated the conscious opposition of catholics to the modern world. In this exaggeration I was very much misinformed by a certain eminent catholic to whom I appealed for information. In his enthusiasm to rope me in, as it seems to me now, he grossly deceived me. He agreed with my views about life and work, probably quite genuinely, but he hid from me what a more scrupulous person would have thought it his duty to reveal — that the catholics of to-day are almost completely corrupted by the world they live in and that, though it is certainly true that 'big business' and the industrial exploitation of the working people are not typically fruits of catholicism, quite the contrary, nevertheless, very few catholics are aware of this and most of them are as enthusiastic about the triumphs of industrialism and the British Empire and money as anyone else. So I was misinformed and deceived. But I do not think any harm was done. I was misinformed as to the quality of mind of catholics to-day, but I was not misinformed as to the main truth. Catholicism was what I supposed, even though neither catholic clergy nor laity were all that my informant would have me think. I was misinformed but not misled. [1]

1 But I owe it to him to record that he had the great wisdom, when I asked him to introduce me to a priest with whom I could discuss my case, not to

And then there is the Gospel. I was never interested in all the stuff my high-church brothers and their friends went in for — Synods and Councils and the thirty-nine articles of religion, and ritual and vestments and the episcopal succession. That all seemed twaddle to me. And I wasn't interested in the anti-catholic stuff either — Pope Joan and Maria Monk and the Spanish Inquisition, medieval corruption, cardinals' mistresses, superstition and pious frauds. I knew, surely everyone knows, that a man can be a holy man, a good man and an intelligent man, and yet be covered with sores, have a shocking temper and be subject to all the temptations of the flesh. If I wanted to join the Holy Roman Catholic Church, I was jolly well going to do so whatever anyone said or did. I told you I invented a new religion and found it was an old one. In effect, I invented the Roman Catholic Church. I didn't invent all those irrelevancies they told me about, but I couldn't believe those things mattered. Of course I know it sounds absurd, and absurdly arrogant, to say I invented the Church. But what, after all does the word 'invented' mean — even in common speech. When you invent a new kind of bicycle pump, what precisely do you do? Do you think that you fish up a brand new article as it were out of the vasty deep? No such thing! What you really do is, taking advantage of the work of thousands of those who have gone before you, you *uncover* or *find* what was potentially there all the time. And that's what I mean when I say I invented the Catholic Church — I found a thing in my mind and I opened my eyes and found it in front of me. You don't become a catholic by joining the Church; you join the Church because you are a catholic.

I say: 'and then there was the Gospel'. I seemed to myself to be in exactly the same case as the centurion at the foot of

send me to some notably cultured person who might have been supposed to understand 'art', but to the parish priest at Ely Place, and thus the first priest I ever spoke to as a father in God was, like one of the disciples, a simple fisher-man, and I a child and a nobody.

the cross. 'Truly this was the Son of God.' I didn't want a
lot of stuff out of books proving this and proving that and dis-
proving the other. Some people revel in that sort of thing.
Well, let them. Don't you see: I saw a vision of the Holy
Church ruling the world in the name of God – ruling the world,
laying down the law, speaking as one having authority, a magis-
terium. How did I know it was the Church of God? Well, as
I have said, there were the fruits – and there was the Gospel.
I had been brought up on the Gospel, so of course I can't say
what effect that book would have had on me if it had been
possible to approach it entirely from outside. It might be more
impressive or it might be less. It is impossible to tell. But the
mere fact that you've been brought up with a thing doesn't
necessarily give it an unfair pull over your mind. I don't see
why it should. It might work just the other way. All I know is
that I felt like the prodigal son. I had been away, squandering
my substance in riotous living – not with women and wine,
though that would have been nice, but with riotous young minds
and the wine of strong words – and now I was, in a manner of
speaking, coming home.

But what takes up only a few pages of a book occupies several
years of a life and the multifarious oddments of daily work and
doings, which make up a life, cannot be recounted in a book.
I did inscriptions and tombstones. I begot three lovely daughters.
I carved all sorts of comic statues – good, bad and indifferent.
In company with Jacob Epstein, Augustus John and Ambrose
McEvoy, I started a society to coerce the world – a simple idea
and a very good one, viz., that if all artists banded themselves
together and refused to work for men of business, the men of
business would be dished completely. A good idea, because
men of business can't do without artists, if only because they
need artists to camouflage their dirty business. But alas! it came
to naught because it became all too clear that Eric and Jacob
and Augustus and Ambrose didn't agree with one another about
what was good and what was bad. But we had grand schemes

while it lasted. And then there was William Rothenstein, the painter. I owe him a great debt of gratitude. He was extremely kind to promising young men and I suppose I was a promising young man. Anyway he was extremely kind to me, and introduced me to a lot of people I was very glad to meet. Moreover he introduced me to a lot of things it was very good for me to know, and he bought my first sculpture in the 'round'. It is very difficult to say either what or how great his influence was. I met a large number of people I should not otherwise have met and meeting a lot of people must make a lot of difference to one's mind. But what difference? One thing is or seems clear to me and that is that I was given the opportunity to become acquainted at close quarters with the leading intellectual and artistic folk of our great Empire . . . and looking back on those days, thirty years ago, the thing that strikes me most is the absence of any clear leading or sense of direction. Rothenstein himself, in the middle of his intellectual salon, sat profoundly on the fence and all the other people seemed to be balancing themselves nicely in the same way. There was no smell of burning boats – burning boats was the one thing no fellow should do. I think it might not unfairly be said that they all believed in beauty, were interested in truth and had doubts about the good. This sounds like trying to be smart, but I am only trying to be brief. I don't want to make too much of this business either way. I was so very much not the artist as they were artists, and though I was an agnostic in those days I was so very much not the sceptic as they were sceptics. They struck me as being superior to all such weaknesses of the flesh as definite belief. The way the Jews wear their blankets when they pray was much more important than what they pray about. Oh my Gawd! It's absolutely marvellous how superior the high art intellectual circles are, and for a few years I was very proud to be received in such circles and share such superiorities. But there were the two inevitable strains – Art and Religion. They most certainly believed in something called Art and I most certainly did not, and I came more and more to detest the whole art world. I believed in religion and was desperately trying to find it, and they seemed to regard religion as being essentially nonsense but valuable as a spur to aesthetic experience and activity. Do I do them an injustice? God knows. Anyway they are all still just where they were, more and more distinguished and more and more impotent. And the strains got worse and worse. You can't have art and religion both together — not art as they meant it, not religion as it seemed to me. The Lord thy God is a jealous God, and there's no doubt about it.

I say I did not believe in Art or the art world. But of course I believed very much in the arts — with a small a and an s — whether it be the art of cooking or that of painting portraits or church pictures. But that's a very different matter and puts the 'artist' under the obligation of knowing *what* he is making and *why*. It ranks him with the world of workman doing useful jobs. And as for the art *world* well, that is even more sickening, especially when all the snobbery of intellectual distinction comes in — the *salon* business, gatherings of 'distinguished' people, invitations to hear so and so sing folk-songs, or someone else to recite his poems, to meet so and so the distinguished traveller ('he's just back from so and so . . .'). Everybody was extremely kind and refined — and distinguished, but, 'I'd rather be a heathen suckled in a creed outworn . . .'

On the other hand, in yet another sense, I believed in art very much indeed. The artist as prophet and seer, the artist as priest — art as man's act of collaboration with God in creating, art as *ritual* — these things I believed very earnestly. But here again I was generally at variance with my high-art friends. Their views were both more simple and more mysterious than mine. They were essentially aesthetes; that was the awful truth. They played about with religion and philosophy and labour politics, but that was all very superficial; what they really believed in and worked for was aesthetic emotion as understood by the art critics. But art as the ritual expression of religion I did indeed believe in and they did not.

The influence of those 'high art circles' was therefore negligible or merely negative — in as much as I was more and more repelled by them, but there was one person, to whom I think William Rothenstein introduced me, whom I might not have met otherwise and to whose influence I am deeply grateful; I mean the philosopher and theologian, Ananda Coomaraswamy. Others have written the truth about life and religion and man's work. Others have written good clear English. Others have had the gift of witty exposition. Others have understood the metaphysics of Christianity and others have understood the metaphysics of Hinduism and Buddhism. Others have understood the true significance of erotic drawings and sculptures. Others have seen the relationships of the true and the good and the beautiful. Others have had apparently unlimited learning. Others have loved; others have been kind and generous. But I know of no one else in whom all these gifts and all these powers have been combined. I dare not confess myself his disciple; that would only embarrass him. I can only say that I believe that no other living writer has written the truth in matters of art and life and religion and piety with such wisdom and understanding. It is absurd to say he has influenced me; that would imply that his influence has borne fruit. May it be so — but I do not claim it.

So I gradually escaped from the high-art world which for a time seemed to be closing round me. Doubtless I never was a serious artist as serious art was understood in that world. I was the son of a nonconformist parson, the grandson of a missionary. Life was more than art. Art in their special sense was, to me, only a fine flower of life and could only be a fine flower if the life itself were fine. In high-art circles they did not agree with that. They managed to persuade themselves that the two things were independent. The spiritual adventures of the studios, though they might be enhanced and enriched by the physical adventure of living, were essentially separate. Chelsea and Hampstead were as spiritually independent of Mark Lane as they were geographically. The history of painting and sculpture and poetry and music was a purely aesthetic history and only remotely if at all connected with the history of capitalist-industrialism. Art was as near as no matter a completely water-tight compartment of human life. Its only connection with human life was the fact that human life offered an aesthetic spectacle for the delight of the artist and, through him, for the persons who could be persuaded to buy his paintings and poems and sculptures and symphonies. The meaning of the universe, if it had any, was no affair of the artist except in so far as the meaning of the universe could be expressed in aesthetic terms, that is to say, in terms of sensation. The Gospel story of Jesus and his disciples, the lives of the saints were no more than pegs upon which to hang rhymes and rhythms. Artists who thought otherwise deceived themselves, though it might often be true, or even generally true that just as artists needed the stimulus of physical necessity, hunger and thirst, the desire of women and the need of clothes and shelter, to make them work, so they needed the stimulus of subject matter to give them an occasion for doing this rather than that. The silly old customer wanted a life-like picture of his wife or mistress, or a recognizable representation of his favourite story or subject, and was prepared to pay for it. Good, that is what the customer is for. And the artist, in so far as he also is a silly old human being, is also interested in such things. But to the artist as *artist* – a being quite superior to the human – all such things are mere frivolities. A factory town may be all that social reformers say it is – a morass, a wen, a powd – but the effects of light and shade and colour visible in such a place obliterate all such considerations – happy was Backhuysen in the shipwreck to have the nerve to clutch 'no board but the drawing board to paint it on.'

And I'm not being too scornful about all this. Anyone can feel the attraction of such a creed. Man is born for happiness –

happiness must, by the strictest logical and philosophical deduction, be his first hope and his last end. And what makes us happier than satisfactory aesthetic emotion. Is not the joy of heaven universally likened either to perpetual love-making or perpetual music. We may laugh at the notion of sitting on clouds playing harps and singing hymns – but that's only because we *visualize* the situation in the terms of Victorian pictures. We all know that music is the one thing which can hold us in pure, disinterested enjoyment. And this not merely a west-end point of view; it's even more an east-end one. So the question is not whether the high-art people are wrong in their aims and objects, but simply whether this is the kind of world in which such aims and objects can thus consciously and deliberately be pursued. If you go for happiness thus directly, do you get it? That's one thing. But, more fundamentally, is beauty something which can be pursued by itself and for its own sake, or is aesthetic satisfaction in reality, the reward of *virtue*? We may be justified in being enthralled by the beauty of factory smoke; for thus we are made. But are we justified in saying or thinking that the morality of industrialism doesn't matter? Many of my high-art friends would have voted 'labour' at the elections, but that was simply because they were human. I voted 'labour' because I held to the view that, in the long run, beauty in human works was the reward of virtue and not otherwise either obtainable or worth having – a delusion and a snare.

This is not a treatise on art, so, thank God, I haven't got to make myself convincing. I've only got to record the things that moved me. An auto-psychography is a work of art and all art is propaganda; but not all propaganda is a business of discursive reasoning. If I fell in love, I must record the fact and hope that the reader will fall in love also. But I haven't got to prove the rightness of my love by algebra. So, in a manner of speaking, I don't mind whether or no I carry my reader with me by the force of my arguments. I only hope to arouse his sympathy. For I was just as much in love with beauty as my high-art friends, but I was more in love than they were with what seemed to me that beauty's Author. And though at that time I had not read St. Augustine, it was his trouble that was troubling me: 'When I love thee, what is it that I love . . . ?' 'About *what* are the sophists so eloquent?' My high-art friends seemed to float on the top of things, both unanchored and unfounded. They seemed oblivious of the precariousness of their position – the lap-dogs of the wealthy with no reason of being but the vapour- ings of art-critics – art-critics whose whole position depended upon the 'art prices' obtainable by the machinations of the art dealers. What a world! No matter how sincere, how passion- ately sincere, sincere to the pitch of martyrdom if necessary, the artists might be and quite commonly were, their whole show depended upon the ability of art dealers, assisted by art-critics, to preserve a hot-house culture in the midst of an inhuman and anti-human industrialism.

God knows, I admired their works and enjoyed their friend- ship. But I couldn't help thinking, I simply could not help thinking that I would rather have brick-laying and turnip-hoeing done well and properly and high art go to the devil (if it must) than have high art flourishing and brick-laying and turnip- hoeing be the work of slaves. How can orchids flourish if daisies don't grow? How can daisies grow while money rules?

Meanwhile the tombstone business continued and I began to get orders for sculptured figures. I began to send sculptures to exhibitions. I had an exhibition all on my own at a gallery in Chelsea. The position was getting dangerous. A tombstone was a sort of stone signpost and if properly made, with due regard to the nature of things – the nature of stone, the nature of chisels, the purpose of the thing, the nature of lettering – would and must give satisfaction to the mind – and the beautiful being that which gives pleasure being seen (you can't get away from that – it simply is so), such tombstones might, like all the old ones, be called beautiful. That's quite all right. You don't make a tombstone for the sake of giving pleasure but in order to put up a record of names and dates. If incidentally it does please you so much the better — nay, more, it will be in some sort a proof that the work has been done properly. All this seems clear and easy. But now how about applying it to sculptured figures? What is a sculptured figure for; what's the good of it? To give pleasure of course, says the high-art world — i.e. the high class and very refined pleasure of those minds which have been well informed by the best art-critics. Obviously the first thing to do is to get round the best art-critics. You won't get far until you've done that. But if, being the grandson of a missionary (etc.) and a tombstone maker, you start trying to find out what statues are for in the same tone of voice, so to say, as that in which you inquire into the rights and wrongs of tomb-stone-making, you will not only find yourself up against the high-art world, the art-critics and the art-dealers,[1] but you will find yourself very much up against your own soul. So now I've come round the circle and there seemed to be nothing for it but that I must sign 'on the dotted line' of the universal Church. *A priori* it was the only thing to do. The only question remaining was: could it be done?

But before I commit myself further I must attempt to describe an adventure I had which very nearly settled my hash altogether. I have said that my friend and patron Count Harry Kessler had given me enthusiastic encouragement when I started sculpturing and that he had previously been my patron in the lettering business. He was the great protagonist in Germany at that time of the use of Roman as opposed to the native German 'Gothic' lettering. He had a Press of his own at Weimar and I used to do engraved title-pages and initial letters for him, in fact it was

[1] I remember the moral indignation of a certain eminent newspaper art-critic and a certain art-dealer when I said in a magazine called *The Listener* sculptures on buildings were simply a kind of furniture. They accused me of lowering and, as it were, betraying the whole profession of art. Definitely, I oughtn't to be allowed to say such things. If only they could have realized that, from my point of view, it was they who were the traitors and degraders. . . .

largely by his encouragement and financial help that I took up
the engraving of letters on wood instead of drawing them on
paper for photographic reproduction, and this led to pictorial
engraving and all my future work for the St. Dominic's Press
at Ditchling and the Golden Cockerell Press, and, later still,
for my son-in-law René Hague's Press. Count Kessler was also
a great friend and patron of the French sculptor Aristide Maillol
and, when I started sculpturing, he was so enthusiastic about it
that he conceived the fantastic project of my becoming a sort
of pupil assistant to that great man. He thought Maillol's
mature and classic power would be a great help to me in my
naivety and that I, on the other hand, with my technical skill
would be able to help Maillol with the carving of his statues.
It's no use burdening this book with a lengthy explanation of
technical matters; it will be sufficient to say that Maillol was
primarily a modeller in clay and that it was his custom, as it is
that of most modern sculptors, to employ hired carvers to convert
his clay models into marble or stone. This is commonly done
by a more or less mechanical method called 'pointing' (because
it is done with the assistance of a machine called a pointing
machine) and the idea was that I could help Maillol with his
pointing and learn from him at the same time. I don't think
Kessler can have appreciated how intimately connected my
notions of sculpture were with the actual process of carving
directly out of the solid block without the interposition of a
full-size clay model. I agreed with him that I could learn things
of inestimable value from Maillol but I was very much puzzled
to know how the kind of work I was doing in England, my
lettering and inscription work, could be carried on if I were to
go away to Paris for a few years to work with Maillol.

However! Kessler was full of confidence and went to the
length of actually getting a house for me and the family at
Marly-le-Roi, where Maillol's studio was, and signing a three-
year lease for it on my behalf! And he arranged for me to meet
him at Paris and go out to Marly and fix everything up, see the

house and see Maillol. So one morning I arrived at the Grand
Hotel in Paris. I got there, after the night journey, at about
seven o'clock. Kessler was not yet dressed but came down and
arranged to meet me later in the morning. We did so and after
lunch we went out to Marly. Of course it was most impressive.
Maillol had no English and as usual I had no French. So Kessler
did all the interpreting and I gathered that everything was fixed
up to their satisfaction. But I was getting more and more
depressed. The house was a typical French suburban villa and
that's nothing to look forward to, in fact you can't imagine
anything worse, even in England. Fancy leaving our beautiful
house in Ditchling village and leaving God knows what else
besides . . . Eventually, after tea with Mons and Mme Maillol,
we went back to Paris and Kessler told me that I was to go to the
Grand Hotel and take a room for myself in his name and that
he would be back later in the evening, as he had a dinner
engagement. (I hope this isn't too boring a story, but it's getting
to the end.) So I went to the hotel and managed to make
myself understood at the Reception Desk. I was shown to a perfectly marvellous and magnificent suite of rooms on the first
floor, with a gilded bed with great red curtains making a canopy
over it and red and gold chairs . . . I thought all this was much
too magnificent for me, but I had told them downstairs what
Count Kessler had told me to tell them, so I supposed it was all
in order and I began to unpack my small bag. I was thus engaged
when there was a knock at the door and an extremely elegant
and polite person appeared who, with really splendid apologies
in excellent English, told me that he feared a mistake had been
made and that, though he made no doubt that Count Kessler
wished me to have a room for the night, he felt sure that
M. le Comte would perhaps not wish to run to quite such a grand
set of rooms as I had been put into – or words to that effect and
of course I quite agreed with him. I thought it most unlikely.
So he suggested that, if I would permit it, the best thing would
be for me to pack up again and deposit my bag at the reception

desk and return later, by which time doubtless M. le Comte would have returned also and would signify his wishes in person. I didn't object. I was feeling pretty rebellious inside, but there's something fascinating about being a lamb in front of the slaughterer. I wanted to suffer whatever indignity the swine might offer. I had a vague idea that it would be sport to see them cringe and apologize when Kessler came and told them off. So I packed my little bag again and went out to get some dinner. I went to some sort of second-rate restaurant and as I ate my dinner I got gloomier and gloomier. I ceased to feel any joy in the thought of the discomfiture of the grand people at the Grand Hotel. The whole expedition seemed mad. The idea of giving up all my work in England, begun so promisingly, and going in for this wild scheme of Kessler's, seemed an impossible idea and I suddenly came to the conclusion that I wouldn't do it. I would go back to England there and then by the night boat. If I delayed to see Kessler I should be trapped; for I couldn't stand up against his over-mastering confidence in his own schemes, or, for that matter, against my sense of his extraordinary kindness and generosity. I must run away now, now at once, or it would be too late. So I hastily went back to the hotel and got my bag. I didn't dare tell the grand people my decision for fear that they would come over all apologetic and beg me to wait for the Count's return. Then I took a taxi-cab to the station and wrote a hasty letter to Kessler on the way, telling him I was off to England for reasons which I would explain at length when I got back home and apologizing for thus running off.

You can't imagine, or can you? the burden that thus fell from this poor Christian's shoulders. I had a miserable home journey after that altogether miserable day in Paris, but I got home to breakfast knowing for certain that I had done the right thing. It would have been madness to throw up all my work in England, madness to become Maillol's assistant and enter a world not only as foreign as France is to England but as foreign as paganism is to Christianity. I must say Kessler was angelic about

it and so was Maillol. And in neither case did I suffer any loss
of friendship. And I had the satisfaction of hearing that the grand
gentry of the Grand Hotel got a proper dressing down for their
snobbish stupidity, though I can't really blame them; for,
according to their lights, I must have appeared an extremely ill-
dressed and unworthy denizen of such a high-class establishment.
There's only one thing more to be said, and I'll say it here
because it may be my only chance, and that is that, in his own
line of business, I think Aristide Maillol is the greatest man in
the world. You'll have to be satisfied with that. One thing
more — years after when he had a show of his sculptures in
London one of them got slightly damaged in transit and the
gallery people appealed to me to effect a repair. It's fun to
think that the thing, which is now in the National Gallery at
Millbank is, in one very small part, my work and no one knows
anything about it; for the gallery people were much too frightened
to tell.

So, it was now somewhere about the year 1911, I seriously
began to consider the practical steps which were necessary if you
contemplated joining the Church. In my own mind I was a
Roman Catholic already — because the Catholic Church claimed
to rule the world in the name of God and I knew of no other
institution that even claimed to do so. The mere claim was a
proof of its justification. No institution could make such a
claim and not be justified. It spoke with authority and not as
the Scribes — not, that is to say, with the faltering voices of all
the schismatical sects, not with the refined tones of the sceptics
who sprawled elegantly in the salons of distinguished persons.
And yet, plainly it was not a one-eyed sort of teetotalism. It
would seem true, in fact, to say that the only way to avoid
heresy was by accepting all the heresies. Charity believeth all
things . . . Moreover 'the Church proceeds confidently in her
doctrine of God', and, not only that, but her doctrine of God
inspires confidence. Perhaps the reader doesn't think so. To
me it was obvious. The Christ of the Gospel was the Christ of

the Church in spite of all the funny stuff – Vatican paraphernalia, 'repository art' and heathen superstition masquerading as Christian revelation. I boasted to myself that I could see the wood quite plainly in spite of the trees.

I think I was very considerably helped in this by reading Browning's poem about *Bishop Blougram*. This was first put before me years before when I was in the architect's office as a pretty conclusive proof of the mendacity and general rottenness of the Church. Tom Bridson gave it to me to read, and George Carter was an ardent defender of the inconspicuous Gigadibs. For several years I accepted that interpretation and I dare say it is the one Browning intended – but I'm not at all sure. Eventually I began to think that whatever his creator might have meant, the figure of Blougram was much more than that of an unscrupulous and sceptical prelate, fat and sleek and contented and cynical. He began to seem to me to represent something mighty big and broad and all-embracing. I began to like the old boy and the more I liked him, the wiser he seemed and so much the more mean and ineffectual and emasculate did poor Gigadibs become. What was put before me as an anti-catholic tract, became a quite powerful influence on the other side. People are not converted by books – nor can books hinder conversion (Good Lord! it's not such a rotten show as all that – it doesn't really matter whether any one can read or write) but if any mere book did do anything to make me a catholic, it is *Bishop Blougram's Apology*.

And a milder example of the same tendency to misunderstand – to take as a compliment what was meant as an insult, to take as evidence for the defence what was meant as evidence for the prosecution – was my reaction to a story I was told a year or two later by Abbot Ford. I think I had made some tentative remark about medieval ecclesiastical corruption and he said: 'The Church is as full of corruption now as then. Last year when I was in Rome I employed a small boy to do a small job for me and I gave him some money out of which he should have brought me some change. But he didn't reappear. A few days later, in Easter week, I ran across him again and I said: "Hallo, you're the young rascal who did me out of threepence last week." And he replied: "Oh, but, Father, that was before Easter".' Abbot Ford told me that story, I now realize, as showing that superstition was still common and that the poor people still regarded religion as a kind of magic . . . But, at the time, I took it to show that even rascally urchins went to confession and expected bygones to be bygones after Easter. Easter! The Rising of the Lord. How could you have the heart to recall small things that happened before that? And isn't it possible that the thief who, in spite of everything, loves God is better than the honest man who doesn't?

But still — I did come over all of a tremble every now and then and resolve to keep out of it. I had done a carving of a mother and child and as they had halos round their heads, I must have thought of them as a holy mother and a holy child — the Blessed Maiden and the baby Jesus even. I had also done several other carvings which art-critics had described as being 'religious'. So one day I got a letter from Louvain inviting me to send works for an *Exposition de l'Art Religieux* to be held in Brussels. I replied to the invitation that while I should be very pleased to send specimens of my work, I did not want to do so under false pretences and that I did not take any responsibility for what critics said. In reply I got a letter saying that was quite in order and hinting that in the opinion of the exhibition judges you didn't have to be a catholic in order to do religious art. Also the writer said that if while the exhibition was 'on' I could come over to Brussels they would be very pleased if I would spend a few days at Louvain. It was a Benedictine Monastery it appeared. Well, this seemed a good proposition. It would be interesting and instructive; it might help to solve some of my puzzles. So I accepted and went off to Louvain for a week.

This certainly was a new experience. The Abbey of Mont

César is a tremendous place.[1] It is a modern building of brick, and though dead and mechanical in actual workmanship, not without architectural quality – not too sham Gothic, even though not entirely free from the smell of ecclesiasticism. My host was one of the monks and I had some long talks with him, but there seemed to be a smell of bad breath about the place. I happened to be the only guest and, in the vast refectory, I sat all by myself in the middle, with the monks at long tables on each side. I was not at all happy. I knew very little French and less Latin. I didn't know what was happening half the time and had no power to express myself or explain my needs or difficulties. Then one day my particular monk had to go away somewhere and he left me in charge of a certain Father Anselm, for the afternoon. We were a comic couple. I couldn't speak French and he couldn't speak English. We had no means of communication except a small pocket dictionary and a very small one too – English-French, French-English. But, somehow, the fact that Father Anselm was a complete stranger and knew no more about me than I knew about him, and the fact that neither of us could even begin to talk nonsense or waste time in unrealities, compelled me to try to get right down to business. So, with the help of the blessed dictionary, which we passed continually across the table – he sitting on one side and I facing him on the other – we started arguing about the divine mysteries. The burden of my song was that I accepted the whole metaphysical and philosophical basis of Catholicism but that when it came to the historical and physical matters – the Bible, the Gospel miracles, the Mass and all the rest of it – I didn't see how it could be acceptable except as symbolical. 'Pas symbolique, pas symbolique,' he kept on replying. I said it wasn't so much that I denied the historicity of the Gospels but that the historicity didn't seem to me to be important. Why not say it was all symbolical? 'Pas symbolique, pas symbolique.' I tried

1 Since this was written the Abbey has been destroyed . . . Soldiers do not revere such things.

to say that I was quite prepared to believe in God and the Church and, in fact, that I did so already, but I didn't believe in the divinity of Christ *because* of the miracles – that miracles were in themselves a bore and the less of them the better. That the divine nature and character and person of Jesus were obvious without a lot of miracle business – that miracles might be true, who was I to say that they were impossible or what was possible or impossible? but why say belief in them was necessary, why not take them as symbolical? 'Pas symbolique, pas symbolique.' A lay-brother brought us a cup of tea and we went on and on. I suppose he said lots of other things but those two words are all I can remember. On the following day or the day after I more or less fled from the place and when I got on board the steamer at Ostend and Belgium receded into the distance I couldn't but quote to myself, as I leant on the ship's railing, the words of Shaw's Captain Brassbound – 'what an escape, what an escape'. My hat! I was glad to get away – in spite of the plain-chant; for, as I have omitted to say, the plain-chant was grand. . . .

I think I ought to say more about that. I dare say that, without my being aware of it, the chant really impressed me more than anything else. One imagines that thinking and talking and argument are decisive in our affairs. One is tempted to put ratiocination very much higher in the list of things which determine our actions and our beliefs than there is any warrant for. One forgets, if one ever knew, that, as St. Thomas Aquinas says, 'The senses are a kind of reason', and that taste, touch and smell, hearing and seeing are not only or merely a means to sensation, enjoyable or otherwise, but that they are also a means to knowledge – and are, indeed, our only actual means to knowledge. . . . At the first impact I was so moved by the chant, which you must remember I had never heard a note of in all my life before, as to be almost frightened. This was not ancient architecture such as the world had ceased to build. This was not the sculptures of Chartres or Easter Island such as the world had ceased to make. This was not the pictures of Giotto or Ajanta such as the world had ceased to paint. This was something alive, living, coming from the hearts and minds and bodies of living men. It was as though God were continuing the work of creation here and now and I was there to hear, to see — even almost to touch. I was lucky, was I not? For, after all, as I have often since discovered, it is possible to sing the chant in such a way as to make you wish that a millstone were around your neck and you in the depths of the sea. But there, at Louvain, after the slow procession of incoming monks and the following short silence when I first, all unprepared and innocent, heard: *Deus in adjutorium* . . . I knew, infallibly, that God existed and was a living God — just as I knew him in the answering smile of a child or in the living words of Christ. As I have said before in this book, there is a palpable righteousness in the things that God has made and that man is God's instrument for making. Emotion follows — of course, inevitably, naturally, but emotion is that which is suffered. It is the suffering that follows knowledge. We may, and often do, forget the knowing and wallow only in the emotion. It is better to forget the emotion. And when I got home from Louvain I did forget it and I remembered only that Christianity was 'pas symbolique'.

But alas! alas! I hadn't been home six months before I was appealing to Abbot Ford, of Downside, to whom my Belgian friend had given me, on spec., a letter of introduction. Somehow or other all the panic of Louvain had worn away. Somehow or other my ratiocinative qualms seemed of no importance. Somehow or other I had come to the conclusion that any doubts I might imagine myself to have must be misunderstandings and that all I had to do was to receive instruction and be received. Psychologically it is a clear case. I did not doubt the efficacy of reason; but I doubted the efficiency of my own reasoning powers. I refuse to believe in human free will and shall support a politics of psychological determinism just because I am not clever enough to prove man's responsibility for his acts beyond a shadow of doubt? That would be absurd. The freedom of the will, whether proved by argument or not, is a fact of human experience, and to be accepted as such. The burden of proof rests with the deniers and they, in spite of the plausibility of their arguments, are more impotent than those who affirm it. It seemed very clear to me that however reasonable a thing might be, and however possible it might be to prove it by logic and historical evidence, it was not by reason of such proof that people believed, but rather that belief was the result or product or consequence of recognition. When you make a friend it is not by a logical process but because you *recognize* friendship, you recognize a correspondence and a harmony. When you 'fall' in love it is not the consequence of your reasonable inquiries into the financial and moral and intellectual and physical qualities of the girl or the man you fall in love with, but because you recognize, as it were infallibly, the righteousness and therefore the delightfulness of a union of your two persons. As it were infallibly! But of course we make mistakes; we are waylaid by our acquisitiveness, by our inordinate concupiscence. We have to be prudent. We do not dare to dash headlong into the intimacies of friendship or matrimony. Our appetites are a bit out of hand. We can't be sure that they are good guides, or rather, though they are good guides to their particular objects, we can't be sure that they serve us in due hierarchy. We are full of prejudices and predilections and our most simple and fundamental instincts have been corrupted by centuries of false education. We hardly know a good plough-field when we see one. Let nothing I say be taken to be a counsel of foolhardiness. Let us look before we leap, by all means. And in this matter of catholicism I cannot be accused of not doing any looking. I hesitated for months and years before leaping; but there came a time when it began to seem obvious that to hesitate any longer would be to be lost. Man is matter and spirit – both real and both good. The Church affirmed this and she affirmed the primacy of the spirit. The industrial-capitalist world of the British Empire (and all the rest of the industrial-capitalist world) also affirmed though with some hesitation and an increasing dubiety, the reality of matter and spirit and their goodness. But though still giving lip-service to God, it affirmed by every evidence of its practice, the primacy of matter. My high-art friends were often in agreement with me about this; but the alternative was not clear to them or, for one reason or another, they were afraid to follow it. One had bought a farm and couldn't come; one had married a wife and she wouldn't let him. One said he couldn't bear 'the smell of the Vatican' (and when you think of St. Peter's and its toy soldiery, and the purple and lace of its fat worldly-looking prelates, and when you think of the subtle intangibilities and intransigencies of its diplomacy, it is not difficult to understand why people run away in panic – what's it all got to do with the Man on the Ass, anyway?). But to me the alternative was too clear to be missed or to be run away from. In fact both alternatives were too clear. The frightful, the truly frightful horror, of the corruption of the ancient Church was as nothing to the essential dirtiness, dirtiness in its very being and nature, of the industrial-capitalist world. In the one case it was as though an ancient ship (very much in need of repairs) were, in spite of much drunkenness and chicanery among passengers and crew, quite obviously being steered to a heavenly Jerusalem, the Porto Fino of our dreams; in the other it was as though, even more obviously, oh! infinitely more obviously, a *Lusitania* or a *Titanic* were being steered, horting and snooting and blind as a bat and deaf as a gramophone, straight to Hell. Heaven and hell! said my high-art friends – the words mean nothing.

Well, fortunately for me, I didn't live in London and I didn't depend on high art for a living. This was partly by good luck, but it was much more by design. We hadn't left London for the sake of 'the beautiful country' but simply that the children shouldn't have to keep off the grass. I had given up architecture

and gone in for lettercutting because I was absolutely determined to have a hold, almost you might say a strangle-hold on
life — a bread-and-butter job, a job that didn't depend on the
fashions prevailing in either Park Lane or Mark Lane circles.
I didn't see it as clearly as this to start with but every month
that passed forced me to see it more clearly. Few of my customers lived in Park Lane — most of them were ordinary
middle-class people and like a general medical practitioner in a
new practice one patient recommended me to another. I had
still fewer customers in the city; such connections as I had with
the business world were through the printing trade. So when
I came to do my leaping I could do it peacefully all by myself
in the country, and no one in London was either consulted or
offended.

I invented the Roman Catholic Church. The more I inquired
into it the more I discovered that, in spite of many necessary
alterations in detail, the thing I had invented and the real thing
were identical. Do not think I take any credit for this, I am not
boasting of my cleverness or perspicacity. I am simply affirming
what I hold to be a fact, that any normal human being who isn't
prudish or squeamish, or, on the other hand entirely devoid of
a sense of sin (as so many of my high-art friends were . . . ), any
normal person can invent, that is to say find or discover the
Church for himself because that is really exactly what it is — a
perfectly human institution, matter and spirit, and the primacy
is of the spirit, therefore guided by the Holy Ghost, therefore
the bride of Christ, therefore a divine institution also.

There was one period, of a few months, just before I took the
leap, when I really tried to be a rationalistic inquirer. I read
books. It was quite exciting. Except Chesterton's *Orthodoxy*[1]
I can't remember what any of those books were, but I remember

[1] In my Fabian days I much disliked G.K.C. Arguing with him seemed like
beating the air. I was quite out of tune with him. But as the years passed I got
past that and came to revere and love him, as a writer and as a holy man, beyond
all his contemporaries. Thanks be to God he also loved and befriended me.

the breathless sort of mountain climbing business it was. Each book was, as it were, a fresh mountain ridge and each time as I climbed it I said: surely this will be the top, this will settle the matter. And each time, when I got to the top, another ridge appeared beyond, another point had to be settled, another ridge surmounted, another book to be read. I began to see that this was absurd. You couldn't settle the matter that way. And just as I could not ask that God should reveal himself to me by commanding all these stones to be made bread nor that his angels should bear me up, so I saw that this mountain was not an earthly one from the top of which I could survey all the kingdoms of the world. I don't think I can claim to have prayed, still less to have fasted. I just asked to be received. This sounds impossibly pious and childlike. Perhaps it was really simple impudence. But I hadn't any qualms because I refused to have any. I refused to have any 'difficulties' because you can't have difficulties unless you make them, and I wasn't making any. When I was 'under instruction' they told me all sorts of things that seemed pretty rum, but I was past that sort of worrying. 'Do you believe all that Holy Church teaches?' That is the all-inclusive and final question; and I could unhesitatingly answer yes. But as to *what* she teaches on all the multiplication of funny subjects that we worry ourselves about, well, at the great risk, or, rather, certainty of being thought both lazy and unscrupulous, I made up my mind to confine my attention to things that seemed fundamentally important and things that intimately concerned me. As to whether or no the sun stood still over Jericho, or whether a real snake tempted Eve, or whether Pope Hormisdas really told a whopper, or whether lions would have lain down with lambs if Adam hadn't sinned, or whether the 'seal' of the confessional had really never been broken . . . well, don't you think these are awfully boring questions? And just think how stupendously learned you'd have to be to answer them with any assurance! In a kind of way they mentally 'turn me up'. Dear reader, you make me ashamed by your look of sad surprise.

I am sorry. But let us turn our attention to more important matters. The bride is in love with her husband and his Bride is in love with Christ. I am a member of that mystical body and share her ecstasy.

So on February 22nd, my 31st birthday, 1913, we went together and were baptized and on the following Saturday the three little girls followed in their parents' footsteps.

# CHAPTER VII

# POSTSCRIPT

## I. THE BUSINESS WORLD AND THE ARMY

A PROPER novel is finished as soon as the hero and heroine get married. There is nothing more to be said except that they lived happily ever after. And in very much the same way the event recorded at the end of the previous chapter should make the end of this book. The present chapter must therefore be regarded as a kind of postscript. No other event of such final importance is to be expected, but some of the implications and consequences of the previous event may be explored.

But first of all for the sake of truth, or even mere accuracy, I should like to rectify the false impression I think I must have given of the character of the author. It doesn't concern me, as I have said often enough, to make a record of what I did or did not. Nor is this book a public confession of sins, or a description of the things I have found pleasant or exciting in my life. It would be a mistake, however, it seems to me, if a false impression of virtue should be given as I think it could be given if I let it appear that practically the whole of my spare time and energy had been expended on religious and philosophical inquiry, and that I were, as indeed quite a lot of people are, a perfectly continent and virtuous person, a very Galahad and respectable don combined. Perhaps, as I hope, I have not given that impression. In that case no more need be said, but if I have done so, I trust the reader will put such a picture resolutely away from him and think of me rather as hiding under a somewhat handsome and kindly appearance a commonplace, mean and vicious nature. I have reason to think that most people could say the same; but that is precisely what I want to make clear. For when

you write a book such as this – a history of religious experience
– there is a considerable danger of making yourself out to be
extraordinarily pious and abnormally intellectual. The human
background of physical life and appetite is likely to take much
too back a place, and yet to bring it forward may so easily bring
it altogether *too* forward. In that respect it is like the ordinary
sentimental church statue. Such things are very important and
an essential part of religious practice, but not to the exclusion
of all else. Yet should you venture into a church, the thing will
perhaps seem to take up the entire landscape and drive you away
from religion for ever. So it is with our physical nature and
appetites. They are an important and essential part of our make-
up and yet we hardly dare to mention them for fear that they
should so prodigiously prejudice our friends against us, in spite
of the fact that the very same friends are victims of the very
same vices, and enjoy the same secret loves and longings.

There is one matter however in which I do strike myself as
being more than ordinarily pious and to hold views which are
shared by an extraordinarily small number of my fellow-men and
women to-day, and that is the matter of what is commonly
called Business. We live in a world which is ruled by men of
business, and ruled therefore according to business men's notions
of what is good. This is a simple fact and it seems to me, and
to the few who think likewise, that it is an insufferably monstrous, iniquitous and vile state of affairs. It seems to us incom-
parably more horrible that men of business should rule us and
impose their foul point of view on the world than it would
be if the whole race of men and women should rot their bodies
with lechery and drunkenness. There is no idolatry so destructive of charity, so desolating; there is nothing which so certainly
obscures the face of God as the desire of money – the root of
all evil. 'The root of all evil'! Did I make up that phrase?
No, it is the word of God to man. The root of all evil, the *root*.
The root of all *evil*. And yet we, in our world of commerce
and finance and mass-production, regard it as the very flower of

virtue. We place those who have successfully amassed money in the highest seats of government and give honour to the rich as to the saints of God. Do I exaggerate? No, it is not possible to exaggerate. No words that the most eloquent could write could make this enormity more enormous than it is. Hence it is that we must go down into the dust disgraced and infamous, with no monument to our prowess but the filthiness of our cheap idols; for even our idols are filthy, having no reason for existence but the money profit of those who sold them. Saleability is the business man's criterion of good.

If a thing cannot be sold, it is no good to the man of business. That is right and proper. I am not complaining or cursing about that. The man who buys in order to sell can only judge of good by the saleability of what he has bought. What will sell is good, because it is good for him. In so far as men of business, taken purely as such, are endurable we must accept the facts of their nature. But there is no reason why we should honour such men as superior beings. From the human and normal and godly point of view the merchant is not purely a man of business; he is the carrier, the purveyor, the conveyor and he is paid for the service he renders in carrying. But the man of business, is the man who, by definition, is only concerned to buy cheap and sell dear, for that is his nature; that is his reason of being; that is what he is for; that is how he makes his living. And it doesn't matter one jot to him what he buys and sells, provided only that the transaction yields him a profit on his investment. The man of business, as such, is a parasite. In the nature of things there is no reason for his existence. There is no reason whatever why there should be any men of business at all. But, be that as it may (and any civilization can endure a certain small proportion of pimps and thieves without succumbing — just as a man can endure a few warts and spots on his body without dying) what is truly monstrous and disruptive and corrupting to our life and virtue is that such persons should be our rulers — that they should have usurped the seats of kings, that their

hideous teaching should have replaced the Gospel. That is what
is unendurable; that is what is unforgivable; that is what God
will neither endure nor forgive.

And we are blind. By far the greater number of our people,
even those who are its most abject victims, are filled with
enthusiasm at the spectacle of the England that is the product
of industrial capitalism. Eccentric persons such as I are not only
voices crying in the wilderness; we are voices crying in a mad-
house. I have written so much on this matter that it is not
necessary to write more here. The thing to record is that
thinking these things and seeing the incompatibility of Christianity
with the industrial world when I was received into the Church
I thought of myself as having joined up with the Christian army
against the forces of the world, the flesh and the devil. It
was of course very fortunate that I knew very few catholics.
Thus I was able to take for granted a general agreement with
what I supposed to be the necessary and inevitable corollaries
of the Catholic faith, and I met no one to disabuse my mind.
I say this was fortunate; for though good things must naturally
be the fruit of truth and cannot be the fruit of falsehood and good
life must naturally be the fruit of charity and cannot be the fruit
of injustice – for injustice must naturally appear where charity
is absent – yet it would be altogether wrong, as well as absurd,
to embrace religion for the sake of 'art' (as many are tempted
to do), or to profess a love of Christ in order to obtain the good
things which come to those who love him. Therefore, for a year
or more, I was able to probe deeper and deeper into the faith
itself, without making the woeful discovery that that same faith
had for most of my fellow catholics no bearings at all on the life
and work of our times.

I am far from claiming that I have succeeded in my probings
and have emerged from those years with any claims either to
sanctity or theological knowledge. The only thing to be said
is that I know, and this can be said without any false humility
but merely as stating a fact, my own worthlessness and ignorance

more certainly. But at least those years supplied a spiritual breathing space and I was not immediately dragged into the vortex of catholic political and social movements. There were indeed no such things to be found. Such political activity as there was appeared to be directed solely to assuring the financial stability of catholic schools and the safeguarding of the religious instruction of catholic children in schools provided by the State. There was also some activity among catholic members of Parliament to promote a Bill for the removal of certain disabilities remaining over from times of persecution. This Bill eventually became law and, as a result, catholics were able to ring as many church bells as they liked and to wear grand medieval costumes in public if they wished to do so. Perhaps there were other rewards for good conduct. But that seemed to be the chief thing in catholic politics — to win the approbation and tolerance of ordinary men and women in our capitalist-industrial society by showing that catholics were after all, no different from their neighbours, just as good and shrewd men of business, just as good imperialists, just as keen on money-making and the application of science to industry, just as keen on machinery and mass-production and the cinema and the wireless and only differing from them in matters of purely private conviction.

This will seem, as it is, an ungracious, inadequate and ungenerous estimate of catholic activity. But it is the quality of this book ('such as it is') that on each page I live again in the mood of the period thereon described, rather than that of the period I am now in. Moreover little harm will be done if I make myself out ungracious or ungenerous. Such is probably more truly my nature than any other. But I am not and was not unaware of the devotion and courage and determination and obstinacy of many individual catholic protagonists and of the catholic body as a whole. The difference between me and them was that, as a convert, I was not prepared to accept without criticism much that they took for granted and were enamoured of. The education given in catholic schools, for example, and the 'atmosphere' which nuns and monkish school teachers seemed to breathe with such freedom and satisfaction seemed to me both narrow and stifling, as well as snobbish and prudish and unreal. The 'penny catechism' of Catholic Doctrine, a grand compendium of Christian teaching (if only by reason of its first two questions and answers and the fact that they *are* the first) is, it is now admitted freely, greatly in need of re-writing, but in the years I am writing of this did not seem to be admitted at all. Everyone, except a few converts, seemed to be perfectly content, and unaware of any blemishes whatever. Complacency! that seemed to be the note of the catholic press and of catholics generally. We alone were good and intelligent, and everyone else was in outer darkness — protestants, heretics, and either fools or knaves. It was assumed that the Church was hated and catholics absolutely basked in that hatred, wallowed in it . . . Here again I am being ungracious and ungenerous — but I do honestly think it will do more good than harm (if it does either). It won't put off the kind of converts who like Farm Street and the London Oratory or Quex Road Church or the new church at —— or the general over-running of England by Irish priests for nothing can put them off. On the other hand, it may do just a little to reassure those who find it more difficult than I did to step gaily over the forbidding doormat.

There were a few matters of difficulty, apart from the question of the schools. For instance, the catholic teaching on the subject of Birth-Control, though, from one point of view, an exceedingly private matter, caused considerable unpleasantness. The economic circumstances of the middle classes and the poor inhabitants of our slum cities are such as to make the artificial prevention of conception seem almost right and certainly necessary. It was all very well for married people in previous periods of history to copulate freely without thought for the morrow, but those 'good old times' are past. And yet people are not going to give up copulation. I mean to say, are they? It is true, beyond a shadow of doubt, that contraceptive methods spoil copulation (if not physically, which they commonly do, then certainly mentally) but, on the face of it, life in a capitalist-industrial world is unnatural and inhuman in any case, and having babies in Glasgow or West Kensington seems no less unnatural than stopping them coming. It is, in fact, as unnatural to have them as to stop having them. It is contrary to the nature of home life and the bringing up of children to live in London or Glasgow at all. But as the catholics could not see these facts any more than non-catholics could, it was inevitable that the arguments of catholics in condemnation of contraception should seem to have very little force. If you more or less openly and heartily applaud a system which drives men to drink, your condemnation of drunkenness 'cuts very little ice' as the saying is. If you approve of industrial-capitalism, then you must follow your neighbours and approve of those practices to which it inevitably leads. If you can't do that then you must turn round and condemn industrial-capitalism as so many of your own more perspicacious writers have done. . . .

Such and such matters disturbed the smooth sky of catholic mediocrity but, in general, no one had any reason to suppose that catholics were different from anyone else. 'They're all catholics round here,' they told me when I went to Preston in Lancashire – 'you wouldn't know if you weren't told,' and, I may add, when I was told I could hardly believe it – there was no reason why I should, though of course I couldn't deny that, in their secret souls, the inhabitants of that dirty and ruined city might be living lives of exemplary sanctity. I only say it didn't appear and that, speaking of England as a whole, the same thing must be said: there isn't the slightest sign that there is a Christian man or woman in the country. There is not. 'My kingdom is not of this world.' Dear Lord, yes, I know. But that is really my trouble ('Eric's trouble' as they used, at 'the Office', to call my special grouse, whatever it was). Anyone would think this world is exactly your Kingdom, so little sign is there that any of your followers thinks anything else.

But, thanks be to God, these presumptuous discontents with the frame of mind of my fellow catholics did not disturb my peace for several years. You see I lived in a country village where there were very few catholics — and none to talk to; for though, not being a very sociable person and having too much work to do to be lonely, it didn't worry me and I don't resent it, converts are not very highly thought of by 'born' catholics. They are regarded rather as interlopers into an ancient and select clique, as indeed they are. I had plenty of work and in that I was exceedingly lucky; for, humanly speaking, lucky is the only word. It was less than a year after our reception into the Church that I got the job of carving the set of representations called 'the Stations of the Cross' in the new Westminster Cathedral. And this was, as near as no matter, pure luck. I was, as I could easily demonstrate, the only possible person for the job, but that doesn't make my luck any less. I was almost unknown in any respectable circles and, I suppose, entirely unknown among catholic ecclesiastics. I believe it is true, as I was told by the architect[1] in charge, that had it not been that I was willing to do the job at a price no really 'posh' painter or sculptor would look at, I should certainly never have got it. As it was, the pious donors were getting restive and as the Cardinal Archbishop is said to have said, if the architect didn't hurry up and do something about it, he would give the work to the first catholic he met in the street. So they gave it to me. But I really was the boy for the job, because I not only had a proper Christian enthusiasm but I had sufficient, if only just sufficient, technical ability combined with a complete and genuine ignorance of art-school anatomy and traditional academic style. Of course they didn't know this. They thought I was carving in the Byzantine style and on purpose! Certainly I was carving in what might be called an archaic manner; but I wasn't doing it on purpose,

[1] To whom I had been introduced by a young man, Gerald Siordet (R.I.P.), whom I had not previously met, but who, having the wit to see that I could do the work, had also the energy and the forcefulness to arrange an introduction.

but only because I couldn't carve in any other way. The result was more or less equally approved and condemned — but it was a *fait accompli* and the Cardinal wasn't going to be bothered to go through all the business again. There were sufficient people to tell him the things were good to outweigh those who said they were bad — especially when you take into account the infernal nuisance of taking all the panels down again. And some of them *are* good, even if some of them are bad; and as no two people agree as to which is which, nothing can be done about it. So my good luck held out. This job lasted for four years. Fortunately I had other work as well, or I couldn't possibly have carried on. Among other things I had a big war memorial to do in Dorset. And this brings me to 'the Great War'.

I suppose it will be clear to anyone who reads this book that I wasn't the sort of person to go rushing headlong to the recruiting station as so many of my friends did. Nor was I the sort to suffer agonies of doubt and indecision as to my duty. War, in my mind, was still the more or less human business it had been in South Africa, and, so little was I acquainted with it, that even the pictures of war (General Gordon, Khartoum — even Zulus and Matabeles) which I pasted all over my bedroom walls as a child still seemed to represent more or less faithfully what I supposed war to be like. So I hadn't connected up in my mind the business of industrialism and the business of war-making. Wars might be just or unjust but they were not, as far as my thinking then went, in any way particularly inhuman. The Germans were reported to talk about 'gun fodder', but I took that rather to indicate their particular tactics of mass attack than to describe the inevitable quality of men's part in war to-day. On the other hand I was under no illusions as to the nature of modern politics and the motives and background of modern politicians. So while I still thought of war-making as a more or less human affair, I wasn't taken in by the war propaganda either of hate for the Germans or of the high ideals for which we were fighting. The atrocity stories were probably as much bilge as the ideals. I read Mr. Belloc every week in *Land and Water* but I had long since given up reading the daily papers and the war didn't induce me to take the evil practice up again. So, though I wasn't at all cold-blooded about it (too many of our personal friends and relations were involved in it), the war really passed me by. It didn't make any difference whatever to my life. I went on with my work and we went on with our endeavours to make a holy and human life for ourselves and for our children. I was certainly not in the least ashamed because I didn't 'join up'. I thought quite simply and quite honestly that it was no affair of mine. I was not a pacifist in the specific sense of that word, still less a 'conscientious objector'. I said quite openly, I will go when they call me up – not before. I didn't ask for exemption and I made no effort whatever to obtain it, but I made no objection when an influential friend, entirely out of the enthusiasm of his heart, obtained an exemption for me until I had completed my job at Westminster Cathedral. I finished it in August 1918 and I was 'called up' in September and was put into the Royal Air Force Mechanical Transport.

My war experience was therefore entirely unheroic. I was conscripted in September and was out of it before Christmas – rather less than four months and all of them spent in home camps learning to drive motor lorries and going round the said camps as a scavenger. Yet it was a monstrous and momentous experience. Four months of desolation that seemed like four years! Of course I was a completely rotten soldier and a still worse motor driver. I was only in the thing as a penance. I had made up my mind to go if called upon and, in the same spirit, I had made up my mind to bear with patience whatever was done to me and to do without hesitation whatever I was commanded. It was exactly like being in prison, and we were treated uniformly as criminals. Whatever we were given to do was given as though it were a punishment – a punishment for something we had done or for something we were probably about to do. It was the end of the war, and everyone, officers and men, were utterly 'fed up'

and discontented and impatient. At the first camp I was in
there were several suicides every week and when I was in hospital
with influenza two would-be suicides were in the same ward
with soldiers on either side of them on guard until such time as
being sufficiently recovered from their sore throats, they could
go before their courts-martial. Oh, that camp at Blandford was
a god-forsaken place and for such a person as I, harbouring such
thoughts as mine (a mixture of willing immolation and patience
and hatred of the institution and a still deeper hatred of the
political and industrial world which had brought the war upon
us) and no one to share them with, it was a period of unrelieved
misery. And there were no counterbalancing advantages. I was
interested in motor engines and there are good moments in
motor-driving, but even such things were poisoned by being
taught us as punishments. The angers and blasphemies of the
drill instructors, the filthy slang of the sergeant who gave us
lectures on how to keep clean after going with prostitutes
(dear readers, imagine yourselves standing 'properly at ease' in
rows, being instructed in the proper way to use a syringe and
how to mix the chemicals), my inability to find anyone to whom
I could talk about anything except matters of interest to recruits
from the suburbs of industrial towns . . . I wish I could write
the book that ought to be written. It wasn't war; it wasn't even
the degraded mechanical slaughter which went on at the 'front'.
It lacked therefore all the compensations of hardships and horrors
shared with faithful and good humoured comrades. It was just
exactly prison – relieved by a few hours off each day in which
the prisoners sought the excitements of women and drink. But
it is no use writing these things. It is impossible, in my experience, to 'get it across'. People who write thus are thought both
despicable and mistaken. It took ten years after 1918 before
the army became articulate and the great spate of war books
which then appeared were compelled by the exigencies of the
publishing business (the need to sell) to be books about the war
as a business of armies and fighting. No public would be expected

to buy a book about desolation and godlessness — even if any writer could have had the nerve and the imagination to write about it. The whole world is doped with the myth of military glory and just as the ordinary war enthusiast never thinks of wounds in the intestines so he never thinks of the spiritual desolation which life in the army actually entails. Moreover he can claim so much evidence to the contrary, so many eloquent and intellectual writers, who themselves went through years of war, are there to maintain the deception, and though many of them wrote critically and bitterly of the horrors of battlefields and the stupidities and fatuousness of the ordinary gentleman commanders, their criticisms were always neatly balanced or rather outweighed, by fine writing and fine thinking about the humours and comradeships and heroisms, and all the novelists' fascinating tricks for bringing a scene home to you. I have never read a more beautiful and serene description of a quiet rolling landscape at evening than occurs in Patrick Miller's *The Natural Man*, where the author describes the distant view of the German trenches just before the outbreak of a barrage. The book is about the war, but it is, in such passages, entirely at peace. So I must leave the matter at this stage. I would love the reader to think of me as an ordinary lover of my country, but I must take the risk of his only acquitting me of being the most despicable kind of knave by my acceptance of the alternative — that I am talking out of my hat. I was wangled out of the R.A.F.M.T. by being transferred to the Admiralty as a draughtsman. But the Admiralty didn't want me. So I was sent home and told to stay there until called upon. I never was called upon and, as far as I know I've never been 'demobbed'.

So I returned to my own work. My experience of the army was brief, but it was sufficient to give me a taste of the sort of life which must be that of three-quarters of our fellow men and women. Life in an industrial town, if you are just a factory hand, is very much like that of the army, and there's very little difference between the non-commissioned officers who prowl around and exercise their small authority in army camps and the police who are perpetually on the watch to see if they cannot snatch promotion from the petty crimes of their brothers and sisters. If I had not had that brief taste of army life I should never have known what it is like to be one of the 'submerged tenth', an under-dog, a person of no use to anyone but as an instrument, a unit on a pay sheet, only to be paid if no disobedience could be proved against him. So I left the army as though I were Mr. Bultitude escaping from school, and, Blessed Martin! I very nearly got caught again in the machine, just as I was being paid off. It was a very near go. They thought I was a new recruit and I only just got out by dodging round the corner.

## 2. T . O . S . D .

I RETURNED to my own work. But this had, during the last year or two, been taking on a new complexion. Under the influence of two friendships my quiet independent existence on Ditchling Common came to an end. First there was Hilary Pepler a recent convert from Quakerism and the L.C.C. and then there was Desmond Chute – a catholic born and in fact my first catholic friend. He was the first friend among those who were catholics not, like myself, simply by conviction and instinct, but by birth and tradition and education as well. And we were also in agreement on all the matters of capitalism and industrialism as to which, as I was now beginning to discover, most of our fellow catholics were in almost complete antagonism. And Hilary Pepler was the same. He had recently set up a printing press at Ditchling village (afterwards known as St. Dominic's Press) and as Desmond Chute had formerly been a student at the London University school of painting ('the Slade') we formed a sort of society of three. My enthusiasm and Hilary Pepler's as converts was equalled by Desmond Chute's and he added a religious experience and knowledge far beyond ours. The result of this association was the idea of a guild or company of craftsmen who should be united not merely by a common desire to further the interests of their work but by the common acceptance of a rule or way of life. We believed that a good life and a good civilization must necessarily be founded upon religious affirmations and therefore that such affirmations and a determination to live in accordance therewith, were the first necessity, for individuals, for societies and for nations. We believed that this was in effect to 'seek the kingdom of God and his righteousness' and that all other things would indeed be added. The beauty and loveliness of the natural world bears its witness to God's love; it is necessary that man's works should bear witness to his love of God. But you cannot have religion for the sake of art and any reform of man's work must be undertaken in a truly and honestly disinterested spirit – so far as that is humanly possible.

Those are pleasant days when young men and men in the prime of their life argue and debate about the divine mysteries and concoct great schemes for the building of new societies, and they were pleasant days for us. There was great love between us and, seemingly, complete agreement. The first thing was to discover what rule of life should be ours and that of the guild we proposed to found. Should we endeavour to devise an entirely new one or should we discover an old one?

Now in these discussions I, being almost entirely ignorant of the religious life, that is to say the monastic life (for the word 'religious' in the phrase 'religious life' does not mean simply a life of exemplary piety and obedience to the divine law but a life according to definite rules of daily conduct in accord with ecclesiastical authority), was in favour of inventing a new rule for ourselves. But Desmond Chute was not so ignorant. He was himself a member of the Third Order of St. Francis and thus able to introduce us to the, to me, almost unknown world of monasticism. Moreover it was at about this time that I had become intimate with Father Vincent McNabb, whom I had

first met some years prevously at the house of André Raffalovich
in Edinburgh, and at whose invitation I had gone to lecture on
'art', according to my lights, at the Dominican house at Hawkesyard in Staffordshire of which he was at that time prior. Fr.
Vincent McNabb was, and for that matter is, a very great man,
a philosopher, a theologian and a man of heroic virtue, a man,
moreover, so very much our teacher and leader in our views
on social reform and industrial-capitalism, on life and work, on
poverty and holiness, that it was natural that we should consult
with him on the matters which were concerning us. And
through him we were introduced to the Dominican Order, the
Order of Preachers, the Order of Friar Preachers founded by
St. Dominic in the thirteenth century of which St. Thomas of
Aquin was a member.

I am writing this and thus for the benefit of my non-catholic
readers. I see no reason to assume that they know more about
these matters than I did. They probably do not know any more
than I knew what the Dominican Order is. They have no more
idea than I had who or what St. Thomas Aquinas was (surely it
is no fault of theirs any more than it was of mine), how great a
man he was and how relevant his teaching is to our own time.
But the discovery we made under the guidance of Fr. Vincent
McNabb was no less than a revelation. I have said on a previous
page how much I am indebted to the teaching of Ananda Coom-
raswamy and I have disclaimed any right to call myself his
disciple — because that would only be to impute to myself virtues
of knowledge to which I have not attained. In the same way I
dare not claim to be a disciple and hardly even a follower of
St. Thomas — the presumption would be ludicrous. Nevertheless it will only be the truth if I say that in my ignorance and
impudence I do and must claim to hold opinions which I learnt
from him through my teacher Fr. McNabb and other Dominicans
to whom he introduced me or whom I subsequently met — Fr.
Austin Barker, another Prior of Hawkesyard, John canon Gray,
of Edinburgh (notable among saints), and Dr. Patrick Flood of

Glasgow[1] – both these last being, like the present Pope, members of the Third Order. It was about this time also that I first heard of Jacques Maritain, the leading lay exponent of Thomism in Europe and perhaps in the world, whose book *Art et Scolastique* had just reached England. 'This little Roman Catholic book on Art' (as a leading literary review with its wonted mixture of public school ignorance and damned superiority called it in the entirely inadequate and non-understanding review they printed of it – but that was in 1920 and Maritain was not then known in England as he now is, so they could know no better) was destined to make a very considerable revolution in intelligent circles – both artistic and philosophical, and we hailed it as a Daniel come to judgment. And yet another person whom we came to know as friend and counsellor about that time was Fr. John O'Connor, then of Heckmondwyke, and he also was of the same way of thinking and helped us greatly by reason of his worldly and other-worldly wisdom. He also it was who undertook the translation of Maritain's book into English and this was one of the first books printed and published at Ditchling. It is claimed by the more pedantic that Fr. O'Connor's translation is not so true to the precision of the Thomistic terms as is the second English translation, but in its rich humanity and humour it is unsurpassable. I hold it to be a merciful and indeed blessed dispensation of divine providence that so precious a book should have first seen the light in English in the rational and beautiful, even if somewhat inexperienced printing of the Ditchling Press.

I have always regarded and shall always regard myself as God's darling and in nothing is his affection more evident than in his choice of my friends.[2] This has I think been clear throughout

[1] And to Dr. Flood I owe an unrepayable debt for his encouragement and help in the writing of this book.

[2] Except perhaps in his choice of my wife – if that is not quite the same thing. I cannot forget the dream in which I was walking in heaven (you can't help your dreams) with Mary and the children. We came upon our Lord . . .

this book and it becomes still more clear to me when I consider the friends who befriended me in these first years after our reception into the Church. I cannot name them all here because I must confine myself to those persons and things which specially influenced me. Among such there were at this time specially these three — Desmond Chute, who himself subsequently became a priest, Fr. Vincent McNabb and Fr. John O'Connor. To them I owe, in the rough way that human beings must necessarily talk, everything. Of Fr. Desmond I shall say little because my love for him is too intimate, too much a matter of daily companionship and discussion and argument, too close a sharing of life and work and ideas and doubts and difficulties — the only man and therefore the only priest with whom I have been able to talk without shame and without reserve. If he should die before me and it should happen that I were asked to write his memorial, I will try to say what I think of his genius and his virtues — but not now. But of Fr. Vincent McNabb and Fr. John O'Connor, though they be very dear friends, it is easier to speak for my relationship is that of son to father. Easier — but not easy; for although the Catholic Church in England is but a small body and suffers much from the sort of sectarianism thrust upon it by reason of its small numbers, and the opprobrium which, by reason of the tragedies of the past and the mistakes, its own and its enemies', it suffers, yet it is a living member of the Universal Church and knows a greatness and a wisdom and a holiness which is entirely unknown to the majority of English people. In writing then of such men as those I have named it will seem to most of my readers as though I were using terms that properly pertain only to members of the Established Church or the professors of our ancient universities. Yet Vincent McNabb and John

And I said to him: 'This is Betty . . . and this is Petra . . . and this is Joanna . . . and this is Gordian . . . ,' and he shook hands with them all. And then I said: 'And this is Mary.' And he said: 'Oh, Mary and I are old friends.' It was a green open hill-side with paths and bushes and a blowy sort of sky with Downland clouds,

O'Connor are in the very first rank of noble minds, and what I learned from them was as from the very fountains of the universal wisdom. Shall I say that from Fr. Vincent McNabb I learnt the truth and, through the truth, the good, and from Fr. O'Connor I learnt the good, and through the good, the truth? This would be an absurd epitome but I think it expresses something of what I must say and something of the truth. They were in a manner of speaking my spiritual father and mother. I am an unworthy son, that is understood, but their son none the less.

So it was with the background of these friendships and under the wings of these guardians that we pursued our design to found a guild of Christian and catholic craftsmen. And it soon seemed to stand out clearly that it would be far better to ask to be received as members of the Third Order of St. Dominic and to found our guild with that rule of life than to set up a new rule of our own. This we did and under that rule, either outwardly or inwardly and sometimes both, I have lived ever since. The fortunes of the Guild of St. Joseph and St. Dominic are not relevant to this book. It still flourishes after twenty-two years, but I am no longer a member. There came a time when, the publicity which overtook it having become, to me at least, unbearable and because of other difficulties also, I fled from the beloved Ditchling of my childhood and found refuge in a hidden valley of the Black Mountains.[1] But quite apart from other difficulties, the publicity was horrible. This was partly our own and partly the fault of our Dominican friends — they told people about us and made us a show place. What we had thought of as a rather secret enterprise, and essentially a company of craftsmen living by their work and earning such reputation as they had by the quality of their goods, our clerical friends thought of as a public spectacle of Christian family life. Those who could bear it remained; ours and two other families fled to Wales.

But I can't leave Ditchling quite so roughly as that. The

[1] And Desmond Chute had gone, to become a priest, two years before.

period between our emigration from London in 1907 and our migration to Wales in August 1924 was, as things go in this book, a very formative period. It was the period, I suppose I shan't give offence by saying it, of my childhood as a churchman, as well as of my childhood as a stone-carver. The two activities, or voyages of discovery (for childhood is such in any case), went along side by side and were intimately entangled. Universal religion was thrust upon me as a necessity as I have tried to explain, by the very fact of my foolhardiness in venturing into the wilderness of the 'fine' arts and the company of London artists. And on the other hand no sooner was I born into the company of the children of God than, as a parallel necessity, I was compelled to consider the nature and conditions of the good life. Thus it was that we became Tertiaries of the Order of St. Dominic. We could not go so far as to say that *all* Christian men and women must, by the simple fact of their being Christians, engage themselves by vow or promise to live according to one or another of the Religious rules, or make new ones, because the same simple fact of being a Christian does in itself imply a life according to religion – I am the Way, the Truth and the *LIFE*. But in the complete mess which the men of business have made of the modern world – for though sinners will make a mess anyway, the particularly beastly and disastrous mess in which we find ourselves to-day is the product of the particular beastliness of men of business – it does seem as though as many as possible should enrol themselves under the disciplines offered by Religion in the special sense of the Religious Orders. I don't know if he invented the saying but it was one of Fr. Vincent McNabb's most impressive doctrines, at least it most impressed *me*, that 'there can be no mysticism without asceticism', and as I am by nature no ascetic and yet by nature yearn almost constantly for mysticism, it was the more incumbent, upon me at any rate, to discover an appropriate asceticism. Perhaps those words need some definition; for they are almost technical terms. Mysticism means a life of intimate union with God. It does not mean a life of vague and cloudy mysteriousness; it has, in fact, only remotely anything to do with the word 'mystery' in its current sense. Mysticism is the doctrine of the 'mystic life'; the mystic life is the life of contact with the Author of our being, with Being himself, and as God is Love and Love is God and as Love is essentially union, thus the mystic life is a life of union with God. And asceticism means training and discipline. It does not necessarily mean, as so many suppose, physical emaciation, starvation, repression and hatred of all sensual and physical goods. It means simply and solely that discipline and training which is appropriate to the particular end or good aimed at. The end determines the means. Asceticism is simply a means. In themselves fasting and abstinence and the avoidance of sensual enjoyment or surplusage of earthly goods are not to be worshipped. There is idolatry in a false asceticism as there is in the worship of money or power. These things being understood, it will I should think be clear that a naturally sensual person, a person tempted by his mind as well as by his body to see in the life of the earth all heavenly goods (so that he could imagine no more desirable heaven than this earth shorn of all its industrial vulgarity and squalor), would, even because of his strong sensuality, seek, ask for and demand a circumscribing discipline if only that he might not be the victim of his own exuberance. The only real enjoyment of life is in the memory. However enjoyable this or that activity may have been or have seemed to be at the time of action – the ecstasy of sensation, the ecstasy of touch and taste and smell, of sight and sound – unless the memory of it be good we must, for our own peace, eschew such action. Peace, that is the word of power! – Peace, in St. Thomas's fruitful words 'the tranquillity of order'. It is only in Order that the mind can find rest. And as, upon inquiry, it is seen so plainly that the beauty without which there is no good memory, is the splendour of order, and therefore of being itself (for being is the antithesis of chaos) does it not immediately become clear that, if only to save sanity, order must be safeguarded and, to that end, the

exuberance and self-centred enthusiasm of the individual be
curbed and restrained, and,

> as music binds into a strict delight
> the manifold random sounds that beat the air,

so a religious astringent must be found to give musical rhyme
and reason to the manifold random exuberances of men and
women.

The Order of St. Dominic supplied this. The Rule of the
Third Order was of course not written for any such circumstances as ours, but it was simple and sufficient and could, by
proper authority, be adapted as required. Perhaps the most
conspicuous part is the daily recitation of the compilation of
psalms and prayers and other readings known as the 'Office of
the Blessed Virgin Mary'. From the outsider's point of view,
this must seem an impossible burden and boredom. I wish I
could show how and why it is not so, but, on the contrary, is a
holy house full of light and music. And who is to tell of the
Communion of Saints, which to the unbeliever is nothing but
delusion and fairy tales?

But the main and grand advantage of becoming Dominicans in
our particular circumstances was and is that the special vocation
of the Order of St. Dominic, the very reason of its being, is
devotion to Truth — and as that is so, it is and must be the Order
of *Preachers*, because it is the truth that must be preached and it
is truth which is the very substance of preaching. And it is clear
that in the circumstances of our time it is the Truth which has
been forgotten. Our industrial-capitalism is *untrue* to the nature
of man. That is the point and it was the realization of that point
which compelled us to become Dominicans.

In this history of influences therefore, the influence of the
Dominicans and of their teaching must take a decisive place.
My life was entirely altered as a consequence. It had henceforth
an anchorage, and not an anchorage only but a port from which
to sail and to which to return. The Church itself, Christ him-

self, is such an anchorage and such a port, but the greater includes the less.

Lord! how I do run on in my pieties. I must leave it to the reader's charitable imagination to see the flesh and blood beneath the black and white habit thus impudently assumed and, by good fortune, a flesh and blood not too unsightly. And as long as the reader does so and continues to do so all will be well, for indeed, however sinful or imperfect or foolish my personal and fleshly life may have been, I was certainly not subject to evil influences and therefore there is nothing of that sort to be recorded in this book.

Apart from persons and things I have mentioned, the chief influence at this time was our daily life as brethren of our guild. In the course of time we built a small chapel and a quadrangle of workshops, and we endeavoured to unite the life of work with the life of prayer. Looking back on those years I find it impossible to think that we were unsuccessful. Such troubles as arose were financial – the difficulty of paying for land and buildings – and those social troubles of which I have already written. But there were no troubles directly arising from any mistaken conceptions as to the nature of the Guild itself. We were of course over ambitious and it was too readily assumed by us that our aims would be understood by our fellow catholics. That was perhaps the chief or only unhappiness (apart from personal ones) of those years. It was the period of disillusionment. We discovered that in spite of the Encyclical letters of Pope Leo XIII and Pope Pius X it cannot be assumed that the clergy and laity are all agog with enthusiasm for social or any other reform and that in general the clergy seem to regard it as their job to support a social order which as far as possible forces us to commit all the sins they denounce. A social order cannot in itself force anyone to do anything, but it can be such as to place many obstacles in the way of those who would live in a human manner. 'A man can be a very good catholic in a factory', our parish priest used to be fond of saying. And he was very annoyed and called us bolshevists when we retorted: yes, but it requires heroic virtue and you have no right to demand heroic virtue from anyone, and certainly not from men and women in thousands and millions.

And when it came to discussing matters of human work, the responsibility of the workman, not merely for obedience but also for the form and quality of what his deeds effect, the ordinary parish priest and the ordinary layman were either not interested or frankly antagonistic to any reform. They were almost as much against trades unions as they were against socialists and communists, and they were generally as enthusiastic about the advances of 'scientific management' as any capitalist could wish. Persons whom you would have thought could hardly exist, catholic bank clerks and stock-brokers for instance, are the choice flower of our great catholic schools. Societies for the promotion of peace among men and nations which you would have expected to be filled with pious catholics are hated and detested by bishops and clergy and laity alike and writers in the catholic press have gone so far as to say that no practising and sincere catholic can conscientiously object to war or to military service!

But though my enthusiastic catholic informant had woefully misinformed me, I had not been misled. If I had the Popes at my back, if I could claim the support of many notably holy men among the clergy and even a few among the laity, I had no reason either to be unhappy or to think myself unorthodox.

### 3. CAPEL-Y-FFIN AND SALIES-DE-BÉARN

MY life at Ditchling came to an end for the reasons I have given, and we went to the Black Mountains, to Capel-y-ffin, on the borders of Brecon and Monmouth. Here began an entirely different kind of adventure and a world of new influences. At first it had been our hope to continue the Guild life in the new place, to form a branch establishment. But this did not prove to be possible. The internal history of the Guild of St. Joseph and St. Dominic is not relevant to this book, so there is no need to say more. And as I was able to continue at Capel the same work I had been trying to do at Ditchling, the fact that I was no longer a member of the Guild did not make any great difference, and I got clear away from the irksome and horrid publicity and from equally irksome and horrid financial entanglements. Perhaps I left the brethren rather in the lurch but that was no fault of mine because the scheme had been for the whole lot of us to leave Ditchling and re-establish ourselves in Wales and by so doing to free not only me but the others also. For good reasons they elected to stay in Sussex, but I was desperate and had committed myself more deeply to Wales than they had done.

But what was a flight from Ditchling had something of the nature of an assault on Capel-y-ffin. The exodus of our family from Brighton to Chichester was nothing to it. Three families left Ditchling – three fathers, three mothers, seven children (of whom the eldest was nineteen and the youngest five years old) one pony, chickens, cats, dogs, goats, ducks and geese, two magpies and the luggage. We hired a lorry at Pandy, twelve miles away (the nearest station at which the pony could be detrained) and arrived at Capel about tea time in a typical steady Welsh downpour. But I have not said anything about our destination . . . and though I should need a separate book to do it properly, I think a brief account of the place is relevant to my story; for it can have happened but seldom in modern family life that four families (for there was one already installed before us) should find themselves the joint occupants of a disused and semi-ruinous monastery.

The monastery at Capel-y-ffin, four miles north-west of Llanthony in the valley of Ewyas, was built in the 1860's by the famous Anglican preacher known as Father Ignatius. His idea was to revive the Benedictine monastic life in the Church of England, but owing to a variety of causes, important among which were his frequently prolonged absences on preaching tours to collect money and the eccentric and fantastic version of the Benedictine Rule which he concocted, the project had been a failure, so that when he died in 1908 there were only three of his monks left and they without money or the approval of their Anglican superiors. These three joined the more recently founded and more successful Anglican Benedictine Abbey on Caldy Island, near Tenby, and so the buildings at Capel became part of the property of that community. The Benedictines of Caldy joined the Roman Church in a body in 1913 and that was how we came to know them.[1] When therefore early in 1924 we heard that they had a disused monastery in the Black Mountains and were willing to consider letting us (i.e. the Ditchling Guild) have the place as their tenants, I and another brother went to inspect and report. It was a weirdly exciting business. We arrived about midnight in deep snow having with great difficulty hired a motor car at Abergavenny fifteen miles away. It seemed as though God alone could know where we had got to, if anywhere. For miles and miles we had been driving slowly and dangerously up a narrow and very rough mountain lane and then we arrived at that dark and almost uninhabited and uninhabitable place. There were two monks in charge and we managed to wake them up.

That night it certainly seemed an impossible proposition, but the next morning, I saw the possibilities – a quadrangle of outwardly miserable but inwardly excellent Victorian sham Gothic buildings and, adjoining, the much too big and extravagant beginnings of a large abbey church. This last was a truly impossible affair, but the quadrangle, though beginning to go to ruin, was just the thing for a small community, if they were prepared to live fifteen miles from a town and without any of the things they call modern conveniences – except water, and of that there was plenitude; for the sound of rushing mountain streams was

[1] Curiously their 'submission' was announced on the same day (Feb. 22nd, 1913) that I and Mary Ethel were received.

on all sides.  And the surroundings would compensate anybody
for anything.  'Montes in circuitu eius et Dominus in circuitu
populi eius', I couldn't help thinking – not that I usually think
in Latin, but that particular verse runs in my head because I, so
to say, collect texts that refer to the heavenly Jerusalem.  And
the mountains above and around and confronting the monastery
at Capel-y-ffin are as good to look at as any in the world – you
know that directly you see them.  But, really! to hear me talk,
you'd think I was a Jew . . . I mean, I'm so Hebraic.  That's
the result of being a Bible Christian – a Christian brought up on
the Bible.

So whatever the rest of the brethren might think, I was
certain that this fastness would make an admirable home for us,
and I did my best to persuade them to the move.  Eventually,
as I've said, only three families found it possible.  But it was a
marvellous thing for us.  And it was a marvellous thing for the
young daughters.  That was in the days before motor cars were,
except as an expensive and extravagant adventure (it was so
rough on your tyres and axles), unknown in the valley, and so
we did all our transport on ponies and with pony carts – milk
floats and gambles.  They used to ride the fifteen miles into
Abergavenny to do the shopping and when I had to go to London,
as happened every month or so, we had to drive the eleven
miles to Llanvihangel Crucorney (the nearest station) with
great nicety of calculation so as just not to miss the train.  Many
a time we would see the smoke of the train approaching us with
another half-mile to gallop.  If we were lucky the porter would
look out at the station gate and see us coming and then he would
hold up the train for us.  Marvellous girls – how hard and loyally
they worked with their mother; it was a big place to run (we
had two sides of the quadrangle, which meant about twenty
bedrooms) and none but themselves to do it – the baking and
brewing and milking and butter-making, the twenty acres of
farm to organize and run as well as all the housework, cooking
and cleaning – and I, except perhaps in haymaking time, no help

to anyone, unless you call keeping a general eye on the whole show helpful.

And I was very busy during those four years; for, although my stone-carving work fell away almost to nothing,[1] I still had a lot of inscription work and lettering and with the assistance of my noble pupil, Laurence Cribb, we got through a lot of tomb-stones in spite of the difficulties of transport. But chiefly I did wood-engraving and it was during that period that the Golden Cockerel Press came to the fore and gave me a lot of work. This was very convenient and the distance from anywhere didn't matter a bit. One of the Caldy monks lived in the house so we were not divorced from Holy Mass and as Donald Attwater, learned authority on Eastern Rites, was also one of the inhabi-tants and also a Dominican Tertiary, we carried on a life of quasi-religious regularity.

Among the lettering jobs that Laurie Cribb did for me at Capel was the painting of a lot of notice boards – to warn off the hundreds of visitors who persisted in coming to see the monastery and Father Ignatius' grave in the big church.[2] These boards were painted in a sort of free sans-serif lettering more or less derived from the type designed for the London Underground Railways by Edward Johnston. We were rather justifiably pleased with these and so when Douglas Cleverdon, a forward-minded bookseller of Bristol, asked me to paint his shop fascia, I did it in sans-serif letters. It was as a consequence of his seeing these letters that Stanley Morison, the typographical adviser to the Monotype mechanical type-composing-machine people, asked me to draw an alphabet of sans-serif letters for the Mono-

[1] But I did a black marble carving of 'the Deposition' which is about the only carving of mine I'm not sorry about. It's now at the King's School at Canter-bury and that seems a decent home for it. This carving, very appropriately, was done in the coal cellar because I had, at the time, nowhere else to work.

[2] You can't imagine, unless you're one yourself, their impudence. They would walk in without asking and you would find them wandering in and out of your bedrooms. And when you asked them what . . . they were doing, they would say: Can we see a monk?

type Corporation. This was in 1927 and that led to lots of other typographical and type-designing business.[1] And I must say, and I hope this is a proper and seemly way to do it, that few associations can have been either more honourable or more pleasant – or, from my point of view, more helpful.

And I hope this is a good place and a good opportunity to say that I hope it will be well understood that just as on a previous page I could cheerfully confess that I had met quite a lot of nice bobbies, so I can with equal cheer, confess that I have met and had dealings with large numbers of nice business men, and business men more than nice. I pray to God that this is understood – that when I am constrained to curse the world that business men have made – the evil world that is the necessary consequence of their domination – I am not accusing any individual of malice or unkindness. And I do not see why offence should be taken except by those who believe that their world is good. When I hear artists accused of temperamental irrationality and loose-living, I do not immediately assume that I am being unjustly attacked. I know that the charges are commonly true, that artists have deserved to be rebuked and I with them. So it is with all forms of patriotism. We must see the baulk of timber in our own eye – and in the eye of our class or profession or nation. Many thousands of men of business have

[1] As being a matter of possible interest to typographers I append a list of printing types designed by me not elsewhere thus brought together.

| | | Punches cut by |
|---|---|---|
| 1925 | Perpetua | Monotype |
| 1927 seq. | Gill Sans-serif | Monotype |
| 1929 | Golden Cockerel | Caslon (for the Golden Cockerel Press) |
| ,, | Solus | Monotype |
| ,, | Perpetua Greek | Monotype |
| 1930 | Joanna | Caslon (for the Hague & Gill Press) |
| 1932 | Aries | Caslon (for the Stourton Press) |
| 1934 | Jubilee | Stephenson & Blake |
| ,, | Bunyan | Caslon (for the Hague & Gill Press) |
| 1937 | Hebrew | Monotype |
| ,, | Arabic (not cut) | |

inherited the traditions of probity and humanity which belonged to the pre-industrial past. Such men are as much the victims (though perhaps more willing victims) of our capitalist-industrialism as are their employees. They are struggling to preserve good traditions of quality and service in spite of all the tendencies towards mere money-making and power; but it is time that they ceased to blind themselves.

And during these years my pamphleteering, or to put it at its most dignified, my essay-writing exuberances, developed a good way further. At Ditchling I had enjoyed the inspirations and instigations of Hilary Pepler and we did a lot of joint work in that way. Now at Capel-y-ffin with the daily companionship and fellow conspiratorship of Donald Attwater I was able to carry on with the added advantage of being a hundred and sixty miles away from the Bedlem Hospital.[1]

And of course during those years, and those before and since, the Child, to use the admirable paranym of the *Arabian Nights*, was seldom asleep, or slept but lightly. I hope this is easily understood and allowed for. I wish I knew, I wish I could find out how much my fellow men and women are, in their secret minds, moved as I am moved by his constant presence. Our working days may be likened to a box filled up, and crammed full too, with a variety of visible and tangible objects — the things we do and which all our companions know we do and see us doing. We wake from sleep and wash and dress. We feed and read our morning letters, eating this and that and talking with our family. We go to our work; we take up and use such and such tools, we make such and such drawings and plans; we put our plans into execution in such and such places and with such and such materials, talking perhaps the while with our companions and assistants, thinking the while about the job in hand or the jobs and other business finished or to be undertaken in the future. At intervals we eat and drink again and in the evening,

[1] Now, as I am informed, converted very appropriately into a war museum (but I really ought to verify this).

when we are tired with the day's work, we sit with our wife and children and read and talk or play games until it is time for bed. Perhaps, if that has been the plan we have made for ourselves, we go to Holy Mass before breakfast (and this was our general rule and practice at Capel-y-ffin) and at intervals during the day we meet, at least some of us do, to say or sing some prayers or psalms. Thus, or in some such way, is the box of our day's doings filled up. But is it filled? No, indeed, for there are innumerable interstices between all these objects, and these interstices are also filled. Perhaps a large number are filled or nearly so by little objects which all may see who look or ask – little thoughts and feelings quite openly exposed if need be. But it is not thus with all these spaces. Many of them are filled with secret thoughts and unacknowledged and unacknowledgeable doings. It must be so. But what I do not know and can hardly guess, what I cannot find out, is how much of this sort of 'ether' which pervades and supports the interstices of our days is composed of the stirrings and awakenings of the Child, his clamouring activity, his felt but not acknowledged presence. I do not mean to suggest that, when all the acknowledged presences are counted and weighed, then all that remains, these innumerable spacelets in which even the minute dust of acknowledged action is invisible, are all filled with that one clamour. There are others equally unacknowledged. There are many other things of which we are too shy to speak – our momentary spasms of prayer, the innumerable awarenesses of loveliness in flowers and birds and beasts of which we have hardly time to speak, even if we are not too decently reticent thus to bespatter our friends and relations with our momentary meanderings. But these things would be acknowledged if we were called upon to acknowledge them. The thing I am trying to reach is the influence of the unacknowledged. Yet I am sure that influence is both great and important, both pervasive and continuous. How many times a day do men think, perhaps only momentarily, of the shape and attributes of female flesh? How many tiny interstices are thus filled? How often and how vehemently do we look forward to going to bed – but not to sleep? And is it the same with women, or are they mostly cold as fishes and as unconcerned and incurious, or only concerned as victims . . . ? They won't or can't tell you. And the few who can and do can only speak for themselves; they don't seem to know what other women think. I must leave it thus. I can only confess that, judging from my own experience and having no reason to think that others are different from me, the thought or memory of that activity of our bodies which is only acknowledged openly between lovers (or alas! when illness gives doctors a polite entry into our too secret life) and which reaches its fulfilment in physical union and orgasm, does in fact occupy, in greater or lesser degree, very many of the interstices of our waking lives and thus colour and inform and perfect or, it may be, mar our doings.

I write these things here because it was at Capel-y-ffin, thus far removed from bedlam, that I was able more dispassionately to review and probe into such psycho-physical problems. If 'Ditchling' may be thought of as the period of my spiritual schooldays (in a quite elementary school I agree) so, 'Capel-y-ffin' must be thought of as the period of my spiritual puberty (is that a bad word? it seems to me more expressive than adolescence). And as in my physical childhood and puberty at Brighton and Chichester I did in a general way live in a mood of thanksgiving – surely I was thankful to our parents and thankful to life itself – so at Capel-y-ffin I learned the spiritual trick (there must be a better word than that, but I cannot think of it), taught me by one of the monks of Caldy, an American with the delightful name of Ambrose Holly, of 'casting all things on the rock which is Christ'. This is straight out of the Rule of St. Benedict – written in the sixth century, and that shows what friends we all are – but it is as true to-day as fourteen hundred years ago. And then I discovered another way of putting it, couched in words perhaps two thousand years older still! 'Who can understand sins? Cleanse me from my secret ones . . , And the words of my mouth shall be pleasing, and my dearest thoughts shall be always in your presence . . .' Suppose you cast all your troubles and sins upon the rock which is Christ, as upon one who is strong enough to bear them and willing to do so. It is good. But suppose you place at his feet, not as trials and troubles merely but as offerings which his love will purify and redeem from the egotism in which perhaps they had their birth, all the wayward sensualisms of thought and secret action which otherwise burden and torment you! Is not that also good? Thus, instead of being occasions of self-condemnation and distrust and self-reproach and self-dislike, they become occasions of thanksgiving. There can be no movement of the flesh or of the imagination which cannot thus be sanctified and turned to sweetness. There is good at the root of all our desiring . . . Appetites which kindle in us the flames of ungovernable lust or wrath were not perhaps ungovernable in their beginnings and if, before too late, we give thanks for the good which is their primary nature, we may, I do not think I deceive myself, turn what seemed sultry and threatening, however alluring, into the cool and friendly. And just as a man who, to use the old simile, drops a drawing pin (which of course rolls away into the darkest corner below his table) may, for the moment, feel inclined to damn the universe and then, on consideration, remember that upon the law of gravity (if there still be such a law) much of our enjoyable activity depends — and may then give thanks for what a moment before had been occasion of cursing, so many a sight or sound, and many a movement of the body which seems to supply only an occasion of sin and therefore to be accursed, may, on consideration, be seen to be occasion of thanksgiving. Would I wish myself different? 'My dearest thoughts always in your presence' — that is the trick. We cannot keep our thoughts secret from him — then let us share them with him. Fling them 'on the rock which is Christ', yes, but not as things to be broken and spurned, but rather as flowers at his feet. And are not those organs which sometimes seem, to ourselves and to others, the very root of scandal, are not they also thus redeemed and made dear. For they are literally our flowers. What are those lovely creatures which we delight to fill our gardens with and to display on our tables? What are they indeed but the sex organs of the plants they adorn. So that it is neither fantastic nor even an exaggeration to say that while from one point of view the country hedgerow is filled with savage creatures armed to the teeth – with poison and thorns and spikes and every sort of offensive and defensive weapon (in this respect perfect models for all modern nations), so, from another, it is nothing but an uproarious exhibition of desire for fruitfulness and multiplication. And having thus become enlightened as to the nature of the flowers of the field, does one then turn round and say: O hell! what a filthy world it is? I can't imagine that such would be the result. Rather, it seems to me, we should turn round on all our previous pruderies and think of ourselves as being adorned, as indeed we are, with precious ornaments. And thus a great burden of puzzlement is taken from the mind. And, what is more to the point, a great wave of cheerfulness breaks over us, and of confidence and that is to say confidingness. It is the confiding that brings the confidence. Isn't that what I said at the beginning – 'my dearest thoughts shall be always in your presence'?

And when I consider the loveliness of our flesh and how, though generally in silence and in secret, we revel in what we timidly call salacity – I say timidly because it is our timidity which makes us pretend to moral superiority and aloofness and hide our delight behind terms of opprobrium – I think it was good for me, useful and salutary that such delight should be balanced in my mind by a reasonable acquaintance with both birth and death. I shall write later about death. Here I only want to recall a thing which influenced me a good deal at the time and which I can never forget – and that was that, in the absence of the doctor, I had the honour to be assistant midwife at the birth of our second daughter.

I do not gather that women have, in general, much of an eye

for the beauty of their lover's bodies. Doubtless there are physiological reasons for this as well as conventional ones. They hunt by trapping rather than by pursuing. They are not inflamed by images; the thought of the sight of a lover's nakedness does not (or am I wrong?) generally provoke them. They do not make or go to see or buy pictures of men as men do pictures of women. They certainly do not. These things being so, and much more of the same kind, we cannot suppose that they carry about with them such vivid and cherished pictures of the male thing as we do of the female. Let it be so. But, the consequence! No one who has not witnessed the almost unbelievable transformation which parturition causes, and witnessed it with seeing eye, can know the truth about human love and sex. When Margaret of Cortona (who died on my birthday six hundred and forty-three years ago, and whose body is still incorrupt – go and see) found the decaying corpse of her lover in the wood, she suddenly saw the iniquity of their illicit love – reverse of adultery's medal. So, with the same kind of shock of revelation, in that chamber of birth I saw, though in this case without fear, the counter-balance of man's desire. I was not horrified; I was simply astonished . . . It was not horrible; it was simply astonishing – that a thing so loved could be thus transformed.

And death! When the husband of our eldest daughter died, she asked me to draw his portrait as he lay in our chapel. For several hours I stood close beside his body looking closely into his face and trying to transcribe his features accurately. That was a revealing experience – before my eyes death took him further from the living world. Even as I watched, the bony structure of his face became more sharp and hard; the flesh contracted on his brows and nose and chin. The nobility and patience of his character became more emphatically visible. It was, as it were, a race between corruption and revelation. On the one hand his spiritual form became more visible as its fleshly shape became more attenuate – on the other the disintegration which death of the body precisely is became more and more woefully and nauseatingly imminent. I was not horrified, I was not even astonished; but it was difficult, thinking of the lips she had kissed, to keep back my tears.

Have you felt the smooth whiteness of the flesh between her thighs and the dividing roundness? Such thoughts are kindling to our fires. Hasten then to cast them on that Rock — and give thanks, give thanks, above all give thanks.[1] 'Adam sinned when he fell from contemplation' — when he saw the treasures of this world as things ministering to *him*. We may recover something of our lost equanimity, our lost integrity, our lost innocence when, instead of seeing things as things to be grasped and possessed, we see them as beings manifesting Being himself.

I need only add that there is a real connection between contemplation and material quietness. The driver of a locomotive must, in duty bound, keep his eyes fixed constantly and without wavering upon the line ahead and the signals and must at the same time bear in mind the gradients and the pressure gauges . . . Yet in his mind quietness may rule. So it is in any life, even in the turmoil of domesticity — most disturbing of all hectic disturbances. It remains true that in a general way we need physical quiet if we are to attain to quietude. In that respect life at Capel-y-ffin was a quiet life. Troubles there were all of our own making and we were not disturbed by the constant petty feverishness of what they are pleased to call civilization in the towns.

I wish I could write a special book all about our four years in the Black Mountains. I did not intend ever to leave Capel. I did not anticipate any reason for doing so. The distance from Bedlem Hospital was no hardship and made no serious difficulties

[1] This is not 'sublimation', for it is not any sort of diversion or transformation. It is plain acceptance of things in their actuality, and reference of them to their Author. In any case, it is vitally important to take no notice of the jargon of Psycho-analysis, just as it is to take none of that of Art-criticism. But it must be added, let nothing I have written be taken to imply that I have not frequently failed, or that sheer sensuality has not often succeeded in hiding under a camouflage of intellectual purity.

to my work, so from my point of view there was no reason for moving – moreover I couldn't imagine how we could ever face so big a job. It had been bad enough moving from Sussex, but now there was another four years of accumulation . . . It was a good life and it was a marvellous training for the girls. For the great thing about it was that we were compelled by mere geographical circumstance to live in a way which would have been fantastically heroic and unnatural and pedantic in any place less remote from industrial civilization. We *had* to do our transport by pony and pony cart. We *had* to bake our own bread – we couldn't possibly have bought enough loaves and got them from the shop. And all our neighbours were doing the same. We were not, as we should have been at, say, Wimbledon, living according to some theory, however excellent, derived from a study of Cobbett's *Cottage Economy*. They could use that excellent book as being what for them it actually was, an up-to-date textbook.[1] We got coal fairly easily from the Welsh coal pits, but we burned a lot of wood which we cut from our own plantation. We did a lot of our own building repairs. The mistress and the girls parcelled the home-work between them. The eldest daughter managed the animals and the farm. Their mother did the baking and the two younger ones did the house and the cooking – but of course they all helped with everything. I don't reckon that I myself did much to help. I had too much engraving and carving to do, but I was occasionally more help than hindrance. I say it was a good life, and it was, and it was a natural life. And Donald Attwater, who was an excellent glazier in the intervals when he wasn't editing dictionaries or writing about Uniat Eastern Churches, repaired all the lead windows, of which there were dozens.

---

[1] A parson magistrate wrote to the Home Office in 1817 to say that he had seized two men who were distributing Cobbett's pamphlets and had them well flogged at the whipping post under the Vagrancy Laws. (Home Office papers, 42, 159) (quoted by J. L. and Barbara Hammond – *The Town Labourer, 1760–1832*, p. 72).

And we bathed naked all together in the mountain pools and under the waterfalls. And we had heavenly picnics by the Nant-y-buch in little sunny secluded paradises, or climbed the green mountains and smelt the smell of a world untouched by men of business. But alas! that is saying too much, for the evil hand, the outstretched claw of the dealer and financier was bringing ruin all around. The valley, the lovely vale of Ewyas, was never afflicted with his evil presence — his petrol pumps and road-houses, his factory filth and his suburban vulgarity. But his evil influence was over all. The population of the valley was but a quarter of what it had been fifty years before. There were twenty ruined cottages between Capel-y-ffin and Llanthony four miles lower down the valley. The young men had gone to the mines and were wandering unemployed in the Rhondda, their fathers could not call them home for the city of London found it more profitable to foster Australian Capitalist sheep farming than to preserve the thousand-year traditions of the South Wales mountains. We were living in a dying land — unspoiled but dying. It is still the same paradise and it is possible that it will long remain so. For by the mercy of geographical accident all the valleys are cul-de-sacs. Let the industrial-capitalist disease do its worst — the Black Mountains of Brecon will remain untouched and their green valleys lead nowhere. God help them! I hope I am right.

And while we lived at Capel we had a great adventure in the south of France. A dear friend bought a small house at Salies-de-Béarn and we conceived the project of sharing it with her. She bought the house and we furnished it. Certainly it was an adventure and I count it among the influential things. You see we didn't just go there for a holiday, we went and lived there all one winter. I can't imagine how one does such things. I suppose if you've got an enthusiastic mistress and three enthusiastic daughters it's not so impossible; but looking back on the affair I wonder we undertook it.

This experience was of course perfectly in harmony with our

life at Capel. The great difference was that the French life was vastly more cultured. It was as though Capel were our kitchen and Salies our salon. And we had the experience, nowhere obtainable in England, of living not only in a civilized town, but a civilized *life* also! Chichester is a civilized town, but it scarcely knows a civilized life. Lincoln's Inn was, in its domestic and semi-collegiate way, a civilized life but it was not a *town* life. There is now no civilized town life in England. It has all long since been submerged in the universal vulgarity of our commercialism. Perhaps the English have never enjoyed such a thing. Maybe our climate has not that benevolence which makes such serenity possible. I do not know — though it is difficult to believe that the beauty and spaciousness of such towns as Beaconsfield and Amersham were not the product of a way of living similarly beautiful and spacious. I say I do not know. What is certain is that life, the town life, in such small places as Salies-de-Béarn, has a quality of goodness and quietness and even holiness which seems to have gone for ever from England.

And this brings me to a matter which I am much concerned in and yet one which is more than most things difficult to describe with justice and balance. We have been so accustomed to the thought that though our very life depends upon the work of our industrial towns, yet that when we seek peace and loveliness we cannot expect them to give it. We take it for granted that beauty 'resides' in the country. The country, thinks the townsman, may be boring but it is certainly beautiful. Life and all the interest of life is in the town, but no one would say that modern towns are beautiful. For the most part the townsman is quite happy to let beauty go. He likes a day or a week or two in the country for a holiday. He will subscribe to societies which make it their business to preserve 'beauty spots'. He picnics in thousands at Burnham Beeches. He founds the National Trust and the Society for the Preservation of Rural Industries (God help him), and his Office of Works spends a lot of money patching up and propping up the ruins of medieval castles and monasteries. But all that sort of thing is not vital to him. It's on the same level as the picture galleries and museums which have taken the place of cathedrals in his towns. He is persuaded that they are important and he has a sort of sentimental veneration for them, but that they have no real importance for him is proved conclusively by the fact that he does nothing whatever to conform his own life to the principles and beliefs which were the inspiration of the pre-industrial world – on the contrary he, with monotonous enthusiasm and energy, continues to develop the commercial-industrialism which is in its nature destructive of all that he thus pays to preserve from disappearance, and which is rapidly destroying the very land itself.

And from one point of view the townsman is right. It *is* a lot of nonsense all this cackle about the beauty of the country. And the cackle would never have been heard if the towns had not become such monsters of indecency and indignity. The right and proper and natural development of human life unsullied by an insubordinate commercialism no more leads to ugly towns than to an ugly countryside. On the contrary, the town properly thought of is the very crown and summit of man's creativeness and should be the vehicle for the highest manifestations of his sensibility, his love of order and seemliness of dignity and loveliness. Man collaborates with God in creating – that, physically speaking, is what he is for. The natural world, following, without the slightest deviation, the line of least resistance, blooms in a million million marvels of natural beauty. The beauty of flowers and trees and beasts and insects, the beauty of bones and muscles and crystals and clouds, is the product of this unswerving but unconscious obedience. Man alone among created things can resist: man alone can willingly obey. Man alone can give thanks: man alone can respond and take a conscious and willing part in the universal creativity. Thus, properly thought of, man's works, alone of all material things, can have the spiritual qualities of tenderness and love, of humour and gaiety: and they alone can, on the other hand, have the qualities of wickedness and pride and silliness.

> Man indeed, one part of thy creation, has the will to praise thee: yes, man, though he bears his mortality about with him, even man has the will to praise thee . . . thou dost stir him up, that it may delight him to praise thee, for thou hast made us for thyself and our hearts are restless till they find rest in thee. . . .

These words, from the first page of the first and greatest auto-psychography, by one of those miracles of coincidence, came into my hand just while I was pondering on what I had just written. I am but echoing their thought — man is that part of creation which can praise his creator. Because he can, he is ordained to do so; and because he is so ordained he is in misery unless he obeys the call.

Now it is right and salutary that we praise God in our hearts — singing canticles. It is no less right that we should praise him in the work of our hands. In its dumb way all creation praises him — *omnia opera benedicite Domino, benedicite omnia germinantia in terra Domino.* Then shall other things praise him and only man keep silence? And as it is in their very springing and germinating that all living things praise him how can it be said that man's works alone need not do so? Obviously I am only writing down rhetorical questions. There is no possible answer but that in the work of his hands man, without any pride or exaggeration of his powers, can add to and indeed improve upon, and that to a literally infinite degree, the creatures of inanimate nature.

The point that I am thus struggling to reach is that clear and heavenly as is the beauty of the Natural world, clear and heavenly as are the mountains and the seas, the forests and the flowers and all the animal world, even when, yes indeed, even when most 'red in tooth and claw', nevertheless the cultivated fields, the farms, the roads, the villages are, when they are the works of men in peace and charity, infinitely more beautiful. And if that be so, the towns and cities where men forgather in the same peace and charity should be and have been and may be again more beautiful still.

I have said that I have a special predilection for texts referring to the heavenly Jerusalem[1] and of course I place as leader among such texts the one which says: *Jerusalem which is built as a city.* I fled from the bedlam of London to discover the lost Bethlehem. But I could not forget that text. Heaven, man's final beatitude, is likened to a place and that place a city. It is not true that the town's primary reason of existence is to serve the country-side, though it must and does do so. The truth is the converse; the country-side exists to support and uphold and nourish and maintain the city. It is only in our gross betrayal of our calling to a house not made with hands that the English town has become a shambles and a brothel and a place of filth and disease. Thus the call to the land, to the earth, is the necessary first call. We must be born again and we must be born again on the land, to dig the earth, to plant and cultivate, to be shepherds and swineherds, to hew wood and draw water, to build simple dwellings and simple places of prayer. But we need not therefore be blinded to what is the truth. Because Babylon is vile it does not follow that Jerusalem is vile also.

I had some such thoughts as these when we fled from London in 1907. I had them even more strongly and consciously when in 1924 we left Ditchling and the community, 'the city' on which we had set such hopes, and fled again, fled to the remotest place we could find.[2] And this is the point I have been trying to get to, I have actually now got to it, about Salies-de-Béarn. At last, at last we had the chance to live for a time in a human city which was in some sort a holy city, and to live a life, a city life which was a holy life. Holy, Holy, Holy, and that means

---

[1] Perhaps that's why my favourite hymn is St. Bernard of Cluny's.

[2] Lest any reader should think I deceive myself, I can refer him to letters which I wrote at that time to the *New Witness*.

hale and hearty and whole and healthy with a mind set heaven-
wards. I exaggerate; of course I exaggerate. The little town in
the foothills of the Pyrenees would be astonished to hear itself
called holy. Was it not 'run' by its local politicians? Had it not
got one of the worst possible memorials of 'the Great War'
with its cock crowing on the front? Was there not the hideous
half-built hotel – the building abandoned because the 'company'
went bankrupt? Was not the parish church almost falling down
and was not the 'altar of Repose' on Good Friday an almost
incredible monstrosity of lace and frills? Were not such new
buildings as there were as bad as any in Birmingham or Edinburgh? Alas! the answer is 'yes' in every case. And yet it
represented and I was properly justified in thinking so the
holy city.

The great thing was that I had a job of work to do – it was
about sixty engravings for the Golden Cockerel edition of
Chaucer's *Troilus and Creseyde*. I had an excellent room over a
chemist's shop (Bourdaguibelle – but perhaps I haven't spelt it
rightly) just round the corner from the *Place*. After Mass at the
Parish Church of St. Vincent I used to go to the café in the *Place*
for Little Breakfast and then to my work till lunch time. Home
to the villa for lunch and then back to work till dusk. Generally
one or more of the girls would come to meet me and we went
to Benediction on the way home to supper. Often in the evenings we went down to the town and sat outside the café in the
*Place* or the café de la Terasse beside the little river, and sipped
the local liqueur. Sometimes there would be a concert at the
parish school. Day after day passed thus, as beautifully regular
and reliable as a good clock. On feast-days we had holidays and
we made expeditions – to Sauveterre with its terrace café a
hundred feet above the rushing Gave, to St. Engrace, right up
in the pass, to Bellocq, to Oloron Ste Marie where there is one
of the best and most vehement sculptures in the world, but
especially to Sauveterre because it was within walking distance
and after a day by the river it was nice to walk the five miles

home (with a good swill of red wine, sitting on the bench outside
the Estaminet at the top of the hill) in the cool of the evening
singing songs along the road. (I haven't told you this: singing
songs was one of their special things; they knew simply hundreds
of songs and sang them in trio — if we were at home I used to
play accompaniments, not always too successfully, on the tin
whistle — songs of England and Scotland, the Highlands, the
Hebrides, of Ireland and France, a never-ending succession, one
reminding of and leading to another and what one didn't remember another would. Did ever anyone ever before have three
such daughters?) Once we went to Lourdes — of which the less
said the better (but there is no doubt about the Grotto). And
once we went to Peyrehorade to buy pots. And once we went
as far as Bayonne because I wanted to buy an oil stone and couldn't
get one at Salies. And once we spent the week-end at Fuenter-
rabia and thus poked our noses into Spain (It was Palm Sunday
and the children came in from all the country round carrying
branches of trees so that the big church was filled with greenery
and you could only just see little faces of children peeping out
between the leaves. And with no other human audience, because
the lazy grown-ups had all been to the low Mass at eight, a small
choir of men sang, and very admirably, all Vittoria's music of
the Passion. Well!). And our little son went to school at the
parish school and learned to talk French like a native (though the
accent of those parts is not Parisian) and to appreciate the fact
that it is possible to describe the battle of Waterloo without
mentioning the name of Wellington . . . And there was the
saintly Marie who cooked for us, and cooked like an angel or
perhaps simply like a good French woman. They learnt a lot
from her; moreover, as I said before, she was a saint. Well,
that is Salies-de-Béarn.

But there is one thing more I must try to describe because it
influenced me very much. I went one day with Elizabeth —,
the dear friend with whom we shared the villa, to a farm at
Castanniede to see her old friends there (she had had her baby

there twenty years before) and we were asked to dinner. It was a big farm owned and worked by the family – grandfather, sons and daughters and their children. But the old grandfather was past work and almost past life. He sat in the chimney corner with his cap on and dribbled. And he more or less minded the baby in the cradle at his feet and the baby dribbled too. Poor old man, the former head of all things, but now fading out in second childhood and scolded and mouth-wiped like the child at his feet (in England he would have been in the workhouse, looked after kindly enough but by paid strangers). And round the table in the big long kitchen-living-room was the huge family. The farmer and his wife and their grown-up sons and daughters and the younger children – down to little boys and girls only just big enough to sit up to table. I think there must have been a married grandson and his wife and children – how else account for such young babies about? And we had, in honour, I think, of the visit of Elizabeth to her old friends, the most sumptuous and tremendous feed. All the food was off the farm – the meat, the vegetables, the bread, the cakes, the wine and finally the *petits verres* of their own cognac. It was a grand example of the patri-archal home and the self-sufficing farm – a grand example of human life in all its vigour and feebleness, its joy and pathos. The two extremes of feebleness, the decrepit slobbery old man trembling and mumbling by the fire with the tiny baby six months old, and, in between, all the grandeurs of human strength and will and courage, the capable craftsmanship of the women and girls, the humble and handsome men hard-worn with the work and the weather – who all disappeared before we finished the vast amount we were expected to eat, to go about their various jobs on the farm. How could I help comparing it with our poor decayed English farm life? How could I help comparing it with the life in our modern towns, the slum life, the suburban life, the life in our smart new blocks of flats? The self-sufficiency and self-reliance of the southern farm, the feeble dependence and syco-phancy of the wretched crowds of wage-slaves and money-grubbers. Such reflections would lead only to despair but for the heartening fact that it is *our* civilization that is doomed, not theirs. It is of the very nature of our life that we should destroy ourselves – either in mutual murder or in physical and territorial barrenness. But the essence and actuality of their life is creativeness and fruitfulness and peace.

And there is one admirable and, as it were, heraldic symbol of that good life which I like to ponder on, for it typifies and sums up the whole difference between that life and ours and that is the ox-drawn wagon. In this particular period of our history wherein we and all our kind have made speed our very God, it must seem not only eccentric but even blasphemous so to think. 'No man ever hurries except when catching flies', says the Arab proverb. And in our industrial world everyone is hurrying and no one is catching anything but flies. It is not only a fever; it is a fever of futility. It is a madness; and, like all madness it means nothing and leads to death. And that, I suppose is why the yoked oxen are so heavenly lovely; they are quiet – like the 'still small voice'; they are slow – like the germination of seeds; they are patient – like the earth. And so they are a symbol of fruitfulness; for it is said of them that hear the word and keep it; that they 'bring forth fruit in *patience*'.

And in the middle of all this agricultural righteousness there was the little town with its little *Place*, overshadowed by green trees, its lovely houses and its little river. It is more than a market town, though it is also that. It is more than a health resort to which people come to bathe in the salt water, though it is that too. It is the centre of worships – the church in which we confess the fatherhood of God and the streets and meeting places in which we confess the brotherhood of men. That I think is why the country must be said to exist to support the town; because the town is the symbol of that heavenly Jerusalem in which men unite to praise God and to love one another. In the town it becomes a corporate praise and a corporate love. But it depends upon righteousness. The country does not exist to support Babylons but *holy* cities — when we say that the country exists to serve the town, God forbid that it should be supposed that we mean it exists to serve London and Birmingham . . . such places are not towns in any human or holy sense.

Nevertheless the salvation of England cannot be brought about by town improvements; it can only come by the land. The town, the holy city, is nourished upon elements drawn from the soil. The modern towns of our industrial England have no such nourishment. They draw their galvanic twitchings and palpitations (for you can hardly call it life) from machines. The modern town is a warren of business men. And though it is still dependent upon the country, it does not desire to be so; for it is slowly but surely turning agriculture into a mechanical or even a merely chemical industry. It will therefore not die only of mass murder (such as is going on this very day as I write — in London and Berlin . . . ) and barrenness but also of poisoning. It will die anyway. So our business is to get back on to the land as quickly as possible.

And that was Salies-de-Béarn. Our longest stay was that winter of 1926 and 1927. Since then we made several similar visits — in fact I've jumbled them all up together in my account of the first — but Salies in its turn became a thing of the past; for I don't see how we can ever get there again. Our dear friend is dead and the villa is sold and all our nice furniture with it. It remains alive in my memory — may the Lord preserve it in the flesh.

I have said that Salies-de-Béarn was to Capel-y-ffin as salon to kitchen. Our expeditions to the south of France were just like going to the family sitting-room after the day's work. We reclined at our ease and, of course without saying anything about it, we contemplated the divine mysteries. It *was* like that. If there had been anything comparable in our native land we should have had no need to take all that immense trouble. Just imagine it! From South Wales and, to start with, fifteen miles to the station; then to London, then to Paris, then the night journey and half the next day. (But the midday Bock at Puyoo was worth all the weary hours between Paris and Bordeaux and through the Landes . . . But on one occasion I remember arguing, or what not, nearly all the night with David Jones and that helped us through the journey – much to the annoyance, I fear, of our fellow travellers who wished to sleep – but how absurd of them!) I don't *want* to go abroad. I don't *want* to go to the south of France to find a human life. But I want to find a human life. And if I can't find it nearer than a thousand miles away, a thousand miles I'll have to go. And it's not merely for myself. I'm burning with desire that *my children* shall know and desire the good. That was what turned the scale – that *they* might be well fed.

And, thank goodness, it worked – you have only to ask them. But we had to go to the south of France to find what we wanted in one way just as we had had to go to the Black Mountains to find what we wanted in the other. And just as Salies came to an end, so did Capel-y-ffin – as our life in Sussex had done. But it is not fair to the land of our birth thus to make it seem that we never knew good days until we went to Wales or to France. There were things about our life in Ditchling, when the children were children, which have the same quality of paradise. I have written, carried away by the ecstasy of memory, of the walk home in the evening from Sauveterre to Salies, but what ecstasy of memory could surpass that of the return in the evening through Poynings under the Downs, along past New-timber and under the round hill of Woolstanbury to Clayton? How often we set out in the morning and climbed the hill by the mills at Clayton and went through Pyecombe and up the Devil's Dyke to drop into Fulking from above. And there their mother would meet us at the Shepherd and Dog with the pony trap and the children and we would have tea with boiled eggs and bread and butter and jam and then, oh God, we elder ones would walk home in the balmy beneficent evening under the Downs. And as I am writing about earthly paradises I must not omit the walk down from Rhieu Wen at the top of the valley back to Capel-y-ffin. That surely is one of the loveliest and also one of the grandest things in this world . . . How blest we have been, and not least, because we have thus seemed to live on the edge of eternity and in places to which we could thus come home.

I suspect all people are agreed about this, I don't feel as though I were being eccentric, but there is something in these home-coming evening walks with children and friends which no other occasion in human life seems to give. I remember, and I have referred to it in an earlier chapter of this book, how as children we enjoyed, and perhaps not less passionately, the same beatitude. It may not strike the reader as having the same importance, but to me it is one of the really important things. We are admonished to see all things *sub specie aeternitatis* and at any moment of the day we may do so. But it seems to me that it is on those home-coming walks that we get nearest to it.[1]

[1] And as I am recalling pleasant scenes I remember the summer holidays we had at Ditchling when we were children, and one in particular. It was in the year 1892 and the twins were in the cradle. We elder ones were more or less mad on 'sketching' at that time (doubtless in imitation of our father) and one afternoon four of us went to sketch Westmeston Church under the Downs. I remember we all sat in a row on the grass on the north side of the little old church and we were pretty busy. Presently, to our astonishment, a smart maid-servant in cap and apron appeared from the vicarage behind us (an exceptionally large vicarage in the middle of a small park with well-trimmed lawns), and bearing tea for four and cakes on a silver tray! Doubtless they had been much affected by the sight of four small children sketching in a row and judged rightly that tea and cakes would be acceptable. We were mightily proud and duly and politely grateful and went home to the farm to tell the tale. We went again the next day to finish our sketches and, I think, hoping for more tea and cakes on a silver tray, and I think we got them. But the sketches being finished we were conscientiously debarred from trying it on again. We never saw the vicar – not even Mrs. Vicar – so you can imagine the psychic effect of bounty and elegant bounty too, thus showered upon us as it were from heaven, for the maid-servant was obviously no more than an angel obeying a mysterious divinity above her. But apart from all that (without which I suppose I shouldn't have remembered it) I like to think of the four small 'artists' thus solemnly engaged in architectural research.

As I have said the main endeavour of this book is to make mountains out of mole-hills. And now I suppose I must somehow contrive to make the exodus from Capel-y-ffin. And most mole-hills really are mountains if you look at them close enough, if you get close enough to them. But I don't think I need explain at great length just why we thought we had to leave Wales. It was not my work or my wish. The first thing was our eldest daughter's marriage. That deprived the household and the little farm of one of the chief workers — because she went away to live with her farmer husband in Sussex. Then the Attwater family went to North Wales and that meant that another large part of the monastery buildings had to be looked after by us. So the physical domestic work and cleaning got very heavy for the mistress and the two remaining girls. But the final blow was the departure of Fr. Joseph Woodford. He suddenly had to be hurried to Switzerland on account of his lungs. So we were stranded without a chaplain and fifteen miles from Holy Mass; for the Caldy monks couldn't spare anyone to take Fr. Joseph's place. Well, you can't live in a place if the women folk aren't happy or satisfied. More depends on the women in country places than the man, or if not more then quite as much. But I believe it's more — in this sense: that if you take a little place in the country and men and women like it equally well, that's all right. If the woman likes it more than the man, that's all right too. But if the man likes it more than the woman, it won't work; it will be misery and a wreck. Because a contented woman is a better thing than any other of God's creatures and will make the most disgruntled man see the bright side of things. But there are no bright sides to anything with a discontented woman about the place. And here, surely, it will be obvious that I don't write with any resentment or complaint. It seems to be simply a 'law of nature'. Of course I know that the feminist ideal is not the contented housewife and mother of children — mother, bed-companion, helpmate and comforter, cook, housekeeper, baker and wine-maker, seamstress and broideress; and very likely farm manager and poultry and dairy-woman as well – no, the feminist ideal is 'the tired business woman' (and tinned food in the cupboard and tailor-made clothes and golf) and of course in that sort of world it doesn't matter tuppence where either of them lives. But I am writing of the ancient and natural (hence 'law of nature') life of men and women outside our commercial-industrialism, outside our big towns. And in that 'natural' world the domestic sphere must naturally be the woman's dominion. The man, whether farmer or craftsman (and that is the normal man, and the normal man has been and will be again the salvation of the world),[1] the man may rule the roost, as a sort or king and bishop, and it may be a real kingship, a real bishopric, he may really represent 'the shepherd and bishop of your souls', but without the woman he will be 'done in the eye' all the time. And if she isn't happy, if she hasn't got the place she wants, or the kind of place she wants, nothing the man can do can make it up to her – no more, in fact, than the woman can make it up to the man if he has got a rotten job – as generally now-a-days he has. If a woman thinks a woman's place is the home then that place has got to be hers, hers to make, hers to love and cherish (let the man guide and guard . . . ) and so it's got to be the place she wants, and that, among other things means that it's got to be a place she can work within her means and strength. Obviously.

I'm bothering, apparently but not truly overmuch, about this because it's one of the uppermost and most important problems of our day. The capitalist-industrial world has destroyed, more or less and rather more than less, the family and family life and the home. And women have succumbed. Men have lost their honour, their responsibility, their crafts, their workshops. Millions of them do not know it or desire anything different; they are happy to be conscript soldiers and conscript labourers.

[1] Farmer or craftsman – or both. The part-time *self-sufficiency* farmer – not the madman who spends his time working for the benefit of town dealers and town shops.

Millions of them have lost their work, their hope, their pride and their faith (do you really think the B.B.C. can comfort them in their souls or that City Institutes can bring 'art' to the masses?). The factory has produced a creature hardly able to be damned. And women have become factory slaves also – in millions. Barrenness is now a privilege. Babies are a curse. Motherhood is despicable. You could still find evidence to the contrary. You could still laugh me to scorn as an evil exaggerator. Your newspapers will support you. Your mayors and corporations and your health centres and your educational institutions will all stand together and tell us how good everything is getting – brighter schools, arts and crafts classes for the children, clinics for the babies . . . But you, reader, in spite of all that, can see which way the wind is blowing.

And the thing, now, is this, that if people, if *any* people, are going to break away from this city of destruction it must be in families. And if families are going to break away, more than half the physical determination, more than half the good will, more than half the cheerfulness and more than half the skill of mind and hand will have to be the woman's – at least as regards the job of breaking away and, still more *staying* away. Because the woman's job is in the home and if she hasn't a will for a home she'd better stay where homes aren't wanted. Of course I knew this as soon as we settled at Ditchling village. I knew it better on Ditchling Common, and better still when we went to Capel-y-ffin. If the women hadn't wanted to go there it would have been no use going. And so when the time came that they no longer wanted to stay, it was no use staying. In this case, of course, it was not at all a case of wanting to go back to Sodom or Bedlem, but simply of wanting a place of manageable proportions and in manageable conditions. So that when I, in a sort of desperation, said: well, it's 'right in or right out', no blooming suburbs anyway – and negotiated for a house with a back garden in Kilburn, it was only because the mistress didn't like the notion of town and no land and no animals, that we settled again in the country. Not that I was sorry, not that *I* wanted to live in the neighbourhood of Park Lane or the Houses of Parliament (though, it's no use pretending, it doesn't matter where your workshop is, so long as you're safely inside it . . . ) but simply that it wouldn't have been any good my buying a country estate if the women hadn't wanted to live on it.

Well, it wasn't such a bad move; for although we gave up a most astonishing fastness in the Black Mountains, as though 'some god had been the guide' we found an equally astonishing fastness in the Chiltern Hills. Suppose I had gone to an estate agent and had said to him: oh, man, find me a place just like this: not more than about an hour from London, because I've been living a hundred and sixty miles away and p'haps I ought to be a bit nearer the architects who employ me. It must be on a hill with a lane up to it, so steep that no one will ever want to go up it unless they desperately want to see us and it must lead to nowhere else. The hill must be a spur of some range, so that it shall be cut off on three sides at least, and the steep hill sides shall be covered with beech forests. On the top of the hill shall be a nearly flat plateau of about twenty acres of grass and arable land and in the very middle of the plateau, thus well separated though still sheltered by the trees there shall be a quadrangle of decent English brick buildings – a quadrangle mind you – because I'm not living in anything else but quadrangles. I had one at Lincoln's Inn. I had a small one on Ditchling Common and a fairly big one in Wales, so I know it's the only decent way to live. And the quadrangle shall consist partly of dwelling houses and party of storehouses, stables, barns and workshops. And when I say 'decent English brick buildings', I mean precisely that. I don't want any of your picturesque half-timbering or side-ways effects – just plain building of a good period of brickwork – as straight and ship-shape as may be. Now get on with it. Do you think he would find it? Well, no. So naturally I didn't do anything like that. We looked at lots of sales prospectuses but the places were either gentlemen's castles or picturesque farm-houses all tumbling down and crooked. That's why I went to Kilburn. Right in or right out – and not merely in a geographical sense, but in every other sense too, something really good and proper, or else something under the wings of the police, cut and dried and the drains inspected.

And there! just after I'd got the lease drawn up, but while it was still unsigned (what a hairbreadth it is between getting off scot free and having to pay three years' rent or what not!) she was told of a place in Buckinghamshire – my future son-in-law told her because his father lived down near there – and so she said she'd go and see it and I said: it's no good, but go all the same; it'll be a nice expedition. And she went, and she came back and reported the very place I'd described to the imaginary house-agent . . . So we sold all that we had and bought it and as it was horribly out of repair and entirely free from any modern encumbrances – and at the top of a hill, 1 in 6, we got it for five hundred down and the rest on the bank.[1]

So in October 1928 we packed up at Capel-y-ffin and having hired two railway trucks and two large and one small pantechnicons from Abergavenny and filled them up and sent them off, we followed ourselves in a Ford lorry with the mistress and the girls and Laurie Cribb and his wife and baby (swung in a basket in the roof of the lorry – the baby, not the wife) and our boy Gordian and Charlie Smith the driver and cats and dogs and chickens and all sorts of odds and ends left out of the pan- (but not completely 'pan') technicons. And of course the tin lizzie wouldn't mount the hill, so we unloaded half-way up and then the pantechniconians and the rest of us all sat down, when it was ready, to a grand supper of bacon and eggs in the new house having unloaded sufficient tables and benches for the purpose. And I remember the first night there – leaning out of the window and hearing the unbelievable silence. In Wales we had

[1] But I would like to record that if Eric Kennington had not just recently bought a statue of mine for an exorbitant price, we should not have had the five hundred high and dry.

never ceased to hear the everlasting streams. Capel-y-ffin, Abergavenny! And now Pigotts, Speen, Bucks. What more Welsh or more English. . . . For the next three years we did repairs, but by June we'd got a chapel made and blessed and approved and the first Mass at Pigotts was said by Fr. John O'Connor on June 7th, 1929.

Thus a certain consummation was reached and a meeting of extremes. And just as physical love is the centre of our life as men and women, so the Holy Mass is the centre of our life as Christians. It is impossible for me to write what ought to be written about the Mass and I shall not presume to attempt it. It is not essential to the purpose of this book that I should tell what others have told much better. I could but make a sort of echo to what Cardinal Newman wrote in *Loss and Gain*. The Mass and the Eucharist are not only the centre of Christian worship[1] they are also the centre of Christian merry-making. I say I shall not attempt to expound this. I can only confess it. From the beginning it was so and it was so from *my* beginning also. I had all sorts of ideas about the Church as ruler and guide. I would, I think, have sought to be received even though I had been living in some place where for some reason or other the Mass was never celebrated. But that was not my lot. And just as, in my mind, the Christianity enunciated by St. John and St. Paul is the necessary counterpart of the Christianity enunciated by the other Evangelists, so the Church as sacrificing priest is the necessary counterpart of the Church as the living voice. And just as Calvary was the necessary consummation of Christ's life, so the Eucharist is the necessary consummation of our life in Him.

Therefore it was that the establishment of the chapel at

[1] And that is why it is, at the present time, so desirable that the altar should be the central object in our churches. Incidentally, such a placing of the altar would revitalize our church architecture. The shape of churches would be transformed and the inside would again be the determining factor.

Pigotts was the consummation of things. Our earthly life is symbolized by the bread and wine. Under the appearance of bread and wine God gives himself to us. Thus we are made sharers of His Divinity who saw fit to share our humanity. Thus man who was made in the beginning with the dignity of God's image, is yet more wonderfully renewed. I am saying these things by way of confession. I would not have anyone think that I became a catholic because I was *convinced* of the truth, though I *was* convinced of the truth. I became a catholic because I fell *in love* with the truth. And love is an experience. I saw. I heard. I felt. I tasted. I touched. And that is what lovers do.

And lest anyone should think that in this devotion to the Mass, to the Blessed Sacrament, to the Holy Eucharist I am devoted to an abstraction, to a purely intellectual and even aesthetic catholicism (not that such things are to be despised or rejected) I must say this: the Real Presence which we affirm is the real presence of the man Jesus. Let no one suppose that because we adore him in spirit we do not adore him in our hearts. Very God, yes. And dear Jesus also. He speaks to us and we speak to him. We kiss the hem of his garment, we also thank him for our bread and butter. He ordained that our bodily motions should be pleasant and gratifying and that the pleasure of marriage should be beyond the dreams of avarice. He ordained the thunderstorms and the lion's voracity; he also blessed the daisies and the poor. He sits in judgment; he is also friend and brother.

And I say it was a meeting of extremes. Because the extreme of God's love of men touched the extreme of my love of myself. It is one of the difficulties of this book that I must always be appearing on a higher plane than that to which I properly belong — or, in case, *per impossibile*, I under-rate myself, at least I must always be omitting the evidence of my sinfulness. And it is a hateful situation. I do not want to appear other than I am — partly because of the untruth, partly because it is all such *nonsense*, this convention, this police convention, this drawing-room convention of reticence in matters which we know are vital to our judgment, and partly because of the unreality. But there is perhaps one comfort. It is this: we human beings are all in the same difficulty. We are all torn asunder, *all of us*, by this disintegration of our flesh and our spirit. And so if in this book I am appearing more spiritual than is credible to some of those I have loved, let them examine their own consciences. I think they will discover, as I have done, that they also are torn asunder and that they also have desired to be made whole.

## 4. JERUSALEM

The removal from Wales[1] to Pigotts, Speen, Bucks, though not undertaken with any such purpose in view, brought about a return to sculpture. At Capel-y-ffin I hadn't had any but small carving jobs, either because architects and people got the idea that I was too far away, or just because there didn't happen to be work for me to do. As I have said, I wasn't worrying, because I had plenty of lettering work and wood-engraving. But no sooner did we get to Pigotts than sculpturing works began pouring in.

From a worldly point of view the most important of these were the carvings at Broadcasting House and the enormous bas reliefs at the League of Nations building at Geneva. The former from my point of view are a failure. I mean simply that I don't much like looking at them. The idea was grand but I was incapable of carrying it out adequately. Prospero and Ariel! Well, you think. *The Tempest* and romance and Shakespeare and all that stuff. Very clever of the B.B.C. to hit on the idea, Ariel and aerial. Ha! Ha! And the B.B.C. kidding itself, in the approved manner of all big organizations (British or foreign, public or private), that it represents all that is good and noble

[1] Two years after we left Capel-y-ffin we bought the place from its Bene-dictine owners and now our eldest daughter lives there.

and disinterested – like the British Empire or Selfridges (and the U.S. Constitution and the Comité des Forges, not to mention our superb and all-powerful and all-pure Nordic race). But wait. Read *The Tempest*. I don't know anything about Shakespeare's intentions, but it didn't seem to me to be unduly straining the poem to see in the figure of Prospero much more than that of a clever old magician, or in that of Ariel more than that of a silly fairy. Had not Prospero power over the immortal Gods? At any rate it seemed to be only right and proper that I should see the matter in as bright a light as possible and so I took it upon me to portray God the Father and God the Son. For even if that were not Shakespeare's meaning it ought to be the B.B.C.'s.

Then I had the amazing honour of the job at Geneva. This was to be the British Government's gift for the adornment of the new building. I don't know who suggested that it should take the form of a work of sculpture – but Anthony Eden seemed to be very keen on it, and I was asked if I would undertake it. So I went to Geneva to see the building and to discuss the project with the politicians and secretaries on the spot. The site chosen (in the foyer of the League Council Hall) was a frieze fifty-five feet long and about eight feet high – and of course, it instantly occurred to me that the most suitable subject in the world, and one which would go very well in the space, was 'The Turning out of the Money Changers'. For as I tried to explain to the Secretary General (whom I afterwards discovered to have been formerly in the French Ministry of Finance) and to other people at the party to which I was invited, that more than anything else was what the League of Nations ought to be engaged upon – the ridding of Europe and the World of the stranglehold of finance, both national and international. It seemed obvious to me and in my innocence I thought the League of Nations would jump to the idea. I didn't mean that international bankers were the cause of all evil, but that the money-making motive was paramount in our affairs so that all valuations other than those in £ s. d. were neglected. Consequently commercialism was not only rampant in every little village hut, as it was in every little heart, but also in all government departments and in international affairs. And so on! The idea was received quite coldly. One American financial delegate said that if such a sculpture were put up it would be 'the last and greatest hypocrisy of the British Empire'. And of course I quite saw that. In the end the idea was turned down because it was 'too Christian' . . . It was ruled that nothing specifically Christian must be represented, for fear of giving offence to the Jews and the Turks and others, but that if I liked to suggest a subject from the Old Testament, that would be acceptable as that book was in good odour with all except atheists and 'we needn't worry about *them*'. So I proceeded on those lines and the result is that there, in the middle of that monstrous exhibition of dead architecture and pseudo-modernity, is a colossal representation of the recreation of Adam with a great text proclaiming the overmastery of God and in smaller side panels children and animals echoing the same sentiment. I fear the American financial delegate still has good cause for jeers. That work took from 1935 to 1938.

But from the point of view from which I am writing this book, the most important sculpturing job I had in these years was the carving of ten panels on the New Museum at Jerusalem—a noble building. This involved my staying in the Holy Land for four months in 1934 and I went again in 1937. Except for our stays at Salies-de-Béarn I have never been away from England so long. I have been to Ireland several times on lecturing business (on one occasion I arrived a week too soon. So I went to Galway and the Aran Islands for the week) and to Scotland on the same business. I had a fortnight in Germany in 1930 when I went to work at Count Kessler's press at Weimar (he took me for drives round the Thuringewald several times, and as we went along the roads under the fruit trees we often saw young men who held out their arms as we passed. I asked Kessler what they did that for. He said: 'Oh, they're followers of a man called Hitler and that's their sign. . . .' It seems odd to think that was in

June 1930 and now it's only June 1940). I went a lot of times to Paris though never for more than a week at a time and I went several times to Italy though only to Rome and Rapallo, and to Rome only for nine days altogether. So, apart from Salies and Jerusalem, I don't consider that I have come much under the influence of foreign parts or foreign people.

I have tried to say what Salies meant to us. I wish I could properly assess the influence of Jerusalem. I was exceedingly fortunate to have the work there. I'm no particular good at travelling – in fact very bad at it, much too worried about the luggage and the tickets and I can't sleep in trains – I don't like sight-seeing or acquiring information and I am no good at foreign languages. So unless I've got a job to do I'd rather stay at home. But at Jerusalem I had work, and a good long job. And it involved my working on the scaffold in the open sun with all the Arab workmen. I wore Arab clothes, which means dressing more splendidly than European kings and princes, and hob-nobbed with Laurie Cribb who came with me, in Arab cafés and suqs.[1] It was altogether splendid – surely it must have been influential.

For Palestine is the Holy Land. That was the most notable and even the most noticeable thing about it, and yet there are people who go there who say they don't notice it. They say they think Jerusalem very disappointing. But to me it was like living with the Apostles. It was like living in the Bible. It was the antithesis of everything our England stands for. You can hardly think of anything which the two countries have in common except our common humanity and in England that is overlaid, corrupted and debauched by every kind of inhuman

[1] And, I must add, we had the most splendid thirst. We broke all the prudent rules (except that we kept off whisky) and drank all we could get – the wine from Latrun, by some held to be Emmaus, and red wine that the Dominicans gave us and lemonade. You can't imagine how like heaven it seemed to drink iced lemonade in a dark cool café in David Street. It was imprudent because we sweated so much, but it was worth it. And after all we were only there for four months. Such a thirst was not made to be wasted.

nonsense, whereas in Palestine, among the Arabs, it is upper-most and unspoiled. I am not saying there is nothing wrong in Palestine. Wherever there are men there is sin and violence and selfishness and disease. Moreover there are poor in Palestine poorer than anything we can conceive in our up-to-date towns. In spite of all that it is the Holy Land and they live a holy life, whereas England is unholy and people can only live holy lives in secret.

I think it is no use my writing thus. I cannot prove what I say. I can hardly find anyone to agree. The English in Palestine and the Jews seem to conceive it to be their mission to reform everything and to turn the Arabs into good Europeans. And there is so much that is irresistible in their reforms. The water supply of Jerusalem is now good and plentiful whereas formerly it was scanty and poisoned. Malaria has been abolished. Ophthalmia is being steadily dealt with. Banditry is being suppressed. The wresting of the land from the selfish grasp of absentee landlords. The agricultural, arboricultural and horticultural work of the young Zionist colonies, as it seemed to me, superb in itself and of great educational benefit to the Arabs. The work of the Hebrew University, and of the Jewish hospitals and clinics . . . These things are good. Are they not? But then, on the other side . . . Except in the old city of Jerusalem, where the streets are only footways, motor cars and motor omnibuses are every-where. Everywhere there is importation of the cheap mass products of Europe and Japan. The smart modern Jews are building smart modern towns and introducing smart modern ways, including smart modern prostitution . . . and smart modern factories, and smart modern clothes. Are these things good? They are not.

But the discussion of such judgments is beyond the scope of this book. I only want to, somehow, make it clear that since going to Palestine my mind is pervaded by a different order of living – an order previously only guessed at, but now experienced – an order not only human but essentially holy. 'Know ye not that you are the temple of God and that the spirit of God dwelleth in you? But if any man violate the temple of God, him shall God destroy. For the temple of God is holy, *which you are.*' Which *you* are! that is the point . . . Oh they are lousy in Palestine. Lousy with disease, lousy with spiritual vermin too. Are we lousy in England? No, no we are not. Are we not lousy spiritually? No, no – the words have no meaning any more. Don't think I saw no bad in Palestine. There was bad everywhere. But the good was not yet dead.

I am not going to write about beautiful things (which I should very likely never have seen at all but for the friendship and enthusiasm of Austen Harrison, the architect – on whom be peace) the beauty of the Judean desert, the beauty of Siloam, the beauty of Justinian's church at Bethlehem, not even the beauty of the Haram at Jerusalem, the Moslem holy place, the most beautiful place I have ever seen and the farthest removed from the Bank of England and all its devil worship, the most civilized, the most cultured, the most quiet and serene, the most spacious, the most spiritually pervaded place now remaining in the whole world. Tell me where there is another. Is it in London, in Trafalgar Square? . . . Is it the Place de la Concorde? . . . Is it on the Acropolis at Athens? They tell me that is very lovely, but at Jerusalem living men worship the living God; at Athens there is but a memory of what was . . . Is it even in the Piazza of St. Peter's? No, not there. That is a grand and solemn place, the gigantic arms inviting the concourse of all the children of men; but it is an impious work – architecture, swagger, human prowess, human greatness . . . The face of Christ has been more defiled by our praise than by spittle – for we have not praised him, but ourselves.

Palestine was the last of the revelations vouchsafed to me. It confirmed and enfolded all the others. And it was a twofold revelation. In the Holy Land I saw a holy land indeed; I also saw, as it were eye to eye, the sweating face of Christ. The half-ruinous church of the Holy Sepulchre at Jerusalem, the half-ruinous church of the Nativity at Bethlehem, these things are symbolical; and we are incapable of renovating them. And that fact is more than a symbol. For what could we do? The government of Caesar could employ learned and sympathetic architects and archaeologians and engineers. We could employ a joint-stock limited-liability company of contractors from Khartoum or Stamboul and they could employ a horde of 'hands'. And American millionaires could subscribe the money – very good men, I dare say, but very bad money – the proceeds of usury and robbery. And then we should have a nice brand-new Holy Sepulchre – very refined and correct according to the style of the Crusaders, and a nice brand-new Church of the Nativity – very correct and refined according to the style of Justinian and Byzantium.

But I don't believe it will happen. By the inscrutable decree of God the sweat is not thus to be wiped from his face. He suffers less if the Copts and the Greeks and the Romans quarrel among themselves than if, having abandoned the Cross, they hand the whole notion of salvation to the sanitary authority. That is what our civilization is seeking to do. That has not yet happened at Jerusalem. They have not yet rendered to Caesar the things that are God's.

Far then from finding disappointment in Palestine I found only good; for I found the divine beauty. And it was a double good; for I saw not only the beauty but the tears and sweat. Illusion fell away. The nonsensical and illusory grandeurs of Rome, Rome, the Holy City, decked out in the finery of Ball Rooms and Banks, the soul-ensnaring magnificence of statistical display, the grand appearance of doctrinal and ethical unity . . . It seemed to me that we should do better to eschew our grandeurs and forget our numbers – and brag less about unity while, to the heathen and the pagans and the infidels, the most conspicuous thing about Christians is their sectarian disunity (and this we symbolize with a diabolical precision by our bloody fights in the Holy Sepulchre itself – fights stopped only by the police and

Moslem police at that) and their only unity is a merely secular
one. For while we fight among ourselves about doctrine we are
united in the common worship of money and material success.
Here I do not exaggerate. That is the awful thing.

But let nothing I say be taken as implying disloyalty to the
Roman Church, mother and mistress, or to the Holy Father,
Vicar indeed of Christ. There is of course a sense in which the
Church and her adherents are one and the same, so that what is
true of one is true of the others, and when they are guilty, she
is condemned. But in another sense it is not so. She wears
the garb of time and place, and that garb is subject to corruption.
As pride and vain-glory afflict us, so is she afflicted. The natural
tendency of all strong institutions to pharisaism cannot be
avoided. Governors and administrators must always see things
from their professional standpoint. Vested interests spring up,
both temporal and spiritual. And how easy it is to deceive ourselves into thinking that the 'precious ointment' has been
provided for his burial, when perhaps it really has been provided
only for our own satisfaction and when, moreover, it is only
precious in the sense that it is cost money and is not otherwise
precious at all, being merely 'made in Birmingham'.

And one thing has become increasingly clear to me and it is
very important. Accusations against the Church can only be
substantiated by Church Doctrine! Do the Christian clergy and
laity side with the rich against the poor? Many seem to do so.
And is it wrong? You may well think so. But how will you
prove it but by recourse to Christian teaching? Is not much of
our worship both vain and vain-glorious? And is not vanity
reprehensible and vain-glory noxious to the Lord of Hosts?
How will you prove these things but from Holy Writ and the
lives of the Saints? And if you are annoyed by the policeman-like
frame of mind of many of the clergy and their apparent conviction
that the spirit killeth but the letter quickeneth (so that you
would think getting to heaven was a business of going 'by the
book') you must still remember that the opposite doctrine is

Christian teaching and that it is the authority to which they themselves appeal who is the judge. And if the Church in Europe and America is full of disease of spirit, lukewarm, pharisaical and subservient to the powers of this world and full of enthusiasm for the material advantages with which science and machinery have seduced us, there is still the Holy Land and, in spite of its poverty, we still think it holy.

What I am struggling to say is that while I never saw or imagined anything more lovely than the Holy Land – whether you think of it as a land or as human habitations, so also I never saw anything less corrupted by human pride and sin. And I understood as never before the virtue of poverty and how peace on earth can have no other basis. I saw a vision of all the peoples of the earth struggling ceaselessly with one another for material possessions and material advantages. And I saw that the greater the material success so much the more frightful must be the struggle. For the competition for riches means a ceaseless spurring of men's powers of invention in weapons and methods of destruction, until in the end, as Pope Pius XII said almost immediately after his election: 'In this age of mechanization the human person becomes merely a more perfect tool in industrial production and . . . a perfected tool for mechanized warfare.' And thus men will perish in the ruins of their degraded cities, perish with curses in their hearts, curses upon a life which was lived in misery and is ending in frightful fear.

And I saw that the only people who lived in holiness and dignity were those who lived in poverty of spirit. Blessed be ye poor; for yours is the kingdom of God. It was in the Holy Land that that lesson had first been taught. It was in the Holy Land that that lesson could still be learned. And it became clear that it is no use renouncing war unless we first of all renounce riches. That is the awful job before us. A whole world crazy for material riches and the Christians as crazy as anyone else – giving secret love to Christ but in their lives contradicting themselves. A whole world doomed to perpetual fighting – and no remedy but to persuade it to renounce riches. What a forlorn hope!

So I came back from Palestine with my mind made up – or at least on the way to it. But this was not going to make things easy. Henceforward I must take up a position even more antagonistic to my contemporaries than that of a mere critic of the mechanistic system. I must take a position antagonistic to the very basis of their civilization. And I must appear antagonistic even to the Church itself. Of course that is all nonsense but that is how it must appear. For the Christians everywhere have committed themselves to the support of capitalist-industrialism and therefore to the wars in its defence, mechanized war to preserve mechanized living, while I believe that capitalism is robbery, industrialism is blasphemy and war is murder.

I had not realized this. I had been misled by the romanticism of my childhood and youth. And I had been misled by the logic of medieval Christian theology. For according to the theologians war is not always unjustifiable and is therefore not always murder. A war of defence for instance, the defence of home and country against an unjust aggressor (like the defence of a man's home and family against robbers) provided it be conducted in a just manner and with a reasonable chance of success, is a just war. But nothing can justify actual sin and direct evil may not be done that good may come. You may not mutilate prisoners, or slay non-combatants. And you may not spread false reports of your enemies' evil deeds or promote a propaganda of hate and ill-will. I had assumed that war to-day was as likely to be just as wars of the past. But now my eyes were opened. And I saw that just as modern capitalism could not justly claim that it merited Christian support because it upheld the sacred rights of property (because for one kind of property it preserved it destroyed a hundred, and the kind of property it chiefly destroyed was the very kind that Christian philosophers were most anxious to preserve – the personal property of the peasant and small craftsman), so modern war had become a totally different business from that envisaged by the medieval theologians.

And just as capitalists see everything in terms of saleability; thus they must naturally see labour also. Labour is something to be bought and sold at its competitive or market price. We are blind to the monstrous, the devilish inhumanity and therefore blasphemy of this theory and the practice founded upon it. How can a man and his wife feed and clothe their family in a human and holy manner if they are thus treated as mechanisms. We do not treat animals thus. A horse must have his proper food and shelter whatever happens but a motor car needs oil and petrol only when it is being used. The capitalist treatment of human beings is like the treatment of machines. Do not think this revolutionary theory is a new thing. It is stated clearly in the Gospel in the parable of the labourers, and we Christians do not merely deny our humanity in supporting capitalism; we also deny Christ. Whether a man works one or twelve hours he lives the *whole* day. It is that division of men into wage-earners and others which constitutes the class division and necessitates the 'class war'. The wage-earners are simply instruments to be exploited for profit, the rest of men are the exploiters. And thus as Christians unjustly hide behind the Christian teaching on war and capitalism, so they unjustly defend the 'wage-system'. For though some men will always prefer to be wage-earners and some will willingly choose to take wages occasionally, a system which deprives the majority of men of ownership of the means of production and drives them to the irresponsible labour of industrialism, is in its nature ungodly and anti-Christian.

And thinking over these things I saw the hypocrisy of my country and its politicians. I remembered the jingo imperialism of my childhood and youth. The wars of petty conquest which we had been brought up to think heroic. And I remembered the condemnation of the Israelitish landowner who sought to 'add field to field', and I saw that the same condemnation was due to the state which sought to add colony to colony. And I saw the hypocrisy of all the blather about 'the white man's burden'. And I saw how the British were not only responsible for the beginnings of capitalist-industrialism and for its monstrous financial developments, but also for the imperialism which was its inevitable result. And I saw the mad foolishness of our British prophets and their racial pride and swagger – Kipling with his 'verily we are the people' and his damned talk about 'the lesser breeds without the law' – the 'traitor clerks' who won fame and riches by pandering to the ambitions of vulgar money-makers. I had long since learned the truth about South Africa, but I had not seen clearly, until I went to Palestine, the dirty materialism which inspired all modern militarism, nor the impossible ungodliness of modern mechanical war-making.

But one thing was clear: I must keep clear of *politics* – politics as the word is understood in our time and in what are called democratic countries. And I must keep clear of politicians – the gang of professional parliamentarians and town and county councillors. For in the first place politics is beyond me. Politics is like foreign languages – something outside my scope, something I can't do. Moreover I do not believe political arrangements and re-arrangements are real. It is all a confused business of ramps and rackets – pretended quarrels and dishonest commercial schemings, having no relation to the real interests of peoples, neither to their spiritual nor their material welfare, and conducted upon no principles other than momentary self-interest. The prestige of parliament is an empty fraud and all its grandiose and clumsy procedure is more outworn and even less venerable than the ritual in Anglican cathedrals. And politics is now a profession! Professionalism is a curse in any trade – the defence of anything, without due consideration of its goodness, on account of pecuniary interest or inertia. Public schools, the army, the law, architecture and, most frightful, the Church, all suffer from the curse of professionalism, though all these are served by trained and honestly devoted men. But politicians, as I have remarked before, can make no such claim to our respect. It is not too much to say that they are trained to nothing but vote-catching, and they are not and they never have been anything but agents for the defence of the monetary interests. Such was the origin of parliamentary representation, such is its very soul. This is no place for even the briefest outline of parliamentary history; it is only necessary to note that all its evils have been grossly augmented since the final and decisive victory of finance which the nineteenth century witnessed. There is now no hope of a reform of our society by parliamentary means.

'Religion is politics, politics is brotherhood,' said William Blake, and, I may add: 'Brotherhood is poverty and poverty is peace'. That is where I found myself and that is where I shall remain.

## 5. ESCAPADES

I seem to have been always escaping from somewhere or something and then crabbing the thing I've escaped from. As though the joy of getting away wasn't enough, I have to turn round and throw stones. It neither looks nor feels heroic. It's nobody's notion of loyalty and patriotism. I think a formal and humble apology is required and I hope this whole book will answer the purpose. But I have a sort of excuse. Though I am sure it was never intended, seven times I've been like a bird in a cage and could only escape by repudiating the kindness of my captors. No, of course, they weren't captors but I was caught all the same.

First of all I was caught in the art-school at Chichester. If I hadn't been really rude, I'd be there still. You can't imagine the trapped feeling I had when I found myself regarded as a promising winner of South Kensington prizes and a likely candidate for the post of art-master. Whether you want it or not you find yourself in the awful position of the recipient of friendship and favours and help and kindness of all sorts who knows that though everything has been done out of pure kindness and good-will, yet, if he rejects it, he will be thought both ungrateful and a traitor. How many candidates for the priesthood have thus been trapped?

It's the curse of kindness. However I did escape and luckily for me, my parents aided and abetted me; for the architectural career seemed much more promising than that of an art-master and our cathedral friends were willing to help with the fees.

But then I landed myself when the time came, in the still nastier business of repudiating architecture. And this time it was really pretty serious. I don't profess to understand myself. There are only bad words to describe my behaviour. Look at the money they spent on me and the kindness in other ways (my fees paid and free board and lodging). And then at the end I didn't even consult them, neither my parents nor the bene-factors. I just, so to say, walked out on them – took up an entirely different line of work and one which they could not, with their conventions and traditions, regard otherwise than a betrayal of my family, my education (i.e. the education I was supposed to have had) and my friends – a workman's job. What a downfall of all their hope and pride! But with unerring (unerring, I say, not inerrant) instinct I did the only thing possible. I knew how impossible it would be either to argue them round or even to argue with them. You do not gather figs of thistles. Then how can you expect Anglican parsons and cathedral prebendaries to understand, still less approve, of an architect turning lettercutter – why not crossing sweeper and have done with it? – and when I said why not indeed? they thought I was simply rude – and mad. But such conversations occurred later. At the time I saw that there was nothing for it but just to go off and do what I had to do. To ask permission would be to ask for prohibition; to explain would be to flout their whole world. I had learned things about the world of work which they, with their gentleman's notions of sitting in offices and telling other people to do things, had not the faintest conception of – not at that date. Things are not, in this respect, quite so bad now, but, on the other hand, other things are much worse. . . .

So I had to chuck architecture and tell the kind friends afterwards and if possible live the disgrace down. And I must say they were exceedingly kind and didn't make half as much fuss as they might have done. (I think I must have rather won them over by penmanship. It's a funny thing, but people are happy to think that writing with a pen is a much more genteel job than inscribing with a chisel.) And their kindness was all the more remarkable because my defection from architecture coincided with my defection from Anglicanism. That was another thing I escaped from. In that case of course there were no vested interests involved, but the toils were toils all the same. Directly any consideration whatever is given to public opinion or the approval of friends and relations you are in the toils and should beware. It's something considered disgraceful, something shameful, something you owe it to *them* not to do. 'Be not a respecter of persons' . . . but don't they make it difficult? . . . and one must not forget that it isn't only the old 'fogies' that thus make your struggle for integrity difficult. There are the young fogies too, and I should think they are almost worse, at any rate they seem more wicked. If the young seem traitors to the old how much more traitorous do the young seem to the young! You can forgive the old, for with a little patience you can see that you can't expect anything different, but with the *young* snobs and the *young* sycophants, the *young* hangers-on of the academies and, above all the young *respectables* there is nothing to be done. And so the young rebels do not only rebel, they also blaspheme.

But though I escaped from architecture I must acknowledge that I owe an unrepayable debt to those three years of pupilage. If it could be arranged I think all young painters and sculptors, and even poets and musicians, should have some years of training in architectural drawing and building work. It formalizes and objectivizes the head and hand and most important of all, it makes evident and constant to the mind the fact that in the art of building all other arts are embraced and entertained.

And though it would be absurd to say that no one can appreciate good building or understand its significance who has not
had that training, nevertheless I think that, having had it, I was
laid open to influences which would otherwise have been less
potent and less salutary. So when I went to Chartres in 1907
and 1908, it was not merely with an eye to the outward appearance of a good building but with some power of appreciating its
structural substance.

And if you sit in front of such a thing and stare at it hard for
a week, probing its very guts, surely it must do something to
your mind for good. I have been to Chartres nine times – to see
the western doorways, the north transept, the sight of the apse
from the eastern terrace, the western windows and, finally, as
embracing all the rest, because it is what all the rest is for, the
sight of the whole interior from beside the western piers.
Beauvais is a more fantastical feat of stone engineering. Le Mans
with its flaming glass commemorating the martyrs, has the most
perfectly poised and leaping buttresses. But I don't see how any
one can say that the Church of the Blessed Virgin at Chartres is
not the most perfectly proportioned stone building in the world,
the holiest work of masonry. How can you judge unless you
have travelled all over the earth and seen all the others? But it's
not so difficult as all that, because only in northern Europe was
the business of building in stone rationally approached and not
much travelling is necessary to see that choice is restricted to a
very small number of buildings in a small part of northern France.
You may prefer round to pointed arches or you may prefer to
have no arches at all. You may prefer the basilica of St. Mary in
Cosmedin at Rome or the little church at Daphne. You may
prefer the church of the Holy Wisdom at Stambul. I am not
saying you would be wrong. But I am writing about *stone*
building – building done according to the nature of stone, stuff
that will stand a lot of squeezing but very little bending – and I
am only saying that among all the holy things that men have made
the church at Chartres is the best of those made of stone. Per-

haps the point is too obscure. It would not be fair to people of to-day to expect them to appreciate the point. They have for so long become accustomed to the use of stone simply as a material for theatrical camouflage and their own work gives them no training in such things. For men of business, shop-assistants, factory hands, lorry drivers, coolies, there is only one technique (apart from cricket and football), that of mechanical engineering, which is matter of common knowledge and enthusiasm. But that should be sufficient. If only they would forget all that art-critics write and all about architectural styles, and look at medieval building as what it was – engineering in the *stone* age, they would be able to understand it. For the enthusiasm which held their minds in medieval Europe must have been very much like our enthusiasm for *metal* engineering, and the development of medieval stone building was, as regards technical method, simply the intelligent application of principles discovered by practical experiment. And then having thus rid our minds of art nonsense we might be in a better position to appreciate the qualities in which that building does really differ from our engineering. We might appreciate the fact that in the absence of commercial domination the criterion of good was not merely saleability and that, though individual men were as sinful and selfish as we are, they were led and moved and even enthralled by a religious conception of man's nature and destiny, while we are led and moved and enthralled by no conception more noble than the material magnification of comfort – how to make more things for sale and how to transport them more and more rapidly away from the coolies who make them in order to sell them to people who will pay more for them. And the proof of these things is to be seen in the works they have left for our reproof.

But again we are in a difficulty, for just as we are unaccustomed to appreciate the qualities of stone building as a technical method, so we are unaccustomed to appreciate the qualities of human work as a religious ritual. Such a notion seems completely and utterly to have departed from our life. How is it conceivable to factory coolies or to city business men that their daily work might be and *should be* as much a ritual as the conducting of a church ceremony? We have the dregs of such a conception in our notions of decency and politeness, but what dregs! The idea that every action is, rightly seen, a ritual action, an action pertaining to worship, and that all things made are, rightly seen, objects of religious use is not only foreign but almost abhorrent to us. And so we talk about art and *religious* art, and music and *religious* music, and we don't see that because all things have meaning, they must mean something good or bad, holy or unholy, and must minister however feebly, however powerfully, either to our salvation or to our damnation. Yet that conception of life and work, far from being eccentric and peculiar and abnormal, is, in the long history of man's life on this planet, the most common and widespread. It is *our* way of thinking that is odd and unnatural. Our boasted enlightenment is, after all, nothing but the cool-headedness of people who don't happen to be in love. Our boasted religious toleration is, after all, only religious indifference. We don't know where we are going and so we don't know a fair wind from a foul one. How can we possibly know the holy from the unholy. That is the point of all this diversion — that somehow some grace descended on me, a grace of knowledge, of apprehension. 'Oh taste and see how gracious the Lord is.' I did taste. I did see. And though when I first went there, in 1907, I was not aware of such things in these words, I was inebriated with more than a sensual delight; for my sensual delight was, as sensual delight should be: an attraction to the truth.

It is not perhaps either seemly or true to say that I escaped from the Church of England, though I fear I have been guilty of crabbing her on occasion, but I can certainly claim to have escaped from Science — science understood as the arch-enemy of religion. I began to be ensnared in my childhood, and that was our father's doing. Like so many people at that time he was a great worshipper at the shrine of the telescope and, though to a less degree, the microscope. Sir Robert Ball was the great popular lecturer. 'He brought the heavens home to you,' as Max Beerbohm said. And our father believed in Sir Robert Ball and took me to one of his great popular expositions at the Dome, in Brighton. We heard a lot about the wonders of the heavens and the immensity of space. And of course we heard a lot about the smallness of the earth and how humble we should feel. The wonders of the microscope were not forgotten, but somehow they took a very back seat – not that they weren't equally wonderful, but that they weren't equally memorable. So I was brought up with a proper Victorian reverence for the great discoverers and their discoveries.

But under the disintegrating influence of 'the chaps at the office', and, a little later, of the Rationalist Press Association, I grew out of and threw off our father's Tennysonian romanticism and became more definitely scientific, Huxleyian, Darwinian, Spencerian. The notion of a divine providence co-existing with material cause and effect became less and less credible – too absurd! And when you consider your fellow men and women, and the millions of them, and how they carry on, it *is* difficult, is it not? H. G. Wells's book called *Anticipations* was very influential in these years and especially the essay called *The Fallibility of the Instrument* (or a similar title) in which Wells demonstrated a truth which it was most important for me to learn, that 'you can't shoot the square-root of two with a gun'. If only the world would get hold of that truth what a different place it would be! But though I saw the point and bore it in mind, it was a long time before It became affective. 1 was still under the spell of the universal non-sequitur: that because man is small in size in relation to stellar space he is therefore relatively unimportant. It was a non-sequitur comparable to that attributed to Galileo: that because the earth turns on its axis therefore the Bible is untrue!

We love to have things big. Sir James Jeans is now carrying on the same campaign of deception and though the wonders of the microscope are no less wonderful than those of the tele-scope[1] men in general are still taken in by the talk of the astronomers. We still fail to see the truth enunciated, as I am told, by Descartes: that we are bounded by two infinities, the infinitely big and the infinitely little. But it did gradually dawn upon me, and at last I saw that all the stuff doled out to us by the Sir Robert Balls was dope, and that the total result to the efforts of astronomers and microscopists was, as regards the importance of man, exactly nothing for,

$$\frac{\text{Astronomy}}{\text{Microscopy}} = \text{as you were.}$$

And so the fact emerges: scientific research as commonly thought of is totally irrelevant to the real problem of man: what is he and why? It is not material measurement that is important but spiritual quality, and sanctity in life and work. The quality in things which makes them beautiful and holy, is the most impor-tant thing and the thing that physical science, by its very nature, cannot touch.

And, in addition to the debunking of Victorian scientific romance (though it is easy enough to understand the prestige of science in that period and our own when you consider the application of science to industry; for who cares whether anyone knows what electricity *is*, provided the electrical engineer can make electric trams *go*, besides, there's money in it), there came the realization that the whole conception of modern materialist thinkage is 'bilge'. We know no more what an inch of space is than what a watt of electricity is. Yet we talk as though it were all as clear as the elementary propositions of

[1] And indeed they may be thought *more* wonderful, for the complexities of anatomical and physiological structure are, at least *humanly* speaking, more to be wondered at than the mathematical evolutions of stars.

theology. We have forgotten that the further a thing is removed from 'matter', the more intelligible it is; and that therefore 'the most intelligible of all beings is God!' We talk lightly about 'solid' fact and yet we have little idea what a fact is and none at all what 'solid' means. The result of all this is to put 'Science' in its proper and very humble place—the devoted servant of industrialism, and nothing to do with anything of any real importance. Therefore however much value we may attach to pure research as enlarging the mind and informing it and as a discipline, we now see that the real things, the really important things, are on another plane altogether. To see all things in their eternal significance, that is what matters. Poor old Einstein, poor old Jeans. So I escaped from the toils and thought myself lucky.

I didn't escape from the Arts and Crafts movement – of course I could not. But the time came when I had to crab it all the same. And that was a good example of the ungentlemanliness to which my desperation leads me. The 'arts and crafts movement', a deliberate effort on the part of a group of persons, of which William Morris was the head, and figure-head as well, to resuscitate the handicrafts which industrialism and commercialism had destroyed, had led to the formation of the Arts and Crafts Exhibition Society, and this society had, since the eighties and nineties of the last century, been holding big national exhibitions of hand-made objects – things for the most part, if not absolutely exclusively, designed by those who made them and made by those who designed them. These exhibitions had won, and doubtless deservedly, a high fame and great prestige. And the standard of works shown at those exhibitions was, accepting their detachment from the common life of our times, a very high one. In furniture and textiles, in pottery and, after Edward Johnston's appearance, in lettering and writing, no better work was being done anywhere in the industrial world – for it was being done in the industrial world even though it was not being done by the industrial method. But what was the result? A considerable number of young men and women, and older ones too, were encouraged to re-enter the common trades and crafts, instead of 'going in for art', and were enabled, as I was, to earn their livings. Surely that was a good thing. But there were two snags and horrid barefaced crags they were. In the first place the sale of the things made was, quite inevitably, almost exclusively, among the rich middle and upper classes. You can't possibly make good tables and chairs and pots in price competition with industrial mass-production, and any argument, such as the kind art-critics wrote in the highbrow papers, to the effect that one good thing made 'to last' is better than a dozen unenduring and unendurable things made cheaply in the factory, had no effect whatever on the masses of the modern poor who were in the first place corrupted, like their masters, to an indescribable condition of vulgarity, ineptitude and sentimentality (for machine-facture necessarily destroys all power of discrimination in both producer and consumer), and who, in the second, did not read those highbrow papers or pay their shillings to visit such exhibitions. And the result of selling almost only to the rich means that you make only 'luxury' and luxurious articles, such as only the rich could want. (See note, p. 277).

That's one thing.

And then the other — the mass and semi-mass producing industrialists were not slow to see their opportunity. They were even urged to do so! For the design (and from the commercial point of view this means little more than the *appearance*) of commercial products was notoriously dull in spite of the Great Exhibition of 1851 and all the South Kensington art-schools, and these Arts and Crafts exhibitions were in effect a free presentation of new and fashionable designs. What a chance! And of course they took it. So there came into existence all the Liberty and Waring and Gillow and Heal tradition of supplying by factory methods, goods which, to the ordinary refined inhabitant of the suburbs and the provinces looked just like the genuine arts and crafts. Thus industrialism got a nice new lease of life among the quasi- and pseudo-educated with incomes from three hundred pounds a year upwards (or whatever it was in those far-off days when we jingled gold in our pokes), and thus they were able to do what it is death to them not to be able to do – make the world look better than it is.

That's the other.

And that was the main result of the Arts and Crafts Exhibition Society – to supply beautiful hand-made things to the rich, and imitation ditto to the not-so-rich. But as for wrecking commercial industrialism and resuscitating a human world – not a hint of it. And so I said the Arts and Crafts movement was a failure and then, when I published an article to that effect in the *Socialist Review* (December 1909) Lethaby said I was crabbing my mother. Dear Lethaby, he said it so kindly and I did feel a pig. But it's no use; those people (not Lethaby, but the others) would not see and could not, they will not and cannot see that no amount of educating the public by means of exhibitions will destroy the moral irresponsibility of the investor or the intellectual irresponsibility of the factory hand. But I never realized that the Arts and Crafts movement was my *mother*! I just took the Movement for granted and thought it only proper to say what seemed true. Just as before, when I deserted architecture, I was quite oblivious, till afterwards, of the kindness of those who had paid for me. I'm no gentleman and I don't understand loyalty to lost causes when the causes deserve to be lost.

Another thing I was entangled in concurrently with my entanglement in the Arts and Crafts movement and from which I had to make a more or less ignominious escape was the socialist movement. I had been a fairly enthusiastic member of the Fabian Society and had even got so far as to lecture to that earnest body of reformers. This was about the time when H. G. Wells was making his abortive onslaught upon it, and I was naturally on his side in the disputes. Indeed I ought to record that Wells was at that time, as he had been for some years previously and was for some years longer, a great influence on my mind and my respect for him was only equalled by my affection. He represented for me and he still represents:

> The struggling soul of man. . . .
> Always dissatisfied, unconvinced at last.

He is typical of humanity in all respects but one – he has never troubled to pretend to conform to principles and practices which in fact he disbelieves in and does not practise. In this respect he is indeed unique, and earns our special respect.

But my mind was moving away from the Wellsian standpoint towards or back to the metaphysical and spiritual bases from which I, like Wells himself, had departed. And I was doing so via Friedrich Nietzsche! There was a great wave of Nietzschean influence among us at that time, and I completely succumbed to it in company with a young Fabian woman with whom, largely on account of our mutual enthusiasm, I fell very much in love. All these things went very much together and formed between them a pretty complicated entanglement. My socialistic enthusiasm was perfectly genuine, so was my enthusiasm for Nietzsche (though *Zarathustra* was the only book of his I ever read – but I read that a great deal and worshipped it as a sacred scripture. And indeed it is a magnificent work, containing much profound wisdom as well as much splendid verbiage). And my love affair also was a genuine mixture of matter and spirit – both real and both good. I lived for a short time in a sort of exaltation, imagining that all things were possible – that jealousy could not exist in such a world and that love was the only passport required. I was undoubtedly wrong, and a week or two of real spiritual agony ensued. I solved the problem in a practical though unheroic manner. I went off with my Fabian friend for a week and thus, having cleared away the passionate side of the matter, was in a clear frame of mind. It was, as anyone who has been through such turmoils knows, a heart-rending experience. I won't attempt to harrow the reader with a description of my agonies – sleeplessness, exhaustion, misery. But I came back with my problems solved – and was reconciled. Perhaps this adventure marked the turning point and I saw that socialism and Nietzscheanism, though they might supply mental pabulum, could not, not for me, supply a practical rule of life. I was too deeply in love with the mother of my children and too deeply in love with the Christian idea of the family and the home and parental love, thus to throw everything away. I could not bear it. I should have broken my own heart as well as hers. It was shortly after this affair that we moved to Ditchling and soon afterwards I resigned from the Fabian Society. It was an escape.

In a manner of speaking our departure from London was an escape, but as we simply walked out, it wasn't much of an adventure. Yet it was an escape because London is undoubtedly a trap – and how many millions get caught in it! And inasmuch as the whole south of England, in spite of the rival wen at Birmingham, is dominated by the city of the bankers and politicians, the shops and the shows, real and complete escape is impossible, except in the spirit, and even in the spirit only by the greatest determination. But we did escape from the parks, and though a large part of my work came from London or from London people I was able to follow the principle that a workman is only responsible for what he does himself and what I did myself might, in respect of material and efficient causes, have been done almost anywhere in the world and at any time – it doesn't owe anything worth mentioning to the capitalist-industrial system. If I travelled by train, well, that was because that was the best the poor old transport providers had got to offer. If I clothed myself in machine-made cloth, well, that was because such cloth is the only kind they have to offer in shops. But my daughter wove me some vests of Assam silk (which looks like hemp), so my clothing was 'all glorious within'. But it is an important principle: that you are only fully responsible for what you do yourself. And when people, poor mutts, ask why, if we so hate the industrial system and mass production, we wear this or use the other machine-made nastiness, we are able to reassure them by saying: well, we do go without as much of the muck as possible but it's not always reasonably possible and, anyway, we can't help what other people do. I make tombstones; I don't profess to make ships and shoes and sealing-wax. When I truly need those things I have to take what is set before me.

So we did, in a manner and to a certain degree, escape from London and of course we crabbed it. But there was no question this time of crabbing my mother, unless we are to say, as many would wish, that the whole of our capitalist-industrialism is our mother and that we owe our life and being to it, and all our freedom and amenities — 'freedom slowly broadening down . . .' and so on. But I can't be bothered with that. You might as well say that bastards born in the public clinic ought to feel the pangs of filial piety towards the Borough Council.

But if it is doubtful whether I escaped from the industrial world I suppose it is still more doubtful whether I escaped from the *art*-world and the art-critics and the art-dealers. And if I displayed disgraceful ingratitude to my architectural patrons and to my spiritual progenitors, the Arts and Crafts movement, I must seem to have behaved even more badly to the denizens of Olympus. I don't know what one is expected to do. It seems to me that even if you slowly and silently vanish away you will still seem to have betrayed those who patronized or pushed you. It's not merely that they want a return on their money, though in the case of the dealers that consideration is not absent . . . I think it must be partly offended pride and partly fear. Your defection offends their dignity and also challenges their complacency. If you would take decently to drink or go off with one of their wives, then you would simply become 'poor so and so' and their world would remain unshaken. But if you cease to believe in them and find their whole business of salons and picture galleries symptomatic of all that seems most deplorable in the world and a lot of it not even genuine – no, I don't mean dishonest, I know nothing about that, but just 'phoney' and 'boloney' and horribly expensive too – well, it's very difficult to fade away without giving offence. That's been my experience. And of course it's been my fault too. You're sure to cause misunderstanding somewhere and some people have absolute genius for being offended.

But how truly abominable the 'art' world is, in all its manifestations. If the war that is now raging does nothing else, surely it will do something towards smashing it up. But I doubt it. The rise of the money-classes to power and to social domination after the breakdown of feudalism and spiritual rule at the end of the Middle Ages had the inescapable effect of secularizing the whole business of production. The idea that production is or should be primarily a sacred and holy activity has completely departed from the world. The mechanization of work seems therefore both right and natural and there are no signs even among those peoples most opposed to the domination of national and international finance, of any wish to abandon the secularization of industry. Therefore, whatever they do about money and the control of credit, there is no likelihood that the mechanization of industry will receive anything but a tremendous impetus from the war – unless the war should be so prolonged and so completely destructive as to destroy this civilization altogether. This must of course happen in the end. Nothing lasts for ever – birth, growth, maturity, decay and death is the divinely ordained sequence for good things no less than bad; but periods of decay have often lasted for hundreds of years and the decay of our mechanical culture may be no exception, although the unprecedented rapidity of its development may presage an unprecedentedly rapid disappearance. Therefore I make no prophecies save only that industrialism will go down in blood and tears in the end. Meanwhile the 'art world' will flourish. Even now, in the very middle of carnage, it is flourishing. I do not mean that large numbers of young painters are selling large numbers of paintings. No, indeed. But there is no breakdown of the universally accepted notion of art as a hothouse flower, of art divorced from meaning, divorced from prophecy, divorced from ritual, divorced from daily life, divorced from the common work of men. On the contrary, even now, in the midst of the struggle for economic and political domination, there are government committees and committees of artists with government backing and prestige, working to preserve the great traditions of the industrial era – the artist, the workman, and 'never the twain shall meet', except of course in the municipal picture gallery.

And there is no breakdown of the universally accepted notion of art as being primarily self-expression, the manifestation of the precious personality of the artist. The rise of this notion was historically inevitable. The decay of the idea of art as being on the one hand *ritual* and on the other *service* (hence the use of the words 'church *service*' for what is essentially ritual) was the inevitable consequence of the commercial and financial domination which characterizes our world. Things are for sale not for service, whether of God or man. And as commercialism naturally blossoms into industrialism, and the division of labour into mass-production, there naturally grows up a wider and wider differentiation between machine-made and man-made. And the special factor which differentiates them being the impersonality of the one and the personality of the other, it is natural that very special value should be attached to those things which bear the imprint of their makers, and therefore of their makers' persons.

And then it must be remembered that though the commercial world is dominated by 'the unfathomable maw of concupiscence' and therefore seeks to hold and control everything, there are some things which do not readily lend themselves to mechanical production. Such are painted images and poems and modellings in clay and musical tunes. Therefore the makers of such things could not be altogether drawn into the maw. The artist is the responsible workman, and these particular kinds of artists were now the only responsible workmen left; so, to-day, they alone are called artists. Thus it comes about that the word 'art' is now confined to their particular arts and the idea of art is now simply that which expresses or manifests the artists' particular sensibility. And of course this is 'jam' for dealers, because nothing is so unique as human personality and therefore nothing lends itself so admirably to the exploitation of 'scarcity value'.

Holding such disgruntled notions, I can quite see what a traitor I must seem, especially when it is their fond belief that I owe everything to them. If my high-art friends hadn't introduced me to such and such distinguished persons, if I hadn't been invited to exhibit my carvings at such and such well-known galleries, if the said works hadn't been noticed and generously praised by eminent art-critics in all the daily papers and the art magazines as well, where, oh where should I have been? Upon my honour I don't know how much weight to attach to such arguments. I don't know. I find it difficult to believe that the art galleries work entirely for love of the arts. I mean, I have heard them talking in those places,[1] and it stands to reason they aren't in the business for nothing. I don't blame them for seeing it chiefly from the point of view of the balance-sheet. But I don't see why I should go so goofy with gratitude as to be blind

[1] In this connection I recall with malicious delight a conversation I had with an eminent American art-dealer. He was endeavouring to persuade me to enter his net and his idea was to show me what a superior dealer he was. People who bought from him, he said, knew they were getting good things because his taste was so exquisite and therefore the artist benefited also. Other men were different. That such and such a thing was bought from Joseph Duveen, for instance, was no guarantee of its quality. 'Now look at Joe Duveen,' he said, 'he wanted me to go into partnership with him, but I wouldn't. Joe was one of the greatest salesmen in the world. He could sell *anything*. But *I* only sell what I *love*. . . .'

to the rottenness of the whole business, or so feeble as to say nothing about it.

*Note.* [See pp. 111 and 269.] I think I have said too little of the influence of John Ruskin. But the only books of his that I ever read were *The Elements of Drawing*, before I went to London [and I did some of the exercises therein recommended], *The Seven Lamps of Architecture* and, in bits, *The Stones of Venice* when I was at the architect's office, and, about 1910, and several times since, *Unto This Last*. So anything that looks like Ruskinism in my subsequent development is chiefly due to the fact that we both accepted the same first principles. And I was able to see that Ruskin's apparently narrow view of Architecture, as being merely a vehicle for sculpture, was not, as critics have thought, purely fatuous but was due to his intuition. That building which did not and could not thus flower was inhuman and subhuman. . . . And it was when I was an architect's pupil that I first read the *Morte d'Arthur*. Perhaps I read it too much, but at least it cured me of Tennyson and balanced my scepticism.

So there it is. This chapter of escapades is not designed to be a chapter of heroic adventures. Its object is simply to record the difficulty I have so often found myself in – the difficulty of the person who is always receiving kindnesses and encouragement and praise from people whose opinions he doesn't really and truly believe in or intellectually respect. He can't very well refuse their kindness altogether – moreover he knows they are not entirely disinterested – he can only try very hard not to get completely into their clutches or the clutches of their world and hope that his seeming ingratitude will not actually break their poor tender hearts.

# CHAPTER VIII

# CONCLUSION

So, it seems, this tight-rope of a life, this altogether too difficult business of living (like giving a child of five logarithms to do . . .) is drawing to an end. And, to press the simile a little further the rope is definitely getting steeper. It was always difficult to keep a balance but now there is fatigue as well. You get definitely tired and desirous of peace and quiet – and there is none to be had. There is no place to which, like a retired seaman, you can go and sit and contemplate your sweet youth and watch the admirable doings of your contemporaries. We have sown the wind and are indeed reaping the whirlwind. We shall have to make up our minds to perish in the storm.

But facing death – that is the chief business of living after all. The soldier, the sailor, the mountaineer and such-like foolhardy persons, miners and air-plane pilots, see death as the normal risk of their trades. But for ordinary people death is not a risk; it is a certainty. Perhaps my forty years as a monumental mason have made this fact uncommonly clear. Perhaps my upbringing as the son of a non-conformist parson gave me a good hold on this thought even earlier. But the grand rush of the modern world to destruction makes it impossible, even if you would, to put the thought aside. How are we going to face up to that? Is death merely the end of all things or is it indeed, truly, surely, certainly and, so to say, visibly and not merely in the conventionally accepted theory, the gate of life? In the former case the less said about it the better, and even the less thought about it; but in the latter . . .

In a general sort of way it might seem a plausible notion that human affairs should be arranged so as to give as many people as possible as much happiness as possible. But as to what does or *should* constitute happiness there is no telling, and there cannot be any real meaning in such words as 'should' or 'ought' – unless you elevate some abstraction like *Humanity* to the position of an absolute value and that is the same as saying that it is God the Father Almighty, which it fairly obviously isn't. So if you don't believe in God, there ain't no 'ought' and then any exceptionally strong and cunning person has as much 'right' to rob and rape as anyone else has to stop him. In fact 'rob' and 'rape' are words without essential significance and are only, as you might say, technical terms – legal jargon. Well, it's not for me to judge other people, though I'm pretty frequently doing it, but that line of thought isn't good enough for me. It seems to me to make nonsense of the universe, and everything in it and, most of all, it makes nonsense of man's life and all his doings. But the alternative is stupendous, stupendous and terrifying. For the alternative is the Cross. That is what we've got to face. The Cross is, in a nutshell, or I should say, in a couple of sticks, the meaning of the universe. To have or have not. To take or to give. You cannot have it both ways. 'He that loses his life in this world shall save it to life eternal.' And therefore he that gains this world is likely to lose his soul eternally. I'm not preaching at you. I'm only recording the dilemma as it appeared to me – as it still appears. Nor am I blaming anyone for taking the modern, and ancient, materialist line. I think people are more or less driven to it. If I hadn't always been lucky in work and life and love I expect I should have taken it also, as I was tempted to do. I think it's a rotten line of thought but an easy one – morally easy though metaphysically difficult – but what are metaphysics in a capitalist-industrial world? I think it is a rotten line of thought, but when I consider how we Christians exhibit our Christianity – making it appear that there's not a ha'porth of difference between Christians and anyone else – neither in our daily life and behaviour nor in our political and economic theory – when I consider this, I say, I don't see how we can expect to convert the world. Perhaps we don't expect to; we are quite comfortable with our accustomed manners and customs. Christian life to-day is not an evangelical or apostolic business; it is attendance at your particular conventicle and indulgence in your particular dope – i.e. ritual of prayers and hymns and preachings. It has no effect on the rest of the world or any appeal to it. So much the worse for the rest of the world. Very true, but such an attitude of superiority is not apostolic. And the situation is worse even than I have made out; for the Christians are not simply regarded with indifference, as curious anachronisms, but as definite enemies of social justice. When there is any outbreak of impatience or despair on the part of the workers, even a legitimately organized strike, on which side will you expect to find the clergy? The Church through her Popes and theologians, supports the institution of private and personal property.[1] The capitalist-industrial world has deprived the great majority of the people of any property whatever – except money (if you call it money) in the Savings Bank which the capitalist financiers control, and what you do not control you cannot properly be said to own. 'As many as possible of the people should be induced to become *owners*,' said Leo XIII. Do the clergy therefore condemn capitalist-industrialism? No indeed. Not a word said, except in condemnation of the desper-

---

[1] Because property is natural to man;

because property is a bulwark against the exploitation of man by man;

because unless you own the means of production you cannot control production;

because unless you control you cannot be responsible;

Because responsibility for his deeds and for what his deeds effect (i.e., both
moral and intellectual responsibility) is the very mark of man.

But note: as freedom is not incompatible with discipline, so property is not incompatible with social justice. The injustices of property owners in the past have only been possible because the few owned too much and the many nothing at all. 'The Law therefore should favour ownership . . .' whereas at present it favours exploitation.

But note also: there is nothing to hinder groups of persons, large or small, owning in common as e.g., Monastic Societies have always done and still do.

ate efforts of the workers to create a new society.[1] Communism started as a movement to overthrow capitalism. It is now, it appears, an equally bloody tyranny. I think the Christians have none but themselves to blame. So it is in many affairs. By our lukewarmness and complacency and blindness we have betrayed our own cause. I think we've got to learn our Christianity again. I think we have succumbed to the prevailing and all-pervading poison of material progress. We think we can get riches and plenty by political and scientific and mechanical trickery. Trickery, that's what it comes to. Press the button and the figure works. They call it the application of science to industry. It's not. It's the application of science to money-making. And the Christians haven't seen through it. No, they think it's 'jolly fine' and that working men ought to be grateful for the higher standard of living and the lower standard of muscular effort.

Well, the point here is not social reform or the rottenness of capitalist culture. The point is that the whole world has got it firmly fixed in its head that the object of working is to obtain as large an amount of material goods as possible, and that with the increased application of science and the increased use of machinery that amount will be very large indeed, while at the same time the amount of necessary labour will become less and less, until, machines being minded by machines, it will be almost none at all. And the point is that this frame of mind is radically un-Christian and anti-Christian. And the point of that is that it is therefore contrary to Nature and contrary to God—as anti-God as any atheist could wish. And that, no doubt, is why our English industrialism is so popular among Russian communists.

The alternative is the Cross. That's the awful fact. And it's not simply a matter of *ethical* behaviour, as who should say:

[1] Need I say that there are many honourable exceptions? The Popes themselves have condemned modern capitalism and many of the clergy have followed their example. But Christians in general, including catholics in general, have quite notoriously not followed the Popes in this matter.

'take up your cross and follow me'. It's also a matter of *intelligent* behaviour, as who should say: 'thou *fool*, this night thy soul shall be required of thee'. Man is made for happiness, not for wealth, and the two are entirely independent of one another and even inimical. A moderate amount of physical health and material wealth is necessary to man, that he may maintain his life. Of course! But even so it is better to give than to receive and therefore better to be given than to take. The whole of our trouble is the secularization of our life, so that we have descended to an animal condition of continual struggle for material goods. By sin – sin, that is to say, self-will and self-worship – by sin man does not descend from the superhuman to the merely human, but from the superhuman to the sub-human. Strange fact! Man cannot live on the human plane; he must be either above or below it. The marvellous feats of our mechanized 'scientific' industrial world are not human feats. They are no more than the feats of highly intelligent animals and the more we perfect our mechanization so much the more nearly do we approach the impersonal life of bees or ants.

And if I might attempt to state in one paragraph the work which I have chiefly tried to do in my life it is this: to make a cell of good living in the chaos of our world. Lettering, type-designing, engraving, stone-carving, drawing – these things are all very well, they are means to the service of God and of our fellows and therefore to the earning of a living, and I have earned my living by them. But what I hope above all things is that I have done something towards re-integrating bed and board, the small farm and the workshop, the home and the school, earth and heaven.

The thing about Christianity, the thing about the Cross, about Calvary, is that it is true to man. Man, not that creature, that biped, known to Science – measured as to his dimensions, his comparative dimensions, for there are no others; dissected as to his physiology; analysed as to his psyche – but man, the person known to himself and to God, the creature who knows and wills and loves, master of his acts (however much he be hindered by and subject to heredity and circumstance), therefore responsible. That is the creature who desires happiness and by the very nature of things, by his own nature, cannot find it except in God. That is why death is the gate of life.

'I have had my time,' says the dying man, and, whatever the men with the magnifying glass may tell him, he believes that the next thing for him is eternity. He finds it much more natural and easy to believe that than to believe the other thing. The other thing seems nonsense, which is precisely what it is — non-sense and non-being. Then they turn round on the poor old man and tell him all his ideas are 'wish-thinkage', and therefore untrue. Of course it is wish-thinkage, but it doesn't follow that it is untrue. I mean, it doesn't follow. So we are as we were. And which do you think is more likely — that the whole show is nonsense, or that it has some sort of final cause? And as neither I nor the poor old man are scientists, we agree heartily with one another that it is nonsense to say it's all nonsense. So if he's been well brought up, he makes his confession, that is to say he admits his responsibility, he proclaims his responsibility, he boasts his responsibility — a creature *able* to be damned — and dies happy. And I hope to do the same.